European security - towards 2000

European security – towards 2000

Michael C. Pugh editor

Manchester University Press Manchester and New York

distributed exclusively in the USA and Canada by St. Martin's Press

Published by Manchester University Press
Oxford Road, Manchester M13 9PL, England
and Room 400, 175 Fifth Avenue, New York, NY 10010, USA

Distributed exclusively in the USA and Canada by St Martin's Press, Inc., 175 Fifth Avenue, New York, NY 10010, USA

A catalogue record for this book is available from the British Library

Library of Congress cataloging in publication data
European security: towards 2000/Michael Pugh, editor.
p. cm.
Includes index.
ISBN 0-7190-3576-7 -ISBN 0-7190-3577-5 (pbk.)
1. Europe–Military policy. I. Pugh, Michael C. (Michael Charles), 1944–
UA646.E943 1991
355′.03304–dc20 91-4025

ISBN 0 7190 3576 7 *hardback*
ISBN 0 7190 3577 5 *paperback*

Printed in Great Britain
by Bell & Bain Limited, Glasgow

Contents

Preface

This book on the future of European security was conceived with university teachers and students of international relations in mind. It draws on the expertise of academic specialists in security issues. We hope that the book reflects the intellectual energy released by the end of the cold war and will also prove of interest to the general reader who is concerned about what happens next, in the years leading to the end of the century.

For ease of reference, notes are gathered at the end of each chapter. A combined list of suggested further reading is provided at the end of the book. The chapters by William Park, Owen Greene and Adrian Hyde-Price are revised versions of papers given at a conference on NATO organised by the Defence Studies Unit of the Mountbatten Centre for International Studies, University of Southampton. The views expressed in each chapter are those of the individual author(s) and do not represent the views of any institution with which they are associated.

The quotations in Chapter 2 (from Kenneth Waltz, *Theory of International Politics*, Reading, Mass., Addison–Wesley, 1983) are reproduced by kind permission of McGraw–Hill, Inc.

I would like to thank Rosemary Morris, secretary in the Politics Department, University of Southampton, for providing administrative assistance; Margaret Curran, who produced an excellent translation from German of Hans-Joachim Spanger's chapter; my wife, Margaret, for the many hours of typing, preliminary editing, proof reading and indexing. Finally, I would like to dedicate my part in this modest contribution to European collaboration to the memory of my father, Charles Pugh, d.30 June 1944, St Manvieu, *pays du bonheur vivant*.

Michael C. Pugh

Contributors

Manfred Efinger is Research Associate in the Peace Research Group, Eberhard-Karls University of Tübingen. He has published on verification and confidence- and security-building measures in the *Journal of Peace Research*, *Aussenpolitik*, and in Volker Rittberger (ed.), *International Regimes in East–West Politics*, London and New York, Pinter, 1990. He is the co-author, with Volker Rittberger and Michael Zürn, of *Internationale Regime in den Ost-West-Beziehungen*, Frankfurt/M., Haag & Herchen, 1988.

Owen Greene is Lecturer in Peace Studies, University of Bradford, and a consultant with the Open University and the Safer World Foundation. He has written extensively on alternative defence strategies and non-military security issues. His most recent publications and co-publications include: *Nuclear Winter: The Evidence and the Risk*, Cambridge, Polity Press, 1985; *The Politics of Alternative Defence*, London, Paladin, 1987; *Science and Mythology in the Making of Defence Policy*, London, Brassey's, 1989; 'Building a new European security structure', in *European Security: The New Agenda*, Bristol, Safer World, 1990.

Bertel Heurlin is Professor-Director, Institute of Political Studies, University of Copenhagen. He was formerly a Secretary in the Danish Foreign Ministry; Lecturer, University of Copenhagen Historical Institute, and Visiting Lecturer at the Universities of Stanford and California. During 1990 he was Visiting Professor, European University Institute, Florence. He has published on Nordic security policy and is the author of *Control of Nuclear Weapons: an Analysis of the Role of Nuclear Weapons in International Politics*, Copenhagen, SNU, 1986, and *NATO, Europe and Denmark: the 1990s Perspective*, Copenhagen, SNU, 1990.

Adrian Hyde-Price is Lecturer in International Relations, Department of Politics, University of Southampton. He was formerly a Research Fellow on the International Security Programme of the Royal Institute of International Affairs, London. He has recently published *European Security Beyond the Cold War: Four Scenarios for the Year 2010*, London, Sage/RIIA, 1991.

Juliet Lodge is Professor of European Politics, Jean Monnet Professor of European Integration, and Director, European Community Research Unit at the University of Hull. She has published widely on the European Community, including: *European Union: The European Community in Search of a Future*, London, Macmillan, 1986; *The Threat of Terrorism*, Brighton, Wheatsheaf, 1988; *The European Community and the Challenge of the Future*, London, Pinter, 1989; and *The 1989 Election of the European Parliament*, London, Macmillan, 1990.

William Park is Principal Lecturer, Department of History and International Affairs, Royal Naval College, Greenwich, and Visiting Lecturer, City University. He has published articles on NATO and maritime strategy, and is the author of *Defending the West: a History of NATO*, Brighton, Wheatsheaf, 1986.

Michael C. Pugh is Lecturer in International Relations in the Department of Politics, University of Southampton. He has published on nuclear deterrence and naval arms control, and is the author of *The ANZUS Crisis, Nuclear Visiting and Deterrence*, Cambridge, Cambridge University Press, 1989. He is the co-editor of *Superpower Politics: Change in the United States and the Soviet Union*, Manchester, Manchester University Press, 1990.

Philip Payton is Senior Lecturer, Department of History and International Affairs, Royal Naval College, Greenwich, and Honorary Research Fellow, University of Exeter. He is a Fellow of the Royal Historical Society and has written extensively on ethnicity and territorial issues. His most recent book has been on the making of modern Cornwall.

Volker Rittberger is Professor of Political Science, Eberhard-Karls University of Tübingen, and Special Fellow, United Nations Institute for Training and Research since 1978. He was formerly Visiting Professor at Stanford University, and Senior Associate Member, St Antony's College, Oxford. He is the co-author with Manfred Efinger and Michael Zürn of *Internationale Regime in den Ost-West-Beziehungen*, Frankfurt/M., Haag & Herchen, 1988. As co-editor and contributor his other publications include: *Mit Kriegsgefahren leben*, Opladen, Westdeutscher Verlag, 1987; *Europäische Sicherheit*, Vienna, Braumüller, 1987; *Theorien der Internationalen Beziehungen*, Opladen, Westdeutscher Verlag, 1990; *International Regimes in East–West Politics*, London and New York, Pinter, 1990.

Hans-Joachim Spanger is Senior Fellow and member of the Board of Trustees, Peace Research Institute, Frankfurt. In 1987–88 he was Research Associate at the International Institute for Strategic Studies in London. He is the author of: *Die SED und der Sozialdemokratismus*, Cologne, Wissenschaft & Politik, 1982; *The GDR in East–West Relations*, Adelphi Paper 240, London, IISS, 1989; and co-author of *Die beiden deutschen Staaten in der Dritten Welt*, Opladen, Westdeutscher Verlag, 1987.

Victoria Syme is Senior Lecturer, Department of History and International Affairs, Royal Naval College, Greenwich. She has written on aspects of defence economics and she is currently conducting research on the problems of economic transition in East-Central Europe and the Soviet Union.

Abbreviations

ATTU	Atlantic-to-the-Urals zone
BAOR	British Army of the Rhine
C^3I	command, control, communications and intelligence
CDE	Conference on Disarmament in Europe (Stockholm Conference)
CDU	Christian Democratic Union (FRG)
CFE	Conventional Forces in Europe (treaty)
CMEA	Council for Mutual Economic Assistance (COMECON)
COCOM	Co-ordinating Committee (on Multilateral Export Controls)
CPC	Conflict Prevention Centre
CPSU	Communist Party of the Soviet Union
CSBM	confidence- and security-building measure
CSCE	Conference on Security and Co-operation in Europe
CSU	Christian Social Union (FRG)
DM	Deutschmark
EBRD	European Bank for Reconstruction and Development
EC	European Community
EDC	European Defence Community
EFTA	European Free Trade Association
END	European Nuclear Disarmament (campaign)
EP	European Parliament
EPC	European Political Co-operation
FDP	Free Democratic Party (FRG)
FOFA	Follow-on Forces Attack
FOTL	follow-on-to-Lance
FRG	Federal Republic of Germany
GDR	German Democratic Republic
GNP	gross national product
IGC	Intergovernmental Conference
IISS	International Institute for Strategic Studies
IMF	International Monetary Fund
INF	intermediate-range nuclear forces
KOR	Committee for Defence of Workers (Poland)
MBFR	Mutual and Balanced Force Reduction (talks)
MEP	Member of the European Parliament
MLRS	multi-launch rocket system
NATO	North Atlantic Treaty Organisation
NNA	Neutral and Non-Aligned (state/s)
NPA	National People's Army (GDR)
OECD	Organisation for Economic Co-operation and Development
PDS	Party of Democratic Socialism (GDR)
RIIA	Royal Institute of International Affairs

SACEUR	Supreme Allied Commander, Europe
SDI	Strategic Defense Initiative
SEA	Single European Act
SED	Socialist Unity Party (GDR)
SHAPE	Strategic Headquarters, Allied Powers, Europe
SIPRI	Stockholm International Peace Research Institute
SNF	short-range nuclear forces
SPD	Social Democratic Party (FRG)
START	Strategic Arms Reduction Talks
TASM	tactical air-to-surface missile
UN	United Nations
US	United States
USSR	Union of Soviet Socialist Republics
WEDC	West European Defence Community
WEU	Western European Union
WTO	Warsaw Treaty Organisation

Note: throughout the book 'billion' is used in the sense of a thousand million.

Tables

1 Michael C. Pugh

Introduction: European security in transition

Observers are generally agreed that European security has entered a period of transition – between cold war stability and an uncertain future. How long the transition will last, and what security arrangements will emerge, depends on the outcome of many issues, including some which are external to Europe itself. This is unsettling, especially perhaps for those who had a vested interest in the cold war system. On the eve of the superpower summit in Moscow in 1988, Georgi Arbatov, Director of the Institute for the Study of the United States and Canada, told American reporters: 'We are going to do something terrible to you. We are going to deprive you of an enemy.'[1] Indeed this deprivation, and the political dramas in Central and Eastern Europe during 1989–90, caused the cold war system to disintegrate. In belated recognition of this, the military structure of the Warsaw Treaty Organisation (WTO) was formally terminated in March 1991. But contrasted with the euphoria of 1989, the *annus mirabilis*, widespread anxiety was being voiced as the new decade progressed.

The passing of communist rule in Eastern Europe was bound to leave wreckage to be cleared up, and to engender political, economic and nationalist tensions. In addition, the hopes for a new European order were dented by two great crises. First, turmoil in the Soviet Union threatened to unbalance the European system by enlarging the power vacuum in the former Eastern bloc. The promise of a reliable Soviet partnership in European and global security was threatened by President Mikhail Gorbachev's rule by decree and deference to conservative and military support to save the Union. The second crisis, Iraq's invasion of Kuwait on 2 August 1990, also threatened to disrupt the progress which had been made in European security. Iraq's aggression was particularly aggravating because it diverted political attention and economic resources when so much in Europe required sorting out. The impacts of these crises are examined in the concluding chapter, but it may be doubted whether the Soviet crisis and the disagreements between the Soviet Union and the West about how to deal with Iraq will turn back the clock towards military confrontation in Europe, though this cannot be ruled out. It seems, rather, that the extension of western assistance to the Soviet Union, ranging from food aid to economic management techniques, is an indication that security within Europe cannot be thought of mainly in terms of military power.

This book examines some of the forces which are changing the landscape of European security. It takes a broad approach to the concept of security and explores the manner in which security through military blocs is giving way to a more diffuse and less militarily-oriented security system.

With both students and general readers in mind, the book is less concerned to establish a theoretical framework than to identify and examine a core of political forces which will shape the future. It was also considered that to structure the book into rigorous categories appropriate to security theory would artificially constrain discussion of the subject matter in each chapter. The subjects were chosen according to their intrinsic importance in affecting the future of European security. They are grouped broadly into those dealing with the roles of key actors (the United States and Soviet Union, NATO, the European Community and reunited Germany), and those which examine key challenges and system developments (security risks in East-Central Europe, the confidence-building regime, alternative security systems, and transnational non-military issues). The purpose of this introduction is to survey security concepts which are relevant to this book and to consider the legacy of the cold war.

Security concepts

In lending his support to an expanded view of security, Barry Buzan remarks that the notion of security is weakly developed, often polarised between 'realist' and 'idealist' perspectives.[2] The realist perspective has traditionally emphasised the assets and military prowess of dominant states as the key elements of security. However, the idealist (or internationalist) tradition was revived as states in Western Europe attempted to implement internationalist principles after the Second World War. Internationalists argue that security is a relative concept and cannot be achieved without addressing the insecurities created by competing state interests. It seems in fact that to reconcile legitimate but competing interests, as in the European Community (EC), requires not just management of interactions but the sharing of sovereignty. This is most easily achieved in non-military affairs. In practice, judgements about military security are made by élites who commonly insulate themselves from the inconveniences of democratic control. Elites claim that domestic democratic rules are inapplicable to the formulation of security policy because secrecy and continuity have to be maintained. But if non-military values become more prominent in European security, then the claims of democrats for greater openness might be more difficult to resist.

This book is concerned with international rather than state security and with the quest for democratic reconciliation of interests. In the academic literature on security, three organisational terms are frequently employed – system, regime and community. A *system* is a complex of relationships encompassing military and non-military issues. Within the system there is a level of interaction, whether confrontationist or co-operative, which constrains the behaviour of participants. The relatively stable, but insecure, environment of the cold war can be described as a system. A security *regime* has been defined by Robert Jervis as permissive co-operation between states, like the post-1815 Concert of Europe.[3] Others take the view that a regime involves explicit rules, norms and processes which are designed mainly to avoid or balance military threats. The European confidence- and security-building regime assumes that there is a potential military threat which should be controlled to render military behaviour predictable and inoffensive. A security *community*, as originally defined by Karl Deutsch, applies to a set of multiple links between members and begins with the assumption that the threat of military conflict between the members is ruled out, as among the Nordic states. Furthermore, a community requires a web of shared values and mutual interests, and the acceptance of peaceful mechanisms to settle their disputes.[4]

In part, the degree of commonality to be expected depends on what constitutes Europe. The 1990 Treaty on Conventional Forces in Europe (CFE) gives a definition of the Atlantic-to-the-Urals (ATTU) zone which is convenient for military purposes, though Turkey and the Soviet Union have substantial territory beyond the zone, and it excludes the neutrals. Table 1.1 shows the membership of various European groups, and it can be appreciated that the main organisation which has a pan-European reach is the Conference on Security and Co-operation in Europe (CSCE) which was vested with a secretariat in 1991. In theory, a security community might be feasible for the territory of all the CSCE signatories. In practice, it will be difficult to endow the CSCE with real powers because the development of common security values is likely to proceed at different rates and with different degrees of intensity from one

Table 1.1 *Membership of various European groups (31 July 1991)*

EC	*WEU*	*NATO*	*WTO*†	*CFE*	*CSCE*	*Council of Europe*
Belgium	Belgium	Belgium	–	Belgium	Belgium	Belgium
–	–	–	Bulgaria‡	Bulgaria	Bulgaria	Bulgaria•
–	–	Canada	–	Canada	Canada	–
–	–	–	Czechos.‡	Czechos.	Czechos.	Czechos.
Denmark	–	Denmark	–	Denmark	Denmark	Denmark
France	France	France	–	France	France	France
Germany	Germany	Germany	–	Germany	Germany	Germany
Greece	–	Greece	–	Greece	Greece	Greece
–	–	–	Hungary‡	Hungary	Hungary	Hungary
–	–	Iceland	–	Iceland	Iceland	Iceland
Italy	Italy	Italy	–	Italy	Italy	Italy
Luxembourg	Luxembourg	Luxembourg	–	Luxembourg	Luxembourg	Luxembourg
Netherlands	Netherlands	Netherlands	–	Netherlands	Netherlands	Netherlands
–	–	Norway	–	Norway	Norway	Norway
–	–	–	Poland‡	Poland	Poland	Poland•
Portugal	Portugal	Portugal	–	Portugal	Portugal	Portugal
–	–	–	Romania	Romania	Romania	Romania•
Spain	Spain	Spain	–	Spain	Spain	Spain
–	–	Turkey	–	Turkey	Turkey	Turkey
UK	UK	UK	–	UK	UK	UK
–	–	USA	–	USA	USA	–
–	–	–	USSR	USSR	USSR	USSR•

Table 1.1 cont. *Neutral and non-aligned countries*

EC	*WEU*	*NATO*	*WTO†*	*CFE*	*CSCE*	*Council of Europe*
–	–	–	–	–	Albania	–
–	–	–	–	–	Austria	Austria
–	–	–	–	–	Cyprus	Cyprus
–	–	–	–	–	Finland	Finland
–	–	–	–	–	Holy See	Holy See
Ireland	–	–	–	–	Ireland	Ireland
–	–	–	–	–	Liechtenstein	Liechtenstein
–	–	–	–	–	Malta	Malta
–	–	–	–	–	Monaco	Monaco
–	–	–	–	–	San Marino	San Marino
–	–	–	–	–	Sweden	Sweden
–	–	–	–	–	Switzerland	Switzerland
–	–	–	–	–	Yugoslavia	Yugoslavia•

Notes: † defunct 1991. ‡ applied for association with NATO. • special guest status. Sweden, Austria, Turkey and Cyprus have applied for EC membership.

Source: adapted from B. Jasani, *European Arms Control Verification From Space*, Institut für Friedensforschung und Sicherheitspolitik and der Universität Hamburg, heft 51, October 1990, p. 64.

country and region to another. Europe is too diverse for a security community to emerge before the year 2000.

The question also arises: what values? The collapse of communist politics and ideology created an opportunity for the West to extend its cultural, political and capitalist values eastward. Few would quarrel with the need to promote the rule of law and democratic rights and freedoms, as defined in the Council of Europe's Human Rights Convention. Other prescriptive rights seem unattainable, even in the West. For example, the Council of Europe's Social Charter, in force since 1965, provides for employment, health and welfare rights, such as the right of all workers 'to a fair remuneration sufficient for a decent standard of living'. Some values will create controversy. It has even been suggested, for example, that the United States should monitor historical education in European states and object to the distortion of 'essentials' as defined in Washington.[5] Furthermore, any dogmatic insistence by the West on market principles, as defined by monetarists, could be unrealistic. Given structural variations in the economies of East and Central Europe, a pluralist approach would seem appropriate. In any case there has been a retreat from 'new right' values in western economies as a consequence of failings in the sphere of social and economic justice. Indeed the problems of capitalism may come under greater scrutiny in the West now that the eclipse of communist rule outside the Soviet Union has weakened the competition against which western capitalism measured its success. The West may also have to tolerate diversity in political values if pan-European security is to be the goal. Eastern political traditions of élitism and vassalage, collectivism and corporatism, authoritarianism and religious obscurantism, will hamper conversion to western political models.

It seems, in fact, that Poland, Hungary and Czechoslovakia are being groomed for economic integration by western institutions, whilst the Soviet Union and Balkan states will remain on the periphery. Discrimination by the West, on grounds of 'worthiness', entails the risk of creating resentment, and could invalidate the West's role in sustaining stability and democracy throughout Europe. As Pierre Hassner has noted, there is a 'North–South' problem within Europe, and punitive discrimination against, for example, the Soviet Union and Yugoslavia, could increase vulnerability to economic and ethnic unrest.[6]

Such uncertainties about the values necessary to achieve stability have revived the policy contest, identified by Joseph Nye, between the quest for *end-goals* and the emphasis on facilitating the *processes* of integration.[7] Some commentators regard agreement on the definition of goals as the key to future security. Gorbachev had a vague vision – the Common European Home – but lacked the means to achieve it, except by removing obstacles to the process of integration. Western visions reflected philosophical and intellectual diversity, as well as diversity of national interests. Ironically, during a dispute over the EC's security competence, sharpened by the Gulf crisis, the British Government called for agreement on goals before establishing machinery to promote co-ordination.[8] The rare spectacle of the British suggesting a teleological approach might be regarded as sophistry, an attempt to hinder forms of European co-operation which might antagonise the United States. Britain's European partners preferred to emphasise the process of cultural, economic and military interdependence, and sought to strengthen decision-making machinery. To some degree, however, the division between ends and process is an artificial one, for their effects are reciprocal. It is also reasonable to suggest that potential partners can agree that a security community is desirable, without necessarily having to detail its precise shape.

The changes in Europe in 1989–90 may have been fundamental, but, obviously, policy-makers were not given a clean sheet to draw upon. It is important, then, to consider the cold war and its legacies.

Cold war stability and insecurity

The worst of the cold war lasted from about 1947 to 1963. In Europe it was marked by superpower domination over the Continent's affairs – though a few neutral and non-aligned states took distinctive, but largely ineffectual, roles in European politics. The apparent durability of the cold war was attributed to the division of Europe and creation of two German states, the conventional military power of the two alliances, and the threat of nuclear war.[9] To cope with the nuclear threat, western strategists constructed a quasi-religious belief system about the effectiveness of untested nuclear deterrence strategies. Its followers considered the gospels of Herman Kahn, Thomas Schelling and others to be self-evidently true – they were patently not susceptible to proof.[10] In both East and West, nuclear weapons and deterrent strategies contributed to what John Herz identified as 'the security dilemma'. Huge investments in deterrence and war merely made the adversary feel less secure, prompting another twist to the arms-racing spiral.[11] Cold war thinking did not encourage policy-makers to contemplate the other side's security interests.

After the 1962 Cuban missile crisis, however, confrontation was mitigated by the development of a management system, comprising communication links, co-operation to regulate arms racing, and reassuring behaviour, including the restraint of allies. The United States actually went further and put into practice a plan for 'graduated and reciprocal initiatives in tension reduction'. The Kennedy Administration declared a unilateral moratorium on atmospheric nuclear testing. In response the Soviet Union cancelled a new bomber. From the military point of view this winding down threatened to get out of hand and was aborted.[12] However, the mixture of reassurance and confrontation persisted and was reflected in the Harmel Report of 1967, *Defence and Détente*, NATO's dual approach to security.

It has become an orthodox view in the West that Gorbachev's election to the post of General Secretary of the Soviet Communist Party in March 1985 was the crucial turning-point in ending the cold war in Europe.[13] The view is simplistic not just because it places too much emphasis on the policies of one man, but also because it overlooks long-term developments which sapped the security system. Although the Soviet Union had proposed conferences on European security in 1954 and 1966 (dismissed by the West as propaganda), the political basis of cold war security in Europe was not shaken until the late 1960s and early 1970s. East–West relations in Europe were put on a businesslike basis by superpower détente, supervised by Richard Nixon and Leonid Brezhnev, and by West German *Ostpolitik* (i.e. 'reassociation' with Eastern Europe), supervised by Willi Brandt. As Charles Levinson revealed in *Vodka–Cola* (1978), it was quite literally 'businesslike', for the ruling élites on both sides conducted economic deals, thereby cocking a snook at the military cold war.

Paradoxically, investment in Eastern Europe in the 1970s was based on the notion that Eastern Europe was one of the most stable areas in the world with which to do business. In effect, western companies could exploit the political stability of everyday repression, the low paid, strike-free labour, and the huge demand for consumer goods. Investment was often wasted by East European governments, fuelling unreal expectations and increasing indebtedness. The experiment failed in the slump of 1979 when East Europeans could not repay debts because of reduced demand for their products in capitalist markets.

German *Ostpolitik*, however, exceeded the mere management of confrontation, and was aimed at revising the European order by stealth. It paved the way for an enduring European détente in the CSCE agreement signed in Helsinki in 1975. In addition to military confidence-building, the Helsinki process played a significant role in reform, by establishing the notion of a standard of human and democratic rights. Although open to wide interpretation, the issue of human rights became a currency in European relations which directly affected domestic politics in communist-controlled regimes.[14] At the same time, from 1979 to 1986, the obsession with competitive security was reasserted in the second cold war.

Relapse and the war scare

The chill was spread by the Soviet invasion of Afghanistan on one side and, on the other, by the pressure from Republican ideologues on President Jimmy Carter, followed by the Reagan Administration's strategic fundamentalism. Conceivably, however, the prolongation of the cold war ran counter to underlying trends in Europe. For example, in the Polish crisis of 1980–81 the imposition of military rule masked a turning-point in European security. To deal with Solidarity, Brezhnev himself ignored 'Brezhnev doctrine' and avoided a Soviet military intervention. The crisis also revealed that the Soviet Union could no longer depend on effective Communist Party leadership in Poland or on the loyalties of Polish conscripts in any war with the West. Such factors were overlooked or discounted, however, and the West imposed economic sanctions against the Soviet Union for *not* invading.

It is worth recalling the widespread sense of insecurity generated by the threat perceptions of the second cold war – lest nostalgia for the discipline of the bloc system re-emerges in the uncertainty and instability of the years ahead. The cold war had kept a country divided and Eastern Europe politically isolated. It produced mind-sets and reduced opportunities for conciliation. The insecurity was manifested by military alerts, and a succession of crises in NATO over burdensharing and nuclear issues. Strategic fundamentalists in the Reagan Administration managed the Western Alliance on the premise that there was a 'seamless web' of extended nuclear deterrence. Yet many of the serious domestic problems in the Alliance were caused by attempts to reinforce the web at a time when the Soviet Union had achieved parity, even regional superiority, in nuclear weapons. In the early 1980s West Europeans demonstrated in their hundreds of thousands against nuclear weapon deployments. Commentators from a variety of political standpoints predicted a new inter-system war – the probable causes of which they then explained to the book-buying public. It did not seem to matter that the central front in Europe had become the most militarily over-insured area in the world and, given the likely costs of conflict, the least likely to experience deliberate large-scale aggression. Soviet and American acceptance of crisis management continued, but it became fashionable to assume that a conflict would result, as in 1914, from a fatal mixture of technical imperatives and miscalculations about intentions.

It can be argued that in the long term, the division of Europe into two camps created stability which facilitated the ending of the cold war. First, the division forged security relationships in Western Europe which outlawed the use of force between states (except between Turkey and Greece), and generally socialised populations into accepting war avoidance as a norm. Second, in the East, Soviet and national communist control smothered potential irredentism among the states of the WTO. Thus with only two blocs involved, the management of relations between states was relatively uncomplicated.[15]

Yet one should not underestimate the impact of divisions *within* the blocs which accompanied the second cold war scare. In the Western Alliance, for example, European perceptions about the seamless web and the nature of détente diverged fundamentally from those of the United States. By the time the INF Treaty was signed in December 1987, the seamless web of nuclear deterrence was embarrassingly tattered. The Europeans regarded deterrence and détente as divisible. The two German states, in particular, protected their own relationship. More generally, Europeans protected détente to safeguard the Helsinki Agreement. By contrast, the United States, under Presidents Jimmy Carter and Ronald Reagan, contemplated ditching CSCE altogether and viewed détente as another instrument of cold war containment.[16]

The strains of the second cold war also spurred new thinking about security. Respected statesmen established two independent commissions: one on International Development Issues (the Brandt Commission), and the other on Disarmament and Security Issues (the Palme Commission). The reports, published in 1979 and 1982 respectively, called for policies of mutual survival and the intensification of détente to build common security. Whereas détente had been loosely based on deals for trading off interests, the Palme Commission offered both broad principles and a specific programme. The broad principles were that: all nations have a legitimate right to security regardless of their ideology; the use of military force is not legitimate to resolve disputes; restraint is necessary in expressions of national policy; security cannot be attained through military superiority; reduction and qualitative limitations of armaments are necessary; linkage between arms negotiations and political events should be avoided because it broadened rather than limited divergences. Above all, the Palme Commission considered that 'greater national military might has not led to a greater sense of national security'.[17]

More specifically, common security advocates addressed the worry that localised inadvertent conflict would escalate out of control. It was important to affect threat perceptions by drawing up codes of military conduct and encouraging policies of defensive defence. These views paralleled those of radical dissenters in the 1980s. Suppressed in the East, reviled and smeared in the West, European dissenters elaborated alternative defence strategies. Such ideas should have been increasingly attractive to NATO states which found themselves in acute dilemmas about matching their human and economic resources to perceived cold war military requirements. But governments emphasised the need for improvement in the political environment before embracing such radicalism. Such a prospect seemed utterly Utopian. Ironically, one of the few people in the West to predict political change and 'people power' in the Eastern bloc was the luminary of the European Nuclear Disarmament movement, Edward Thompson.[18] By 1990, however, the common security precepts of the 1970s and 1980s may be said to have been partially achieved, mirrored in NATO's London Declaration and the CFE Treaty.

In spite of the exaggerated claims for Gorbachev's role in ending the cold war, it would be churlish to deny that his incoherent policies were far-reaching. Indeed Gorbachev and his Foreign Minister Eduard Shevardnadze (1985–90) played a weak hand with skill in conducting relations with the West. Gorbachev's policies reflected changes in the global power balance which has seen economic crisis in the Soviet Union and retreats by Marxist-Leninist ideology, even in Albania. As Michael Cox demonstrates, the critical situation in the Soviet Union owed more to a fall in the oil price, the increasing economic burden of Eastern Europe, and the Chernobyl accident than to American actions under Reagan. When a prominent US congressional leader complained that the 'strategy of spending the Soviet Union into oblivion worked, but we also spent ourselves into oblivion', the second half of his remark was probably truer than the first.[19] Perceptions of war in Europe receded and the rush to political pluralism and military independence in most of Central and Eastern Europe and many of the Soviet republics brought about a major shift in the geopolitical balance.[20] But establishing a new security system is likely to be a much more gradual process than destroying the old.

Continuities

At this point it is useful to recognise that elements of the cold war system survived after the demolition of the Berlin Wall. First, powerful military structures have survived. Soviet military capability, even after implementation of the CFE agreement, will remain considerable, though the subtraction of other Warsaw Pact (WTO) forces puts it in a generally inferior position to NATO. Germany after unification remains heavily militarised, with an armed serviceman for every fifty or so inhabitants.[21]

Second, many threats to security persisted, such as terrorism. Other threats, which had either been overshadowed by the cold war (as in the case of ethnic unrest and irredentism), or detached from military considerations (such as environmental pollution), became more prominent.

Third, the war against Iraq reminded Europeans that their security could be complicated by conflicts beyond the Continent. Many European countries continued to rely on imported energy, petrodollar investments, and Middle East commercial contracts.

Fourth, cold war values persisted beyond the cold war itself. Although Italy and the Federal Republic of Germany took Gorbachev at his word and reacted positively to his initiatives from 1985, the response of many NATO countries might be characterised as 'wait and see'. In Britain and the United States, particularly, the view until the end of 1989 was 'let's wait' until Soviet forces pull out of Europe and 'let's see' if Gorbachev survives. Even after the 1989 revolutions, vested interests in the old system continued to emphasise Soviet military capability and untrustworthiness. Indeed in the Soviet Union, military and conservative forces rallied in the autumn of 1990 and fortified their arguments with cold war rhetoric against the West. The potential for a revival of cold war attitudes in the West was signalled by the hostility in the United States towards Gorbachev's handling of the Baltic republics, his diplomacy during the Gulf war and Soviet delays in bringing nuclear and conventional arms control negotiations to fruition. Indeed the US Secretary of Defense, Richard Cheney, and the Deputy National Security Adviser, Robert Gates, remained cold warriors long after threat assessments by the Central Intelligence Agency, Defense Intelligence Agency and the State Department contradicted their stance.[22] European governments tended to be more tolerant of Gorbachev's diplomatic efforts and his difficulties in maintaining the Union. But the prevarications and ambiguities in western policy merely emboldened orthodox communists and the demoralised military interests in the Soviet Union who openly opposed Gorbachev's 'retreats' and 'submissions'.

Finally, a legacy of zero-sum thinking can be detected in the view in some circles that the West had won the cold war and could therefore dictate the peace. In sponsoring economic reform, for example, western decision-makers, no doubt guided by the experience of the 1970s, concluded that to support Central and Eastern European government agencies would merely subsidise inefficiencies. However, political pluralism has altered the governing contexts since the 1970s, and the aim of economic assistance should be to underpin political gains, not to jeopardise them. Negative effects of enterprise culture have ranged from the collapse of the lively Hungarian film industry, to the devastation of Zeiss production in Jena, and the International Monetary Fund's interference in Polish politics by threatening to cut aid if Jan Bielecki's Government did not re-employ a former monetarist Minister of Finance.[23] It is plausible to argue that, in order to minimise impoverishment and social disruption, some Eastern and Balkan economies need efficient *dirigisme* as well as entrepreneurs.

Arms control provides another example of the cold war prism at work. Conventional arms control, properly implemented, has been something of a triumph for NATO. Certainly, the CFE Treaty was as unbalanced as the military situation in Europe: the WTO needed to reduce its levels of key equipment by about 60 per cent, whilst NATO's will reduce by about 15 per cent. By some accounts Gorbachev had to struggle against his military advisers to secure an agreement of conventional forces. But the refusal of US officials to discuss naval measures in any European forum, and the elimination of a tentative reference to naval confidence-building from the draft of NATO's London Declaration of 6 July 1990, demonstrated a degree of insensitivity about Soviet security concerns which the Soviet military establishment repaid by evading the spirit of the CFE Treaty.[24]

Nevertheless, the United States and all European states began disarming in 1990, consistent with budgetary pressures and reduced threat perception. There seemed little doubt that Europe would face instabilities, of a different order, which could not be dealt with by armed forces. To a large extent, then, the biggest challenge which the peoples of Europe confront is how to think differently about security.

A changing landscape

The chapters which follow examine elements which will shape the European security system of the future. First, although Europe has been liberated from the strait-jacket of the bipolar system, the roles of the

Soviet Union and United States remain significant. In Chapter 2, Bertel Heurlin discusses the change in the global power balance which has left the United States in a pre-eminent position. Yet there is bound to be a shift in relations between North America and Europe, partly because Europe is developing its own economic clout and partly because the United States faces challenges, not from a single rival state but from non-state actors and transnational interdependence.[25] True, in 1991 the Americans gained enormous self-esteem by 'kicking the Vietnam syndrome' and winning a war in the Middle East. But dealing with the aftermath of military success, including the relief and protection of refugees, has proved extremely taxing for the United States. Nor were the 'advantages' of lifting a psychological restraint on US military intervention universally welcomed. Further, during the war against Iraq, budgetary constraints forced the Pentagon to cut deployments elsewhere, especially in Europe, and reduce military programmes.

The Soviet aim, as defined by Gorbachev, was to partner the West in achieving joint security. It may be doubted whether such a partnership is feasible when the legitimacy of the Soviet Government is itself challenged and its economy lurches from one crisis to another. But the Soviet crisis, discussed in the concluding chapter, is also the most problematic part of the European security framework.

By removing the West's worst security fears, Gorbachev solved some of NATO's manpower, expenditure and strategic problems. It is questionable whether NATO is an appropriate institution to tackle broad security issues, but it remains the pre-eminent military structure and will not be dismantled whilst Soviet policy is in disarray. William Park's chapter considers the requirement for NATO to reconstitute its strategy. In military terms such a strategy will emphasise the need for integrated forces and lightly-armed, mobile units, plus an ability to mobilise reserves. In political terms it will emphasise reassurance and crisis avoidance, whilst preserving the North American link and providing international regulation of German security policy – which would include the creation of multinational units for service in Europe.

In Chapter 4 Juliet Lodge assesses the prospects for increasing the European Community's role, as suggested in March 1987 by Jacques Delors, President of the European Commission. Ironically, as the EC was considering proposals for closer political and security co-operation, the Gulf crisis opened up rifts between member states. The specific positions which they adopted certainly reflected national outlooks. But it is worth remembering that members of the EC were also constrained by consultations and collective pressures. The Germans wrote cheques and the

Coalition remained intact. The process of further integration in Europe, especially if the United States reduces its European commitment, will inevitably include security measures. Perhaps the most intransigent problem, however, is that of generating economic growth beyond 1992 through deeper integration among existing members whilst decreasing the economic gap with non-members.

Germany naturally claims a leading role in shaping the new Europe. As Hans-Joachim Spanger indicates in Chapter 5, dealing with the former German Democratic Republic will take enormous energy and expenditure through to the end of the decade, the Kohl Government having underestimated the costs of unification. On account of its own 'stability complex' and historical memories of 'the German question', Germany cannot comfortably take a more extensive role without accepting the demands by France and others for the Europeanisation of security. Germany will have to settle for the relatively modest function of acting as a bridgehead for promoting western values in the East.

In Chapter 6 Victoria Syme and Philip Payton consider the ethnic and economic issues in Eastern Europe and the external problems which these pose. Speaking on New Year's Day, 1991, President Vaclav Havel of Czechoslovakia commented that what had looked like a neglected house a year before was actually a ruin (which could not be rebuilt purely on market forces). Externally, Czechoslovakia, Poland, Hungary and even Bulgaria were concerned about a security vacuum in Central Europe. Indicating their vulnerability to disintegrating trends in the Soviet Union, they sought protection within NATO. But NATO politely refused to extend its guarantees because there was no intention of antagonising the Soviet Union. A solution proposed by Wim van Eekelen, President of the Western European Union, was to offer links to the WEU, whilst at the same time merging the WEU with the EC Heads of Government Council.[26]

In a transition period the strengthening of the confidence- and security-building (CSBM) regime is doubly important to reassure the states of Europe about the peaceful intentions of neighbours. In Chapter 7, Manfred Efinger and Volker Rittberger argue that it is easier for states to reach a *modus vivendi* about procedures than to bargain about power. Consolidating the CSBM regime will absorb the energies of the CSCE states in the 1990s and will be a prominent feature of the post-cold war period, not least in monitoring implementation of the CFE Treaty.

Alternative systems and 'ideal' visions of European security are analysed by Adrian Hyde-Price in Chapter 8. This overview juxtaposes an 'Atlanticist' model, a West European Defence Community, a pan-European collective security system and a more fragmented system based on nation-states or regional arrangements. New institutions, such as the Centre for the Prevention of Conflict (CPC), have been established. But the most likely structural change will involve the adaptation of existing institutions which have proved serviceable in the past. Thus the WEU or the CSCE could play more of a role in stabilising Europe after the cold war.

Owen Greene argues in Chapter 9 that transnational processes should be encouraged in keeping with the changed environment. In essence, Europeans are losing their deference to realist military values and identifying with transnational non-military values such as human and political rights, environmental health and safety, non-violence and economic well-being.

This book focuses on Europe itself, though clearly European security is also dependent on the treatment of broad global problems. These include damage to the environment, the arms trade and proliferation of weapons of mass destruction, poverty and famine in the Third World and the fragility of the international trading and financial systems. Indeed the conflict in the Middle East underlined the extent to which a crisis beyond European shores could affect developments within Europe. But there is also a sense in which the European experience of security-building among diverse political cultures has global importance. This is not to say that a European security system could necessarily offer a model, or stand by itself (given the former dependency on superpower leadership). But Europe has had a long history of building security among diverse political cultures. After the disastrous failure of liberal internationalism in 1939, Western Europe pioneered new forms of conflict-avoidance through regional integration. By 1991 visions of European security, previously geared to prevent defeat in an East–West armed conflict, had broadened to encompass more states and a more diffuse and variegated security agenda.[27] In analysing security issues in the remainder of the twentieth century the authors disavow any millenarian intentions to provide a blueprint. Our task is to identify and analyse developments in the belief that there is a need for open discussion in uncertain times.

Notes

1 Cited in US Department of Defense, *Soviet Military Power 1990*, Washington DC, USGPO, 1990, p. 21.
2 Barry Buzan, *People, States and Fear: The National Security Problem in International Relations*, Brighton, Wheatsheaf, 1983, pp. 3–9.
3 Robert Jervis, 'Security regimes', *International Organization*, XXXVI, no. 2, Spring 1982, pp. 357–78.
4 Karl W. Deutsch *et al.*, *Political Community and the North Atlantic Area*, Princeton, NJ, Princeton University Press, 1957.
5 Stephen Van Evera, 'Why Europe matters, why the Third World doesn't: American grand strategy after the cold war', *Journal of Strategic Studies*, XIII, no. 2, June 1990, pp. 14–15. See also Vilho Harle, *European Values in International Relations*, London, Pinter, 1990.
6 Pierre Hassner, 'Europe beyond partition and unity: disintegration or reconstitution?', *International Affairs*, LXVI, no. 3, July 1990, pp. 469–71.
7 See Joseph S. Nye, 'The long-term future of deterrence', in Roman Kolkowicz (ed.), *The Logic of Nuclear Terror*, Boston, Mass., Allen & Unwin, 1987, pp. 245–7; Ken Booth, 'Steps towards stable peace in Europe: a theory and practice of co-existence', *International Affairs*, LXVI, no. 1, January 1990, pp. 32–4.
8 See Ole Waever, 'Three competing Europes: German, French, Russian', *International Affairs*, LXI, no. 3, July 1990, pp. 77–93; 'Hurd falls out with EC on defence', *Guardian*, 11 December 1990, p. 10.
9 See, e.g., Anton DePorte, *Europe Between the Superpowers*, New Haven, Conn., Yale University Press, 1986 (2nd edn).
10 See, e.g., John Lewis Gaddis, *The Long Peace: Inquiries Into the History of the Cold War*, New York, Oxford University Press, 1987, pp. 215–45.
11 John H. Herz, *Political Realism and Political Idealism*, Chicago, Chicago University Press, 1951.
12 Charles E. Osgood, *An Alternative to War or Surrender*, Urbana, Ill., University of Illinois Press, 1962; Anatol Rapoport, 'Conflict escalation and conflict dynamics', in Raimo Väyrynen (ed.), *The Quest for Peace: Transcending Collective Violence and War Among Societies, Cultures and States*, London, Sage/International Social Science Council, 1987, pp. 175–6.
13 See, e.g., Walther Stützle in SIPRI, *Yearbook 1990: World Armaments and Disarmament*, Oxford, Oxford University Press, 1990, p. xxi.
14 Michael R. Lucas, *The Conference on Security and Cooperation in Europe and the Post-Cold War Era*, Institut für Friedensforschung und Sicherheitspolitik, heft 48, Hamburg, September 1990, p. 9; Jan Urban, 'Czechoslovakia: the power and politics of humiliation', in Gwyn Prins, *Spring in Winter: The 1989 Revolutions*, Manchester, Manchester University Press, 1990, pp. 112–13; Karl E. Birnbaum and Ingo Peters, 'The CSCE: a reassessment of its role in the 1980s', *Review of International Studies*, XVI, no. 4, pp. 305–19.
15 Pekka Sivonen, 'European security: new, old and borrowed', *Journal of Peace Research*, XXVII, no. 4, 1990, pp. 388–9; Kenneth Waltz, *Theory of International Politics*, Reading, Mass., Addison-Wesley, pp. 194–210.
16 Lucas, *The Conference on Security and Cooperation in Europe*, p. 84.
17 Independent Commission on Disarmament and Security Issues, *Common Security: A Blueprint for Survival*, New York, Simon & Schuster, 1982, p. 4.
18 E. P. Thompson, *Beyond the Cold War*, London, Merlin/END, 1981.
19 Ronald Dellums, House Armed Services Committee, *Hearings on National Defense Authorization Act, FY 1990, HR 2461 and Oversight of Previously Authorized Programs*, 25 April 1989, p. 176; Michael Cox, 'Whatever happened to the "Second" Cold War? Soviet–American relations: 1980–1988', *Review of International Studies*, XVI, no. 2, April 1990, p. 164; Fred Chernoff, 'Ending the cold

war: the Soviet retreat and the US military buildup', *International Affairs*, LXVII, no. 1, January 1991, pp. 111–26.

20 See Renée de Nevers, *The Soviet Union and Eastern Europe: The End of an Era*, Adelphi Paper 249, London, Brassey's/IISS, 1990.

21 Dieter S. Lutz, *Brauchen wir noch deutsche Streitkräfte?* [*Why do we need German forces?*], Proceedings of the August Bebel Circle for a European Collective Security System, Bonn, March 1990, p. 3.

22 'Webster and Cheney at odds over Soviet military threat', *New York Times*, 7 March 1990, p. 1. Former US Defense Secretary, Robert McNamara, condemned the obstinate cold warriors for failing to seize opportunities to create a new security system: Senate Committee on the Budget, *Hearing on 'After the Thaw: National Security Objectives in the Post-Cold War Era'*, 12 December 1989, Washington DC, USGPO, 1990, p. 6.

23 'US veto nails Poland to tough regime', *Guardian*, 8 January 1991, p. 9.

24 Article 13, draft London Declaration on a Transformed North Atlantic Alliance, 6 July 1990, German text; interviews with arms control officials in London, Brussels and Bonn. Among other 'violations' the Soviet Army transferred three European-based divisions with their armour and artillery to naval coastal defence units.

25 David Allen and Michael White, Western Europe's presence in the contemporary international arena, *Review of International Studies*, XVI, no. 1, January 1990, pp. 19–37; Joseph S. Nye, Jr., *Bound to Lead: The Changing Nature of American Power*, New York, Basic Books, 1990.

26 'NATO may reject Eastern Europe, warns WEU chief', *Guardian*, 16 February 1991, p. 9; Jan Urban, David Davies Memorial Lecture, London, 28 January 1991.

27 Paul Eavis (ed.), *European Security: The New Agenda*, Bristol, Safer World Foundation, 1990.

2 Bertel Heurlin

The roles of the United States and the Soviet Union

An epoch in Europe came to an end in 1989. This epoch began in 1945, when Europe was liberated and then dominated again in different ways by the non-European great powers (labelled superpowers), the United States and the Soviet Union. Unable to manage its own affairs, Europe became a divided centre in the global polarisation between the two giants. This partition, affecting most European states, was maintained firmly until the Federal Republic of Germany promoted *Ostpolitik* in the late 1960s and détente became well established in Europe.

The healing process proper began in 1990. The immobilism of the cold war is over – provided Soviet leaders do not revert to a fortress mentality or continue to defy the principles of the Conference on Security and Co-operation in Europe (CSCE) in their handling of nationalism in the republics. Over, too, is cold war stability, the price of which had been general insecurity and, in Eastern Europe, suppression of freedoms. With the opening up of new instabilities as well as new opportunities, political scientists and commentators have tried to offer convincing interpretations of what happened and why, and what is going to happen. Assessments have ranged from predictions of revolutionary change with deep structural implications, to concern that the cold war will revive, to the premature announcement that history has ended – not with a bang but a whimper.[1] In examining the role of the superpowers in Europe we need first to analyse changes in the international system as a whole.

The transformation of the international system

The point of departure for this chapter is that in the early 1990s the international system entered a transition period, in scope and effect very much like the period immediately after the Second World War. In the first two years after that war there was speculation about whether there would be change from a multi-power system (which in wartime had been structured in a polarised way between the two coalitions) into a uni-, bi-

or tri-power system. By 1947 it was becoming clear that the international system would be a bi-power system, which turned out to be extremely polarised. The point is that a world war had initiated a system transformation. Two aspiring world powers – Germany and Japan – had been virtually reduced to non-states, experiencing complete domination by the conquerors. Other great powers, notably Britain and France, had been weakened rather than strengthened by their wartime roles. Now in the 1990s we have a similar situation. A 'war' is over and Europe has entered a period of transition.

We are witnessing a move from a bi-power structure into a specific uni-power structure. The United States is emerging as the dominating state in terms of its capability and influence. Its leadership is, however, of a specific kind, namely that of a *primus inter pares*. The Soviet Union has lost its political role as a superpower. Thus the structure is transformed from a two-power system to a 'one-plus-four' system: the United States plus the Soviet Union, Japan, China and Germany (or a united Europe). But the factor which will prevent this evolving into a hegemonic regime is the political and military role of nuclear weapons. In military and strategic terms, largely defined by nuclear weapons, the Soviet Union will still be able to balance the United States. Otherwise, the Soviet Union is in a process of absolute decline, perhaps even dismemberment. The United States is either in a process of moderate relative decline, or is merely holding its own.[2] New great powers, Germany and Japan, are emerging, but for different reasons are confined to play primarily economic roles. Although Western European integration might promote European unity there are also severe disintegrating forces with which to contend, in particular with regard to the Soviet Union itself and Yugoslavia.

The ending of East–West polarisation has entailed a new geopolitical, regional, military and economic situation for Europe. The role and capabilities of the main actors have changed, both objectively-speaking and in their own perceptions. The United States managed to use the United Nations to engineer world-wide support for pressure to expel Iraq from Kuwait, and itself demonstrated a political influence and military capability second to none. By contrast, the economic foundations of the Soviet Union were revealed as extremely weak. The exclusive dependence of Soviet economic and political management on command structures produced inefficiency and malfunctioning on a near-catastrophic scale.

The Soviet Union as an international actor

Soviet economic growth had been impressive in the 1950s, and we were offered a rather exaggerated view (from the Soviet Union itself and from the outside world) of the general condition of the Soviet economy and its prospects. Despite 'minor problems', the Soviet Union was presented as forging a change in the international correlation of forces in favour of socialism. But the objective reality by the late 1980s was of a Soviet Union in deep economic and political crisis. Economic weakness and discrepancies between official statistics and reality, stemming from the lack of honesty and transparency, were exposed by *glasnost*. The new circumstances also revealed the lack of coherence inside the Soviet empire, raising doubts about the continued existence of a Soviet state. The standard cold war picture of the Soviet Union in the West, as a threatening and gloomy, politically stable and militarily strong communist state was revealed as largely fake. The Soviet Union has the potential for expanding its power, even in the economic field, but this was hardly the image it projected on the international stage in 1990.

It is difficult to argue that the main objective of Soviet foreign policy in the 1990s should be to maximise power, which realists in international studies consider as the goal of all major international actors. What we have seen, on the contrary, is a demonstration of the renunciation of power in order to protect the most vital factor in a self-help system – the survival of the Soviet Union as a unit in international politics. Assessments and interpretations of the Soviet role in world politics have had to be radically revised.

The question is: how can the Soviet Union, given its domestic difficulties, conform to the sound theoretical goals of state actors – namely, to preserve its sovereignty and enhance its autonomy, power and influence in the international system? To analyse, explain and predict Soviet foreign policy is of the utmost importance for Europe. On the one hand, Soviet foreign policy can be seen as a reaction to internal pressures and defections which threaten its position and power in the international system; and on the other hand, it can be seen as an attempt to cope with the effects of a transformation in the international structure.[3] How, then, can one best analyse Soviet policy?

A reasonable interpretation seems to be that there was a voluntary surrender, a capitulation without direct defeat, in a global East–West confrontation. Likewise the western position can be described as a victory achieved without coming to military blows. But how can one talk of 'victory' and 'surrender' if no real war has been fought? The answer –

that the cold war was something akin to a real war – is of crucial importance to the general argument of this chapter.[4] Adapting the Clausewitzian theoretical and analytical framework, one can interpret the cold war as a 'world war', based on polarisation and confrontation using all means, bar one, in order to throw the opponent to the ground. The exception was the specific use of military force to shed blood directly between the superpowers or their European allies. Bloodshed everywhere else was allowed. It is usually deduced that this was a consequence of the advent of nuclear weapons. Regarded as the ultimate weapons of mass destruction which could neither be used nor defended against, they were assigned political functions though were continually prepared for use.[5]

The cold war was fought by political, economic and military means but in important areas and circumstances was a non-violent 'war'. On the military side it involved provocative exercises and deployments, high alert states, wartime-oriented, centralised and integrated command structures among allied forces, provocative global strategies directed against the opponent and arms racing with considerable investment in the research and development of new weapon systems. The last of these was a key factor in ending the cold war. With SDI, the mere political decision to set up a comprehensive research programme, a new Manhattan project on an even larger scale, was sufficient to confound Soviet policy-makers, even though the United States itself could not afford to deploy it. The Soviet Union took up the challenge with limited means, and lost. In effect the technology revolution, manifested spectacularly in Japan's economic performance, forced the Soviet Union to surrender and reduce itself to a regional power – though with international aspirations and a superpower capability in the nuclear-military field.

In what sense can one speak of a surrender, even of an unconditional surrender? Quite simply, virtually all the most extensive American and western goals were complied with. The Soviet Union attempted to change its political, economic and military policies. Moreover, from 1985 to 1990 the Soviet leadership seemed to be genuinely aiming at a liberal, market-orientated economy through the initiatives of *perestroika*. Until the crackdown in the Baltic republics in January 1991, the Soviet Union had taken over practically all western international norms, such as freedom for the individual (human rights), the international rule of law, democracy more or less western style and the concept of global interdependence (taken over from a US policy of the late 1970s).[6] Although the concept of communism was still upheld, the one-party system was abolished, and a revival of dictatorship was less likely after the failed coup of August 1991.

With the Soviet Union yielding as a world model, what used to be called the Socialist Commonwealth, as an alternative to the capitalist world, ceased to exist. In the military area, what American hardliners could only fantasise about – a roll-back from Eastern Europe – was set in train and in the future this could be followed by looser control over the Baltic states and possibly other parts of the empire. The import of these geopolitical and geostrategic changes cannot be overestimated. The Soviet Union conceded German unity within NATO, most of the Soviet troops are expected to be out of Eastern Europe by 1994, and the Warsaw Pact languished as a paper organisation without military significance. By the early 1990s the Soviet Union had begun a comprehensive unilateral disarmament, and made one concession after another in accepting practically all western proposals in disarmament negotiations. Finally, although continuing to supply arms to Third World countries, the Soviet Union drastically scaled down its Third World activities, once considered to be a cause of confrontation and polarisation in the cold war. In practice the Soviet leadership accepted its former adversary's predominance, and lent diplomatic and military intelligence support to the anti-Iraq coalition in the Gulf war of 1991. The former East–West confrontation thus gave way to the prospect of a new order in which aggression would be met by collective security to protect international law and the sovereignty and integrity of states. These developments and the long-term structural trends in the international system have important implications for Europe.

Implications of the transformation

For Europe, freed from its pivotal role in the cold war, the so-called new order promised new possibilities. The superpowers had functioned, though in rather different ways, as pacifiers and managers within their spheres. In the West, although transatlantic relations have frequently been in disarray, a perception of common interests has survived and will be a decisive factor in the creation of the new Europe.[7] Indeed very few responsible, representative American, Soviet or European decision-makers would question the continued importance of the United States in Europe's future. At the same time there needs to be an understanding among the western powers not to exploit and push the Soviet Union too hard. They need to take into consideration fundamental Soviet interests which, not least for security reasons, impinge upon Europe. This has to be recognised not only for geostrategic reasons but also to avoid the emergence of a 'Versailles complex'. In the long run, western triumphalist claims will be considered humiliating and illegitimate by the Soviet Union.

In terms of power relations, Europe will operate within an international system based on a uni-power structure (with the United States as *primus inter pares*), a bi-power nuclear-military balance between the United States and the Soviet Union, and an economic reordering of the hierarchy of power. The last of these is being marked by the rise of Germany and Japan, by the Soviet Union's absolute decline, and by uncertainty about American economic strength. Within Europe, the power and leadership of the Federal Republic of Germany has been enlarged; the status of the Soviet Union has shrunk as it claims integration with the rest of Europe; and most East European states, strengthened politically by the adoption of democratic principles, seem doomed to economic subsistence. Possible continuities in the European power structure include the European Community states enlarging their common sovereignty through comprehensive political and economic integration, and the NATO states enlarging their regional and external security through comprehensive military and political co-operation.

In such a context, changes are to be expected in the policies of the main actors in Europe – the United States, Germany and the Soviet Union. What restraints and possibilities arise from their structural situations? They all have very specific positions; none of them is a 'normal' state.

Germany is unique, firstly because of the completeness of its defeat in war and its historical burden of identification with Nazism. Secondly, it derives advantages from its central position relative to its competitors on the periphery, France and the United Kingdom. Thirdly, Germany probably has the world's third largest economy, after the United States and Japan, and ahead of the Soviet Union (depending on which estimates for Soviet GNP one believes). Fourthly, irrespective of the fundamental security changes in Eastern and Central Europe, Germany will remain vitally important in the internal defence of Western Europe and in maintaining the NATO military balance with the Soviet Union. Finally, it is surrounded by territories dominated by German language and culture.

These unique features have a considerable influence on German policy, accentuating self-censorship and restraint. Any policies of German nationalism are internationally stigmatised, whereas nobody reacts with hostility to expressions of, say, British or French nationalism. Two approaches to this problem are being attempted in parallel, albeit in contradiction. By integration in the EC and NATO, Germany will be *eingebunden*, i.e. embedded, in order to ensure a European Germany. To avoid a German Europe the parallel approach is to restrain Germany through discrimination and singularisation in security policy. Germany's exceptional position in NATO is well known. There is no German general staff in the usual sense, and German combat forces are under NATO command. Organisationally Germany is more controlled than her NATO partners. This remains the case after reunification, the ending of occupation rights, and loosening of the German constitution to allow German forces to operate outside Europe. In the long run the concept of singularisation cannot form the basis of a sound policy, though Germany's NATO role will continue for some time in view of its unique strategic position. As discussed in the next chapter, implementation of a new NATO strategy to replace flexible response, and proposed organisational changes, such as the introduction of fully integrated divisions, will take at least five years.

Germany will continue to play a key role in the European policies of the United States and the Soviet Union. Germany's ambitions in the Second World War, and predicament afterwards, were incentives for the United States to abandon isolationism. Germany will be America's main European partner. The Soviet Union not only considered the Federal Republic as a platform for western confrontation policy during the cold war, but also perceived it as a real security threat. In the 1990s the Soviet Union will continue to watch Germany carefully for signs of recidivism, but in 1991 the Government of Helmut Kohl was the most anxious of the European governments not to allow the independence struggles of the Baltic republics to interfere with restructuring East–West relations. Germany, of course, will be the main European source of aid and investment for the Soviet Union and is likely to be much courted. But, as the French Foreign Minister noted in 1990: 'Her economic potential will be superior [to the French]. But her constraints will also be heavier.'[8]

Integration will stay firmly on the agenda, though it is unclear what the end result will be. Will Europe act as one unit, as a new great power? Or, perhaps more likely, will it continue to be dominated by nation-states operating in a co-operative network which requires some transfer of sovereignty? The result will depend on the international setting as well as on inter-European relations. These problems are surveyed in subsequent chapters. Here the future role of the superpowers is considered in the light of their unique positions *vis-à-vis* Europe.

The Soviet Union: shrinkage or resurgence?

Is the Soviet Union part of Europe? In spite of, or even because of, grim historical experiences, the Soviet Union will always place Europe in the centre of its foreign policy. But what is the Soviet Union's European policy? Apart from the structural considerations already discussed, there seem to be two main and contrasting interpretations: the 'continued shrinkage' interpretation, whereby the Soviet Union continues to adapt to its reduced role in world politics, and the 'attempted resurgence' interpretation, whereby the goal is to restore the bipolarity.

The 'resurgence' interpretation emphasises the Soviet objective of returning to the world stage as a complete superpower. This assumes that it can gain time to benefit from a revived economic base. According to this view Soviet military leaders have a vision of a modern defence establishment like NATO's – 'leaner and meaner'. Based on cool calculation the Soviet Union realised that global polarisation was unfavourable to its interests. It was confronted by too many adversaries, not only the western allies but also in East Asia and the Middle East. Also, Eastern Europe's economic ineffectiveness and political illegitimacy became increasingly burdensome to the Soviet Union. The only sensible policy was to turn opponents into partners and collaborators. This could be done by a gigantic international striptease show in which the Soviet Union presented itself as more peace-loving than ever, divesting itself of military strength, a threat to nobody. The Soviet Union is nevertheless modernising its nuclear arsenal. In the long run, relieved of the burden of Eastern Europe, it will take its place in the mature nuclear age, when these weapons have even less military importance but remain politically significant.

Maybe the show has already had an effect. An old Soviet dream, modernised in the Gorbachev concept of a Common European Home, could in the foreseeable future create a situation where, if the Americans leave Europe, a new strong grouping emerges, the Soviet Union–Europe with the Soviet Union being the potential hegemon. The neo-realist, Kenneth Waltz, made the following prediction in 1979 in accord with this interpretation:

> The emergence of a united Europe would shift the structure in international politics from bi-to tri-polarity . . . A newly united Europe and the Soviet Union would be the weaker of the three great powers. In self-help systems external forces propel the weaker parties toward one another. Weaker parties, our theory predicts, incline to combine to offset the strength of the stronger. The Soviet Union would work for that result,

> and Europe would benefit because weaker parties pay more for support that is given . . . The Soviet Union and the new Europe would cooperate in ways that we [the USA] would find unpleasant.[9]

The 'continued shrinkage' interpretation arrives, however, at a somewhat different conclusion (though using the same broad theoretical approach). Faced by a choice between competition or copying, the Soviet Union took its weak position into account and chose emulation. Western social, economic and institutional norms are copied. However, the paradox for Gorbachev and his successors is that in a country with vast resources and economic potential, they operate an internal structure different from that of other empires in history – namely one consisting of an economically weak centre and a stronger periphery.

Indeed the focus is now on the ability of the Soviet Union to survive as a unit in the international system, the most sacred goal of a state. The threats are not external but internal, affecting the unity of the state, the coherence of society, government legitimacy and, fundamentally, the condition of the economy.

For these reasons the Soviet Union desperately seeks co-operation with the United States and Western Europe on western terms. It has nothing to do with an earlier concept of a superpower condominium. The Soviet Union aims to reassure the West and be rewarded. But it realises that if there is a Soviet future, it will depend mainly on Europe simply because of geographical contiguity. The idea of the Common European Home is more a signal than an exact concept, though none the less important as an indication of fundamental changes in Soviet European policy. The signal is an invitation to accept the closest possible co-operation.

These changes are convincing, for although Gorbachev acted repressively in the republics to maintain the Union, he condemned former interventions in Europe, halted coercion abroad and abandoned the traditional anti-EC posture. Moreover, the Moscow leadership has not pursued a policy of getting the United States out of Europe. Although the Soviet Union makes continuing references to its Asian connections, Europe, *with* American involvement, is considered the most important arena for ensuring its survival and economic recovery. The Soviet Union's demonstrable weakness means that it has to accept a new European structure, whereas the United States is allowed to play a role of its own choice relatively unconstrained by the Soviet Union.

As to the possibility of hidden Soviet intentions to lure European states into a zone of Soviet dominance, maybe they exist as a long-term goal. But such a goal seems remote from the reality of the new international structure. The Soviet Union aims to be a European power, not in order to dominate but in order to adapt and integrate. It favours the CSCE regime as the best framework for giving it the European role which is necessary for security and economic reasons. There are clear indications that the Soviet Union perceives itself as a genuine European power and not just as an external controlling power like the United States. At the CSCE meetings the Soviet delegations emphasised what they called a single European area in legal, humanitarian, cultural, economic and environmental issues. The Soviet Union expressed an eagerness to seek 'practical ways of building a peaceful, democratic and united Europe'.[10] This is not possible without American co-operation, even though in the Soviet conception the United States cannot be integrated into a united Europe. The Soviet Union projects itself as the natural partner to the rest of Europe, as a non-threatening balancer, a partner trading energy for technology, a nation which has decided, in the words of Gorbachev, 'to return to the mainstream of civilisation'.

The 1990s will show if the 'attempted resurgence' or the 'continued shrinkage' interpretation will be the correct one. The former would imply a return to cold war bi-power structures. In line with this chapter's predictions of a 'one-plus-four' power world, probably followed by a multi-power world, the 'continued shrinkage' scenario is considered the more likely of the two.

The United States: a pacifier in Europe?

The position of the United States is, for obvious reasons, quite different. Western Europe is still a zone of American dominance in the sense that the United States is the unchallenged leader of the Atlantic alliance. The Western European states will still need an alliance offering military guarantees, given the Soviet Union's military capability. Unable to act as a unit, they will still require a 'pacifier' – as Joseph Joffe terms it – to regulate and organise competition between the powers of Europe.[11]

The question is whether the West European states will fundamentally change their internal organisation from an anarchic into a functional, hierarchical structure, i.e. to continue to operate as equal, similar units or to specialise and completely restructure the units. From the beginning of the cold war the United States pleaded for restructuring. Regardless of predictions about an emerging European superpower overtaking American world leadership, US policy has consistently supported comprehensive European integration. No doubt this reflects confidence in the American model, but it also reflects a confidence that pooling resources would facilitate transatlantic co-operation. A united Europe would produce a fairer solution to the pertinent problem of burdensharing.

The need to create an image of an Atlantic community with a common destiny and common values in opposition to aggressive, oppressive, expansionist evil forces in the international system, was a factor in America's avoidance of a simple divide-and-rule concept *vis-à-vis* Western Europe. Obviously the declaratory enthusiasm for extended European integration can be interpreted as a necessary and wise response to the declaratory policies of the leading European states, recognising full integration as the ultimate goal, but at the same time appreciating that the goal is more ideal than real.

However, the strongest reasons for arguing that the US role in Europe will continue are:

- Europe is still important in American forward defence. By early 1990 Congress realised that there had been an overstretch of its military power and that foreign bases and defence spending could be curtailed in line with the reduced Soviet threat. The huge and costly imbroglio in the Middle East and the effort to restore Kuwait's sovereignty, as well as the proposed CFE cuts, will reduce the American military presence in Europe, perhaps to between 50,000 and 100,000 troops. But the war against Iraq demonstrated the importance in American military and political thinking of having a European base to call upon. Naturally, any deterrent to a Soviet use of force such as an attempt, however unlikely, to re-establish Soviet control over former Eastern Europe (or over newly-established independent countries emerging from a dissolution of the Soviet Union) must have its base in the European arena.
- The United States remains pre-eminent. Although there are three emerging rival centres, with actual as well as perceived potential to threaten the United States economically, none of them can pose as an alternative to US leadership. In spite of its economic and technological prowess, Japan will not have the status in the international system to play any significant global, political or military role in the foreseeable future. Germany will be in a similarly restrained position. Despite far-reaching integration, the EC will have the fundamental deficiency of not being a sovereign unit in the international system.[12] The United States remains the only power with global range and presence in all political, military and economic realms, though its ability to meet the long-term costs of the Gulf war may be in doubt.
- The United States requires Europe's support. The Bush Administration increasingly spoke of sharing the burden of world leadership

with its closest allies and therefore will continue to stress its position in Europe. Although the European powers (or an emerging European bloc) will be mainly regionally oriented, the Middle East crisis reminded Europeans that there continue to be interests outside Europe which can be best tackled in co-operation with the United States, though distrust of American diplomacy was expressed by Germany, France, Spain and Italy in promoting separate talks with Iraq before the war began.

- A European–American community in values remains intact. Although the United States and Europe have many divergent interests and the United States–EC relationship has been characterised by bitter and harsh competition resulting in trade wars, there exists a common ground of democratic, capitalist and pluralistic values unequalled in the relations between other corresponding units in the international system.[13] However, the early days of the cold war, when the United States acted as the hegemon, using the Marshall Plan as an important political tool, have long gone. A repetition of the Marshall Plan, dispensed to the Soviet Union and Eastern Europe to reward and strengthen liberal and pluralistic values, is not a realistic possibility. The United States is no longer the economic power it was, and is likely to be reduced further by the Gulf war. Besides, the United States may have 'missed the boat' to underpin Soviet liberalism, a danger demonstrated when Gorbachev was briefly deposed by hardliners in August 1991.

Although alternative security systems are possible, one which envisages a continued American presence in, and American impact upon, European affairs should be judged as most probable.

Conclusion: Europe and the new international structure

The role of the superpowers in Europe has been transformed. Only one superpower remains, the Soviet Union withdrawing to leave Eastern European countries to determine their own destinies. The Soviet Union remains a formidable military power, though it has shown no inclination to use it externally. But, weak in economic, political and ethnic cohesion, the Soviet Union has assumed the role of a regional power and, in seeking European integration, the Soviet Union has become a supplicant. As indicated in the final chapter, the struggle for power within the Soviet Union and the implications of a hardline reversion to isolation, or of a regime collapse, give cause for great anxiety. A key difficulty for the rest of Europe is to understand the Soviet Union's security problems, external as well as internal, in order to avoid creating a 'Versailles complex'.

As the remaining superpower and leader of NATO, the role of the

United States has not ceased, as one might imagine, as a consequence of a vanishing enemy. For Europe one important question will be whether the United States, still functioning as a guarantor of European military security, will extend its military deterrence to include East European countries – as hoped for by Poland, Czechoslovakia and Hungary. Extended deterrence will continue to be a very delicate problem, and no-one expects a situation to arise which will put the matter to the test. The United States may leave some military and political role for the Soviet Union, assuming Soviet policy-makers do not fundamentally violate the terms of the CFE Treaty and the CSCE accords. A continued American presence would benefit the whole of Europe including the Soviet Union, not least in upholding a regime in which Europe can be comfortable with the stronger Germany.

Europe also has to adapt to a transition in the international system, which might include having to take on a more global role. As stated by Kenneth Waltz, the transformation from a multi-power to a bi-power system in the 1940s 'created a situation that permitted wider ranging and more effective cooperation among the states of Western Europe. They became consumers of security.'[14] In other words a new situation arose where it was possible to work effectively for European unity, even though this was difficult to achieve. The fundamental change was the end of conflict among the Western European states. Competition between them continues, of course, not least in the EC, as might be expected in an organisation which still functions in many respects as a self-help system. There are differing policies on integration and unity, betraying strong national interests. However, the policies of Western European states amount to more than EC policy, and in many ways the emerging international structure will enhance European integration. Building on German unification, the development of a 'one-plus-four' system could in theory encourage further pan-European co-operation to tackle the non-military security issues which confront the continent.

Notes

1 See Joseph S. Nye Jr., 'American strategy after bipolarity', *International Affairs*, LXVI, no. 3, July 1990, pp. 513–21; Michael Cox, 'Whatever happened to the "second" cold war? Soviet–American relations: 1980–1988', *Review of International Studies*, XVI, no. 2, pp. 155–72; Francis Fukuyama, 'The end of history?', *National Interest*, no. 16, Summer 1989, pp. 4ff.

2 For a survey of the decline controversy, see 'Introduction – the debate on decline',

in Michael C. Pugh and Phil Williams (eds.), *Superpower Politics: Change in the United States and the Soviet Union*, Manchester, Manchester University Press, 1990, pp. 1–8.

3 The description of Soviet developments is primarily derived from the official statements of President Mikhail Gorbachev and Foreign Minister Eduard Shevardnadze.

4 For further elaboration see Bertel Heurlin, 'Sovjetunionens frivillige kapitulation' ['The voluntary surrender of the Soviet Union'], in Morten Kelstrup (ed.), *Nyere tendenser i politologien III*, Copenhagen, 1990, pp. 71–100. See also Peter Sager, *Der politische Krieg. Die reale Gefahr*, Bern, 1985; Charles Reynolds, *The Politics of War: A Study of the Rationality of Violence in Inter-state Relations*, New York, Harvester Wheatsheaf, 1989.

5 Steve Weber argues that 'the widespread deployment of these weapons led to nuclear deterrence, a system-wide condition that does constitute a particular kind of structural change', 'Realism, détente, and nuclear weapons', *International Organization*, XXXXIV, no. 1, Winter 1990, pp. 55–81.

6 See 'The Global 2000 report to the President of the United States. Entering the 21st century: a report prepared by the Council on Environment Quality and the Department of State', I–II, New York, 1980.

7 Among important analyses of the US–European relationship, see Jack Snyder, 'Averting anarchy in the new Europe', *International Security*, IV, Spring 1990, pp. 5–41; Robert E. Hunter, 'The future of European security', *Washington Quarterly*, Autumn 1990, pp. 55ff; Glenn Palmer, 'Corralling the free rider: deterrence and the Western Alliance', *International Studies Quarterly*, XXXIV, 1990, pp. 147–64.

8 In Lawrence Freedman (ed.), *Europe Transformed: Documents on the End of the Cold War*, London, Tri-Service Press, 1990, p. 467.

9 Kenneth N. Waltz, *Theory of International Politics*, Reading, Mass., Addison-Wesley, 1979, p. 202.

10 Eduard Shevardnadze, speech at CSCE meeting, 1 October 1990, text from the Soviet Embassy, Copenhagen, p. 3.

11 Joseph Joffe, *The Limited Partnership: Europe, the United States, and the Burdens of Alliance*, Cambridge, Mass., Ballinger, 1987.

12 See Pierre Hassner, 'Europe beyond partition and unity: disintegration or reconstitution?', *International Affairs*, LXVI, no. 3, 1990, pp. 461–75.

13 The idea that the United States had no comparable interest in the Third World was argued (before the Gulf war) by Stephen Van Evera, 'Why Europe matters, why the Third World doesn't: American grand strategy after the cold war', *Journal of Strategic Studies*, XIII, no. 2, June 1990, pp. 1–51.

14 Waltz, *Theory of International Politics*, p. 70.

3 William Park

Political change and NATO strategy

The cold war offered NATO an unusually clear-cut, unambiguous military threat from the Soviet Union and its allies. Now, the quite phenomenal political transformations within the Warsaw Pact in recent years are threatening to deny NATO its *raison d'être*, and have raised the core question of whether it will be possible, desirable or necessary to sustain NATO – at least in something approximating to its present form. Does an alliance need a threat? Part of NATO's official retort to this question, according to the 'London Declaration on a Transformed North Atlantic Alliance' which emanated from the meeting of the North Atlantic Council of 5–6 July 1990, is to stress the intention to enhance its 'political component'.[1] But what of its military component?

The problem of change and NATO's fragile consensus

Although the cold war has been pronounced dead even in the most respectable circles, what is to replace it remains unclear. In the wake of the Gulf war it clearly cannot be automatically assumed that any comparably stable, predictable, ordered system of international relationships must inevitably supersede the relatively crystalline, if unpleasant, simplicities of the last forty years. It is also not clear whether the Middle East conflict will have a lasting impact on NATO's military preparations. We are in a transitional period, from which the new shape is yet to emerge. Indeed, a 'shape' as such may not emerge, and we could be in for a prolonged, messy, and even violent period of turbulence. In any case, Soviet capabilities are still formidable, and Gorbachev is not immortal, politically or otherwise.

Be this as it may, in the current climate the maintenance of NATO's military and doctrinal status quo is proving to be impossible and indeed undesirable. Impossible, because the political pressures for a so-called 'peace dividend' are irresistible in political democracies observing genuine reductions in the capacity of the Soviet Union to spring large-scale military surprises and the clear disappearance of any immediate aggressive intent. Undesirable, because negotiated and unilateral cuts in force levels, and a readiness to shift towards more defensive, less provocative strategic concepts, constitute useful levers in the endeavour to encourage threat reduction and desirable political change. However, the intellectual and political problems involved in the responsive military reform of NATO are formidable. Identifying the desirability of moving away from forward defence, flexible response or a high reliance on nuclear weapons is relatively easy. Outlining what it is that NATO should move towards, or even is moving towards, is a far more complex task. Maintaining strategic coherence whilst managing an orderly shift from the old to some new posture is already proving problematic for NATO's political, military, and strategic review committees which have been tasked to devise a new strategic formulation.

Participatory alliances cannot avoid some degree of fuzziness, of incoherence even, where their military preparations are concerned. This is because. in an alliance of sixteen sovereign states, harmony will be more easily achieved towards the lowest common denominator, or where agreements are vague or obligations weak. NATO is a 'bottom-up' rather than a 'top-down' organisation, and politics are dominant. Thus, flexible response should be seen as a political compromise, as a device to paper over cracks, at least as much as it is a military strategy. This duality explains why, in 1983, Robert McNamara was able to note that: 'The substantial raising of the "nuclear threshold" as was envisaged when "flexible response" was first conceived, has not become a reality.'[2] It is also why, in the same year, the then Supreme Allied Commander (SACEUR), General Bernard Rogers, characterised NATO's operational, as distinct from declaratory, strategy as akin to the 'trip wire' it was supposed to have replaced.[3] The adoption of flexible response did not produce increased conventional force levels, it intensified anxieties about the credibility of the US nuclear umbrella, and it failed to clarify the role of battlefield and theatre nuclear weapons deployed in Europe.

In more recent years, unease concerning the place of nuclear weapons in NATO strategy had deepened still further, most crucially in the Federal Republic of Germany. One author has cited 'a growing sense of concern about the risks and costs associated with the traditional transatlantic bargain'.[4] Another has detected a 'specter of denuclearisation', ultimately traceable to the emergence of strategic nuclear parity between the superpowers during the 1960s, as 'haunting Europe'. He asserts that: 'The fabric of flexible response has frayed over the years because its underlying logic is weak; it is periodically patched and propped up because nothing better is able to replace it.'[5] Such assessments are fairly typical. In other words, Gorbachev came to power at a time when the consensus which had underpinned NATO's strategic posture was perhaps facing its most severe challenge for two decades, when the policy of 'patching and propping up' was arguably approaching its nemesis. As a result, such military changes projected in NATO for the 1990s stem not simply and crudely from the need to respond to the remarkable turnaround associated with Gorbachev's initiatives and 'new thinking', but rather from their interaction with an underlying internal erosion of NATO's status quo.

Thus, even before 1985, we were already witnessing the emergence of a range of trends, proposals, and policies reflecting some dissatisfaction with the existing state of affairs. For example, there was a renewed interest in enhanced West European self-reliance in security matters, as symbolised by: the resuscitation in 1984 of the Western European Union (WEU) and the efforts to improve Franco-German defence co-operation through, for example, the creation of the Franco-German brigade; the proliferation of ideas for non-nuclear, defensive defence; the intensification of traditional American interest in mobile, 'offensive' warfare to exploit the West's presumed technological advantage (often presented as a means to raise the nuclear threshold, and to make up for the conventional force level shortfall); more calls for, and attempts at, an improvement in NATO's conventional force capabilities; and London and Paris maintaining and even strengthening their determination to possess credible, nationally-owned nuclear deterrents. Perhaps above all we should not forget the series of domestic political crises associated with the 'neutron bomb' debate of the late 1970s and the deployment of Cruise and Pershing II missiles in the early 1980s. These shook the defence establishments and undermined political consensus. In short, the western strategic landscape in which we must locate the changes associated with the Gorbachev era was already fragile.

Nuclear dilemmas in the wake of the INF Treaty

The signing of the Intermediate-Range Nuclear Forces (INF) Treaty in December 1987 did more than eliminate all US and Soviet land-based nuclear missiles with ranges of between 500 and 5,500 kilometres. It also weakened what had come to be regarded as a central tenet of NATO's strategy of flexible response, and in so doing threatened still further the broad strategic consensus within NATO. It served to focus attention on those nuclear systems of less than 500 kilometre range – the majority of which were deployed in or would, if used, fall on one or other of East and West Germany. It skewed NATO's tactical nuclear arsenal towards the shorter range in precisely the opposite direction from that sought by Bonn. In particular, for Germans of all political persuasions, one consequence of the INF Treaty was that it represented a shift towards so-called 'singularity' – that is, away from an equal sharing of risks within the alliance and towards a disproportionate burdening of Germany with those risks. Certainly, by leaving NATO with fewer options between the use of short-range battlefield nuclear weapons on the one hand, and general strategic nuclear response on the other, the effect was to de-couple in some degree the United States from the European battlefield.

The story behind the INF Treaty reveals how arms control processes can develop their own, quite irresistible, internal dynamics. Having proposed the removal of the missiles in the Brezhnev era, NATO could hardly spurn Moscow's unanticipated acceptance in the Gorbachev era. Yet the logic which had required that the missiles be installed in the first place did not disappear with the missiles themselves. As a result of the treaty, NATO now felt itself to be so exposed as to warrant the consideration of the deployment of a variety of air- and sea-launched nuclear systems to seek to make up for the gap left behind by the withdrawal of Cruise and Pershing missiles from Europe. On the other hand, Bonn now felt itself to be so exposed, both to anti-nuclear sentiment among its own electorate and to nuclear 'singularity', that it began drifting inexorably towards the so-called 'third zero' option, the elimination of the short-range systems deployed so predominantly on its own territory.

What followed, therefore, were intense and not infrequently acrimonious discussions within NATO on the modernisation of nuclear weapons. Not surprisingly, Germany led the way in arguing for early talks on the 'third zero' option, or at least for deep reductions in short-range nuclear force levels. Although Foreign Minister Hans-Dietrich Genscher acquired a high profile on this stance, it had support across the German political spectrum and not least from the right. The Belgian and Dutch Governments took similar positions. The American, British, and French Governments tended to see in this the whiff of de-nuclearisation and neutrality. In public at least, the British took the most uncompromising stand, and were disinclined to accept even the principle of negotiations on the short-range nuclear forces (SNF), let alone countenance their eventual complete elimination. Whereas Bonn sought to downplay the 1983 Montebello commitment to, and any immediate necessity for, nuclear modernisation, London regarded an early decision on modernisation as essential both to stop the rot of de-nuclearisation and because the maintenance of a whole range of nuclear capabilities was seen as essential for the preservation of flexible response and nuclear deterrence.

As time passed, however, Washington moved in the direction of a compromise position which accepted the principle of SNF talks, but which sought to delay them until sufficient progress had been made at the Vienna talks on conventional forces in Europe (CFE). In addition, any SNF talks would aim at reductions rather than elimination. Furthermore, although development work on modernised SNF systems could continue, there was no immediate need to set a date or deadline for their deployment. This in fact was the compromise reached at the Brussels summit of NATO heads of government in May 1989. It was widely interpreted as presaging a shift by Bush towards the German perspective, and indeed just twelve months later Bush had moved still further towards Bonn's inclinations. The political and strategic landscape had, in that short time, been transformed by the revolutions in Eastern Europe; the real and even imminent prospect of German unification; the continuing progress in Vienna and at the Strategic Arms Reductions (START) negotiations; the increasing fragility of the Soviet domestic political and economic system; the remarkable improvement in East–West relations all round, and the agreed withdrawal of Soviet forces from Eastern Europe.

By May 1990 President George Bush felt able to announce the cancellation of the follow-on-to-Lance (FOTL) programme to develop a ground-launched nuclear missile. This missile would have had a range of about 300 miles and would have been fired from dual-capable Multiple Launch Rocket Systems (MLRS) already being deployed in Europe. It was being developed in accordance with the 1983 Montebello Agreement to continue to modernise NATO's nuclear capability, and specifically as a successor to the shorter range (seventy miles) and less accurate Lance missile, which it is anticipated will have to be scrapped by the mid-1990s. Bush also announced the cancellation of further modernisation of US nuclear artillery shells in Europe. The majority of these shells, which numerically form the bulk of NATO's SNF capability in Europe, have a range of around fifteen miles, are relatively inaccurate, and in some instances have inappropriate yields. A modernisation programme has, however, been under way in the wake of the Montebello Agreement, and there are some hundreds of newer thirty-mile range and more accurate shells already deployed.[6]

In addition, President Bush expressed his willingness to enter into SNF arms control talks as soon as a CFE agreement was signed. The western proposal covers land-based systems only, and will thus exclude air-based nuclear warheads. However, given reports that the German and Dutch Governments sought to persuade Washington to withdraw the nuclear artillery shells unilaterally,[7] given too that the July 1990 London summit declared NATO's readiness to eliminate all nuclear artillery shells from Europe, and given reports that Moscow is willing to eliminate all nuclear artillery capabilities, including those located in the Soviet Union and the United States,[8] there is now a genuine possibility that SNF will eventually disappear as an element in NATO's overall force structure. In any case, the imminent obsolescence of the bulk of NATO's nuclear artillery shells could leave the Alliance with land-based short-range systems numbering no more than a few hundred, and no medium- and longer-range systems. Although the French, outside the military structure of NATO and thus not bound by NATO's collective decisions on force deployments and arms control, are to go ahead with deployment of their 480-kilometre-range land-based Hades nuclear missile, Paris has announced that the eventual deployment will be less than the 80–120 originally envisaged.[9]

The TASM issue

These decisions point to the proposed tactical air-to-surface missile (TASM) as the major element of NATO's future nuclear posture in the European theatre. These would replace the approximately 1,400 nuclear gravity bombs, soon to be phased out because of their obsolescence and the likely toll of NATO's manned bomber force in encountering the Soviet Union's air defences. The missile, with a range of around 240 miles, would be required to suppress the Soviet air defences, to destroy air bases, and to target Command, Control, Communications and Intelligence (C^3I) installations – roles similar to those for which Cruise and Pershing missiles had been earmarked. It was partly for this reason that the TASM issue was put before NATO's Nuclear Planning Group at its meeting in Scheveningen in October 1988, and partly for the same reason that it caused controversy there. The Belgians led the way in arguing that, given that the ink on the INF Treaty had not yet had time to dry, it was too soon to be considering the deployment of systems which were bound to be seen as alternatives to the Cruise and Pershing missiles. There was also an assumption that those countries which had been ready to host INF – Belgium, the Netherlands, the United Kingdom, West Germany, and Italy – might also be expected to take the aircraft allocated to deliver TASMs. However, any such deployment would be bound to raise a domestic political storm in most if not all of these locations. Hence, although Washington had taken the decision to press on with the development of the system, the decision to deploy TASM in Europe was deferred.

The TASM deployment issue became the most sensitive confronting NATO planners, and it was made more sensitive by the decision to cease modernisation of ground-based SNF. NATO's future as a nuclear-capable alliance could rest on the deployment of TASM, for which the position of Germany has become crucial. Thus far, most of the indications are that Bonn is reluctant to upset either its own electorate or Moscow by agreeing to TASM deployment on German soil. As a result, the atmosphere at the North Atlantic Council gathering at Turnberry, Scotland, in June 1990, was marred by unmistakable German discomfort at British Prime Minister Margaret Thatcher's contention that effective deterrence required TASM deployment in Germany. And although the London Summit the following month committed the Alliance to 'maintain for the foreseeable future an appropriate mix of nuclear and conventional forces, based in Europe, and kept up to date where necessary', no deployment decision was made. Indeed, there were reports that NATO was considering the possibility of storing TASMs in the United States in peacetime, and deploying them to Europe in times of crisis only.[10] In October 1990, congressional leaders signalled that they did not regard TASM development with any particular urgency by almost halving the Administration's funding request for the project.[11]

By early 1991, the balance of assessment seemed to be that a German agreement to take TASMs was unlikely. The same could well be true of Belgium and the Netherlands. This would render full deployment of the planned 450 TASMs improbable.[12] In addition to any American systems which may eventually appear in Europe, France has already begun deploying its own TASM. The British Government, too, is seeking to acquire TASMs under national control to replace its ageing stock of free-fall nuclear bombs. The American system appears to be the option preferred by the Royal Air Force owing to its longer range, but there have also been discussions with the French covering the possibility of jointly developing a long-range missile.

An additional option for the modernisation of NATO's nuclear capability is the dedication of sea-based cruise missiles to SACEUR. Such systems would have the advantage of low visibility as far as problematic western electorates are concerned, and although some might argue they would be contrary to the 'spirit' of the INF Treaty, like TASMs they would not be contrary to its letter, which was to ban the deployment of land-based systems only. A further attraction of the sea-based deterrent derives from the vulnerability of the air bases which would host the TASM-equipped aircraft. As a result of all these factors, the possibility of some form of sea-based alternative has been under consideration for some time now. Although the idea of a NATO force of surface vessels carrying nuclear missiles has been mooted[13] – echoes here of the Multilateral Force concept of the early 1960s – the most likely form of such a force would be US surface or sub-surface vessels equipped with Tomahawk cruise missiles. A figure of 200 such missiles has been suggested and it has been admitted that agreement is already in place to hand over control of the missiles to SACEUR in a period of tension.[14] Given the likely peacetime presence of US sea-based nuclear systems in or around NATO waters anyway, such an arrangement would avoid the political controversy which would probably result from a public, peacetime and permanent assignment of such a missile force to SACEUR.

The kind of strategic rationale which could be developed to explain and justify any future Europe-based NATO nuclear capability will to some degree depend on the form it takes. The emphasis would have been moved back towards delivery systems with longer reach, the size of the force would be smaller than it has been hitherto, there would be relatively little or no forward basing of nuclear weapons, fewer dual-key arrangements and more direct American control, and a severe reduction or complete elimination of NATO-dedicated land-launched systems. The detailed configuration of the force will depend on the arms control process, the outcome of the TASMs deployment debate, and the form any sea-based dedication might take. It is unlikely that such a force would reflect the preferences of NATO's military planners, who would surely prefer a fuller and more diverse array of systems, a higher numerical total, greater survivability, and a more evenly distributed pattern of deployment.[15] For similar reasons, NATO's likely future arsenal of nuclear weapons will not please flexible response purists, who believe the efficacy of deterrence rests on the capacity to conduct a protracted, controlled escalation passing through a number of stages before general nuclear response is arrived at. It might especially irritate those resentful of the need to tailor military preparations to special German political sensitivities.

On the other hand, it should satisfy those who believe in existential deterrence, particularly in circumstances of reduced Soviet threat, provided some kind of linkage with the US strategic nuclear arsenal is preserved. It should stand a greater chance of being accepted by those sections of western electorates who disapprove of over-visible nuclear weapons deployments, and dislike talk of nuclear war fought in their own homelands or of targeting new-found friends in Eastern Europe. The London Summit declaration that nuclear forces should be 'truly weapons of last resort' will have laid the groundwork. The planned use of nuclear weapons will be deemed to be later than has generally been the case so far, and the targets will be further away. The force, whatever form it finally takes, will be regarded as compatible with the requirements of 'minimum deterrence' or 'war avoidance' in a situation of reduced threat. It has in fact been reported that MC 14/3 will be rewritten as MC 14/4, and presented as a modification of flexible response – a term which is literally difficult to disapprove of but which has acquired a cold war, nuclear age connotation – a modification already promised by the London Declaration.[16]

A conventional threat?

Because nuclear weapons had also functioned as substitutes for NATO's presumed conventional force inferiority in Europe, the INF Treaty had the additional effect of refocusing attention on to the conventional balance. Seeing, realistically, that there was little prospect of a substantial improvement of NATO's forces, many now turned to détente generally and to the Conventional Forces in Europe (CFE) talks in Vienna specifically, in the hope that Warsaw Pact levels could be brought down to approximate those in the West. On this score, the omens looked better than at any time since the advent of the cold war. This tendency was again particularly marked in Germany, where it served to reinforce the existing policy of preserving intra-German détente against external buffeting, and where the frustration and unease at the nature and depth of the American commitment to Europe was at its most marked.

Even this early post-INF thrust towards further détente was dramatically bypassed by the events of 1989. The very likelihood of any NATO resort to the use of nuclear weapons through conventional force inferiority has been massively reduced anyway by the collapse of the forward-based threat of surprise attack on the inner-German border, and also on the eastern border of united Germany. In the future, NATO will be able to plan for a much longer warning time of Soviet attack, and a numerically less formidable adversary.

Thus, to complete the emerging picture of NATO's new military posture, we need now to turn to current thinking with respect to the Alliance's conventional force preparations. This thinking is being driven by more substantial developments than a mere change in threat perception and atmosphere. The US–Soviet agreement early in 1990 that the two superpowers should reduce to 195,000 troops each in the central treaty area – a remarkable achievement in itself – was in effect bypassed by Moscow's pledge to withdraw all its troops from Eastern Europe; by the agreements already signed to withdraw Soviet troops from Hungary and Czechoslovakia; by the reunification of Germany, which led to the dismantling of the East German Army and the pledged withdrawal of Soviet troops from the former GDR by the end of 1994; by the CFE agreement to cut Warsaw Pact–NATO tank levels to 20,000 each, requiring the Pact to reduce by around two-thirds; by the agreement that no one country should account for more than 33·7 per cent of its alliance's total of tanks; and by the projected partial withdrawal of British and American troops from continental Europe as a result of new budget cuts.

In any case, the Warsaw Pact has ceased to function as a military alliance. There is also continuing consideration in Moscow of still deeper cuts into the defence sector, and a real prospect of an eventual switch to an all-volunteer force. If the CFE process goes to a second stage, it will explore the requirements of defensive, or territorial defence, and will seek to produce cuts in the armed forces of the smaller allied states. But CFE began looking superfluous, as both NATO and, to a greater extent, the Warsaw Pact implemented unilateral reductions in defence spending and capabilities in 1990. The terms of German unification, which abolish the East German armed forces and limit those of a united Germany to 370,000, also have a substantial impact here.

In effect, the threat of a surprise attack along the lines formerly envisaged, has disappeared, as General John Galvin among others has himself conceded.[17] By the mid-1990s it is clear that there will be no Soviet troops in Eastern Europe. It is also evident that East European states will for the most part either be acquiring a neutral or semi-neutral status. They have been clamouring to join western institutions, including NATO. Eastern Europe will have become an active or passive barrier through which Soviet forces would have to move to launch an attack on the West. Barring a major political reversal or crisis in Moscow, the prospect of such an attack looks absurdly unlikely. Of course, the threat, in the form of capabilities, has not receded to anything like the same degree on the flanks, and especially in the North. But the flanks are a less likely target of aggressive action if there is little scope for more or less simultaneously taking the war to the European centre. On the other hand, as Turkey's role as a forward base in the Gulf war indicated, the southern flank blurs into a region which could involve NATO in meeting out-of-area threats. This then is the background, the 'threat', against which NATO's conventional forces are to be restructured.

A reorganisation of defence

Defence reorganisation is not an easy task, not least because actual, planned and contemplated unilateral defence cuts are already threatening to deny NATO's military planners the capabilities properly to implement even their scaled-down proposals to put NATO's defences on to a new footing. Throughout NATO, politicians and electorates are finding it difficult to give priority to military reform. Nevertheless, proposals are being considered at Strategic Headquarters, Allied Powers Europe (SHAPE), and a future outline which takes into account a reduced peacetime presence and a lower state of readiness is beginning to emerge. The removal of the forward threat from Warsaw Pact forces will permit NATO, in the words of the London Summit communiqué, to 'prepare a new Allied military strategy moving away from "forward defence", where appropriate, towards a reduced forward presence'. The smaller NATO forces which will emerge from CFE, German unification, and unilateral defence cutbacks, will be spread more thinly across the area to be defended. This will put a premium on mobility, and on surveillance and intelligence.

Once Soviet forces have finally departed from Eastern Germany, the extension eastwards of NATO will comprise a German corps, despite anxieties that this would be unacceptable to NATO and would be provocative to the Soviet Union. The notion that a German-only presence to the east of the former inner-German border would probably be as unwelcome to Germany as it would be to Poland and the Soviet Union, proved unfounded. In May 1991 NATO Defence Ministers decided, also, to create forces based as far as possible on multinational units integrated at the lowest practicable level.[18] Even if, as seems intended, nationally-based army divisions combine to form multinational corps,[19] the history of the European Defence Community in the 1950s, and the limited progress made by the Franco-German Brigade in the 1980s, advise caution. In addition to the obvious problems of language and command, NATO would have to make substantially more progress in the future than it has done in the past with respect to common funding, standardisation and interoperability, if multinational forces are to be militarily viable. On this issue, it seems certain that military logic could clash with political commitment, for it is the latter which is driving these developments. As one senior NATO defence planner has put it, multinational forces 'have considerable political value as symbols of the cohesion, solidarity and interdependence of the Alliance'.[20] On the other hand, the political difficulties should not be underestimated either, particularly in the light of the call by the Secretary-General of the Western European Union, Willem van Eekelen, that multinational units should be based in more than one country.[21] The Germans appeared to have taken this suggestion to heart, but the French are known not to be keen to play host to such units.[22] In fact, the most likely outcome is that such 'multinationality' as emerges from NATO's current deliberations will be located no lower than divisional level, and even then that it will be implemented only in crisis and war.

Six multinational corps will be located roughly speaking in the forward defence areas of 'West Germany'. A Rapid Reaction Corps would be deployed (70,000 men under British command), which could have contingency arrangements for multinational planning, and could even form the basis of a NATO reserve force for use on the flanks or out of area.[23] The Gulf crisis following Iraq's invasion of Kuwait, and the withdrawal from Germany of US and British forces for redeployment in the Gulf, will surely lend support to this possibility. Indeed, it would seem politically desirable to replace the specifically eastward-facing orientation of NATO's defence forces with a 'multi-directional' threat assessment.

The final part of this proposed new defensive system consists of forces made up of mobilised reserves as well as reinforcements from the United States, obviously not permanently stationed in peacetime but temporarily deployed for in-theatre training and available for introduction in periods of tension. This reconstitution strategy would form a prime element of the new defensive structure. With the halving of the British Army of the Rhine (BAOR), announced as part of the 'Options for Change' exercise in the summer of 1991, the planned removal of French forces from German soil – a development neither welcome to the Germans[24] nor self-evidently compatible with the professed French preference for a more Eurocentric defence structure – and the very real likelihood that the peacetime American presence in Europe will fall substantially below the 195,000 agreed with Moscow, NATO in-place forces in Germany will be proportionally more German than is currently the case. On the other hand, such a 'reconstitution strategy' – as it was dubbed in 1990 – would place less reliance on in-place forces, and more on reinforcement capability. Whether there will be sufficient enthusiasm to maintain the requisite heavy forces and lift capability only time will tell, but Saddam Hussein's sudden emergence as a heavily-armoured and out-of-area adversary might help. In fact, it is far from self-evident that any sharp distinction between the characteristics of the elements of the new forces will prove practicable or desirable.

An additional feature of this proposed new strategy could be its continuing reliance on the 'smart' long-range weapons systems associated with the Follow-On Forces Attack (FOFA) concept, adopted by NATO in 1984 as a Planning Guideline.[25] Indeed the distance from the battle area at which Soviet forces would be obliged to concentrate, and NATO's increased reliance on mobilisation and reinforcement, could render deep strike capabilities and enhanced C^3I even more desirable and effective.

To some extent, of course, FOFA was driven by the emergence of technologies capable of implementing it. Accuracy and speed of reaction are likely to continue to improve as a result of incremental technological drift. Thus far, however, the record of deployment has not been impressive. The weapons have disproportionately originated in the United States, thus undermining attempts to create a two-way trans-atlantic street in arms sales. In some instances, promised technological breakthroughs are still to materialise, have not lived up to their promise, or have been prohibitively expensive. In the 1990s a slump in the West's defence industrial sector, and the widespread curtailing of defence budgets, are likely to hit expensive research and development programmes severely. These downward pressures might be counterbalanced by the savings to be made in force size and readiness, but the prospects for significant high-technology rearmament do not look bright in the evolving political and financial climate.

Furthermore, although FOFA capabilities are neutral in the sense that they are appropriate for defence as well as for offence, the ability and incentives to strike deep and early which these systems offer will be problematic for any future arms control negotiations which aim to make both sides structurally incapable of waging offensive warfare.[26] Yet NATO's commitment 'to limit the offensive capability of conventional armed forces in Europe' at the CFE follow-on talks was reaffirmed in paragraph 13 of the July 1990 London Summit Declaration. Squaring an effective and plausible alliance strategy with the broader objective of developing co-operative European structures to enhance stability and security for the whole of Europe will surely be difficult. It will be interesting to see whether there is sufficient intellectual agility in NATO to come up with semantic solutions to the problem of describing a new strategic doctrine.

The London Declaration also stressed that, as we have noted, 'NATO will rely more heavily on the ability to build up larger forces if and when they might be needed' – reinforcement and mobilisation (paragraph 14). However, much might depend on the propensity for instability of Europe's new political order. Reinforcement and mobilisation would of course be unequivocally essential in the event of unambiguous preparations for large-scale war on the part of the Soviet Union. Is such a contingency the only, or most likely one against which NATO should plan? And would NATO's largely German, albeit multinationally configured in-place forces be adequate and appropriate to deal with the possibly numerous but lower level of crises which could occur? Would they be enough to deter a possible reintroduction of Soviet forces, for whatever reason, into Central or South-Eastern Europe? Would mobilisation and reinforcement of continental Europe be exercised frequently and seriously enough to deter any such action on the part of the Soviet Union? The days preceding the outbreak of war in 1914 revealed the dangers of military and security arrangements left dependent on competitive mobilisations.[27] Even in the case of a crisis containing the prospect of a profound challenge to the European order, the decision to order large-scale mobilisation and reinforcement of NATO would be fraught with political difficulties and could undermine attempts at 'graduated conflict control'.[28] These problems would be even more acute if NATO were to rely on the reintroduction of nuclear weapons into Central Europe.

Change and cohesion?

It is, in truth, too early to say what shape the new European order will take, and how durable it might be. It is also too early to say precisely what form NATO's military rearrangements will eventually take. That it is not too early, however, for NATO's defence planners to start thinking about the alliance's post-cold war military arrangements constitutes NATO's current core difficulty. Change there must be, but how can NATO ensure that it takes place in an orderly, agreed fashion? Is Europe heading towards a period of stable peace, based on all-round satisfaction with the prevailing order? If so, what should the limit to all-round disarmament be? Or is Europe heading towards an unstable peace, characterised by tensions, challenges and crisis punctuations?[29] What form might such crises take, and what would be the appropriate response to them?

In conclusion, then, we can see that political change begets military change, but that the correspondence between the two is less than perfect. This is in large measure the result of NATO's current unavoidable attempt to respond to an ongoing process of political change rather than to some new, but relatively unambiguous, environment. There is, too, a tension between the 'official' desire to develop military structures predicated on the basis of a continuing, though reduced and restructured, threat, and the deeper sensitivity to the problems of maintaining coherent force structures and alliance relationships in the face of a collapse of the threat. At what point is a 'threat' so reduced, in either capabilities or perceived intention, as to have ceased to exist? Above all, NATO will have to decide whether 'the threat' will necessarily emanate from Moscow. If NATO planners consider the Soviet Union to be potentially dangerous in the longer term, politicians and electorates will need persuading of the necessity to prepare now for something which is not around any immediate corner. The answers to such problems matter less, perhaps, than recognition of the difficulties involved in maintaining a coherent alliance posture for as long as such questions have currency.

Notes

1 Reprinted in full in *Survival*, XXXII, no. 5, September/October 1990, pp. 469–72.
2 Robert S. McNamara, 'The military role of nuclear weapons; perceptions and misperceptions', *Survival*, XXV, no. 6, November/December 1983.
3 General Bernard W. Rogers, 'Greater flexibility for NATO's flexible response', *Strategic Review*, XI, no. 2, Spring 1983.
4 Douglas Stuart, 'NATO in the 1980s; between European pillar and European home', *Armed Forces and Society*, XVI, no. 3, Spring 1990, p. 433.
5 Richard K. Betts, 'NATO's mid-life crisis', *Foreign Affairs*, LXVIII, no. 2, Spring 1989, pp. 40–3.
6 See Hans Binnendijk, 'NATO's nuclear modernisation dilemma', *Survival*, XXXI, no.2, March/April 1989; William D. Bajusz and Lisa D. Shaw, 'The forthcoming "SNF negotiations" ', *Survival*, XXXII, no. 4, July/August 1990.
7 *Jane's Defence Weekly* (*JDW*), 19 May 1990.
8 See Bajusz and Shaw, 'SNF negotiations', p. 336.
9 *JDW*, 28 July 1990.
10 *JDW*, 14 July 1990.
11 'Blow to hopes for new NATO missile', *Independent*, 18 October 1990.
12 'Bush finalises NATO summit proposals', *Independent*, 27 July 1990.
13 Lewis A. Dunn, 'NATO after global "double zero"', *Survival*, XXX, no. 3, May/June 1988, p. 207.
14 Binnendijk, 'NATO's nuclear modernisation', p. 142; 'NATO in secret pact on naval cruise missiles', *Independent*, 4 June 1990; Otfried Nassauer *et al.*, 'Sea Launched Cruise Missiles in NATO Nuclear Planning', BASIC Report 90.2, London, June 1990.
15 See Binnendijk, 'NATO's nuclear modernisation', pp. 145–7, for a consideration of possible alternative nuclear force postures.
16 *JDW*, 14 July 1990.

17 'New scenario for NATO forces', *JDW*, 17 March 1990.
18 'Ministers agree to shake-up of NATO forces in Germany', *The Times*, 29 May 1991.
19 'NATO; still the best guarantee of collective security?', *JDW*, 14 July 1990.
20 Michael Legge, 'NATO defence planning after CFE', *NATO's Sixteen Nations*, XXXV, no. 3, June 1990, p. 33.
21 *JDW*, 5 May 1990.
22 'End of an era for Paris and Bonn', *Independent*, 17 September 1990.
23 'Mourning after the hype before', *Guardian*, 1 October 1990.
24 *Independent*, *op. cit.*, 17 September 1990.
25 See comments by Deputy SACEUR General Eberhard Eimmler, *JDW*, 19 May 1990.
26 The point is made by Manfred R. Hamm, 'NATO strategy and arms control in Europe', *Comparative Strategy*, VII, no. 3, 1988, pp. 201–4.
27 For arguments similar to this, see Paul Bracken, 'The changing nature of deterrence in Europe', in Ted Galen Carpenter (ed.), *NATO at 40: Confronting a Changing World*, Lexington, Va., Cato Institute, 1990, pp. 153–67.
28 For this concern, see Karl Kaiser, 'From nuclear deterrence to graduated conflict control', *Survival*, XXXII, no. 6, November/December 1990.
29 See Ken Booth, 'Steps towards stable peace in Europe; a theory and practice of co-existence', *International Affairs*, LXVI, no. 1, January 1990, for a discussion of these and other concepts.

4

Juliet Lodge

European Community security policy: rhetoric or reality?

It has long been commonplace to argue that the European Community (EC) has a very restricted role in international politics. Indeed, until the Single European Act came into force in July 1987, the dominant view was that the EC had a role in external relations but not in any aspect of international affairs impinging on the traditional diplomatic endeavours of the member states. The military aspects of security were certainly considered taboo.

Broadly speaking, an artificial distinction was made between the economic and political aspects of external relations. Defence and security matters were seen as the prerogative of NATO and the Western European Union (where appropriate) and of the member states. By contrast external trade was seen as falling under the competence of the EC Commission. In so far as the EC had an 'external profile', it was linked to its position as a major world trader and its self-image as a 'civilian power' devoid of imperialistic or territorial ambitions backed by military capacity.

However, not all the international trade that EC member states engaged in was regulated solely through the Commission. Nor can it be credibly argued that the EC's external relations consisted solely in external trade. Trade was certainly the starting point but additional issues such as human rights crept into agreements with other states and organisations. The attempts to extend the Lomé Conventions and to link the granting of aid to countries willing to forswear safe havens to fugitive terrorists, for example, illustrated how easily trade and aid packages could be adapted in the context of other pressing political issues. Moreover, the Single European Act's extension of assent procedures to the European Parliament in these spheres gave Members of the European Parliament (MEPs) a powerful political weapon to wield in pursuit of political objectives – as MEPs demonstrated in denying their assent to the financial protocols of Israeli and Turkish association.

The Act was to break the taboo about the legitimacy of the EC discussing, and more importantly acting in, security matters broadly conceived. It did so by two means. On the one hand, articles explicitly condoned such developments. On the other hand, European Political Co-operation (EPC), which had run parallel to the EC but which had not been fully integrated into the supranational decision-making structure, was brought into the EC treaties system.

The Single European Act and security

The Single European Act (SEA) grouped together a series of amendments to the existing treaties. Title III on *Provisions on European cooperation in the sphere of foreign policy* constitutes an important landmark in the evolution of the EC's role in security matters. Article 6(a) explicitly sanctioned readiness 'to coordinate . . . positions more closely on the political and economic aspects of security'.

However, the importance of Title III must not be exaggerated for several reasons. Firstly, while it brings EPC into the EC treaties, it does not give supranational bodies, notably the Court of Justice and the European Parliament, rights in respect of foreign policy matters comparable to those they enjoy in respect of other EC activities. The Court lacks any jurisdiction whatsoever under Title III. Secondly, military/defence aspects of security are circumnavigated even though MEPs and EC political élites have argued persuasively over the years that the EC's economic security (and notably its trade routes) cannot be secured without appropriate military backup. Thirdly, even though EPC is strengthened through the establishment of a small secretariat, which leases premises from the Council of Ministers for a peppercorn rent,[1] its distinctiveness from the supranational system remains. Fourthly, this separateness and the concomitant implications it has for the sovereignty of its participants is underlined by the reference throughout Title III to 'the High Contracting Parties' rather than to the 'member states' as is the norm elsewhere in the SEA.

There is another facet of the EC's external relations which sits uneasily with attempts to venture into security realms: namely, its profession to be a civilian power lacking military might and ambitions and possessing, *through its member states*, only a defensive military capacity. The civilian power imagery cultivated over the past twenty years was designed principally to show that the EC had a non-threatening face; that it lacked militarily-based aspirations and capabilities; and that the EC was concerned not with defence issues – which were left to other bodies, notably NATO and to a lesser extent the Western European Union (WEU) – but with trade.[2]

This chapter focuses on the evolving debate in the EC about its attempt to commit the member states to a common foreign and security policy. It concentrates on the current deliberations of the Intergovernmental Conference (IGC) on Political Union and the advocacy of a linkage or merger between the WEU and the EC in defence and security matters.

EC institutions and security

As far back as 1973, the Copenhagen summit referred to security possibilities under the aegis of the embryonic EPC. This was taken up by the Genscher–Colombo initiative for a European Act in 1980–81, the London Report 1981, and the Solemn Declaration of 1983. EC involvement in the security realm remained contentious even after both the European Parliament's 1984 Draft European Treaty establishing the European Union and the fudged references to foreign and security policy in the SEA.[3] As with so many unanticipated areas of the Single Market programme, the SEA was to catalyse thinking on security and the EC's role in effecting it.

As early as May 1986 the Subcommittee on Security and Disarmament of the European Parliament (EP) put a question to the Foreign Ministers' meeting on Political Co-operation, hinting that it hoped that the EC would embark on 'a European project for strategic defence'. This failed to secure the EP's approval and six other resolutions on security also fell. The EC's competence to discuss security was hotly contested by MEPs. The then chair of Political Co-operation, Dutch State Secretary Wim van Eekelen, insisted that the EC did have the legal right to discuss such matters. Eekelen also insisted that contrived distinctions between economic, political and military aspects of security were pointless and that a minority of states opposed to EPC discussing security were not to be allowed to prevent the majority from going ahead.[4] The historical juncture at which the security debate took off is also important, coming as it did during the Libyan crisis, and at a time when the US SDI initiative was under the microscope. It is instructive that MEPs accepted the need for European Union to embrace security and defence and that some saw European competitiveness in the new technologies as vital if Europe was to avoid finding itself one day 'with no defence at all'.[5] Reticence to discuss SDI and to move towards a European strategic defence project was condemned, and anxiety expressed, lest the US policy of limiting technology transfer inhibited Europe's future development and rendered it dependent on the United States. The member states divided into an Atlantic or Euro-camp (with the former to some extent mirroring their self-interest in SDI involvement and a privileged relationship with the United States, and the latter consisting of those opposed to Euro-SDI involvement lest it endanger Europe's information technology base).[6] There was wide agreement that Europe's technological capacity be strengthened all round (and thus also from the point of arms production) through competitive research in Eureka, and pre-competitive research in Esprit, the European Space Agency and other schemes. In short, the linkage between industrial and information technology policies and security was clearly established although its consequences were sidestepped.

EC encroachment into policy sectors, traditionally seen as the realm of sovereign nation-states, remained highly sensitive, and this accounts for the various attempts to find alternatives to the EC developing an independent, supranational security policy. The development of EPC parallel to, rather than as an integral part of, the EC was consistent with member states' anxieties that the EC Commission might ultimately usurp them in the definition of objectives and introduction of initiatives likely to deviate from national goals and priorities. Limiting the Commission's role in non-trade aspects of external relations has been of paramount importance to the member states. Maintaining this limit effectively has been far from easy, given outside expectations of the EC's role in international affairs that outstrip the EC's capacity to deliver. Moreover, the member states themselves remain divided over the issue in general, and over any roles that might be given to the Commission and the European Council in the definition and pursuit of a common EC foreign, security and defence policy in particular.

The Gulf crisis highlighted the imperative for improving the EC's competences in the security sector. There was some cohesion among the Twelve, but their weak capacity for common action was equally emphasised. *Anti-communautaire* commentators quickly interpreted this as the death-knell for political union but the consensus was that this merely accentuated the need to revise EPC and political union to enhance the EC's capacity in foreign and security matters.

The Intergovernmental Conference and foreign and security policy

In preparation for the IGC on Political Union, several inter-institutional meetings between the Commission, the Council and the EP were convened (the first on 17 May, the second on 23 October and the third on 5 December 1990). The delegations were led by their respective presidents who, between these meetings, met among themselves.

The Presidency issued a document on the subject of the four main themes of the IGC on Political Union: foreign and security policy; extension of Community competences; effectiveness of the Union; and democratic legitimacy.[7] All indirectly impinge upon the EC's competence in the foreign and security realms and it would be a mistake merely to suppose that only specific foreign/security policy revisions to the existing treaties resulting from the IGCs later in 1991 will be of relevance. While the focus of this chapter will be on foreign and security policy, a brief note on each of the relevant points under the above headings is warranted.

- *Foreign and security policy.* There was broad agreement on the principle that 'the Union' (namely the EC) aspires to competence on all aspects of foreign and security policy through a process of constant evolution. To this end, it was envisaged that the EPC secretariat and that of the Council be strengthened and the Commission's tasks reinforced. Most delegations (and member governments) agreed that the aim must be a common foreign and security policy but that defence issues give rise to specific problems. Commission President Jacques Delors was quick to differentiate, however, between a *common* and a *single* foreign policy.
- *Extension of EC competences.* While all favour widening EC competences, the areas of central concern to this chapter relate to the internal and external aspects of security broadly conceived. They therefore encompass areas currently under intergovernmental control. Because of the requirements of the Single Market and the removal of internal borders and the reinforcement of the external frontier, many additional areas must become subject to supranational regulation (e.g. immigration and visa controls, drugs, and external border controls). Moreover, these particular areas are problematic because they relate to the completion of a supranational goal, normally subject to the usual supranational legislative procedures, but also impinge on sensitive areas where intergovernmental co-operation has been fostered in parallel to the EC but not always under supranational guidance. The Trevi and Pompidou groups are important in this respect. Moreover, there has been increasing work within working parties of EPC on security (including internal security issues) and more recently suggestions that the WEU and NATO foster co-operation in the very same fields. Since co-ordination between the various groups is poor, overlap and contradictory policy directions may create further problems.[8]

• *Effectiveness of the Union.* The Union cannot be made effective unless appropriate mechanisms for elaborating a foreign policy are devised. The role of the European Council is central to the idea of the effectiveness of the Union. The European Council comprises the Heads of Government or State of the Twelve. It has a specified and limited role *vis-à-vis* security and foreign policy under the SEA. The IGC deliberations showed that the member states disagreed as to the development of the Council's role. Some, notably the Dutch, felt that the EC Commission rather than the European Council should be empowered to initiate policy in this area. Others felt that the European Council should offer general direction and guidance. Some qualified this by observing that the European Council lacked the mechanisms to go much beyond declaratory statements of principle. It was suggested therefore that the General Affairs Council should have an enhanced role in this area and *vis-à-vis* the sectoral councils. Italy suggested that the European Council should progressively and gradually define foreign and security policy sectors without excluding *a priori* any issue. The General Affairs Council would, on the basis of the guidelines, then formulate and conduct the policies and ensure coherence in them. A secretariat for foreign policy within the Council Secretariat was mooted whose role would also be to liaise with the Committee of Permanent Representatives and the Political Committee. The Commission, which is present at EPC meetings, was to be fully associated with the formulation and implementation of the foreign and security policies and be given a non-exclusive right of initiative.

The extension of the European Council's role mooted by the IGC deliberations raised the spectre of the EC slipping back into intergovernmental co-operation dominated by the most vociferous and intractable of member governments. An augumented role for the European Council could only confirm such a trend. However, Delors demurred. He saw the European Council playing a more general role giving direction to European Union specifically in the foreign policy arena but leaving implementation and arbitration to others such as the General Affairs Council. It is hard to reconcile this hands-off approach with past experience of the European Council arbitrating when the Council has become deadlocked. Mindful of this, Delors added that the European Council could not become a supreme body extending its reach and 'directional role' into additional or new areas of EC policy-making. Reticence to put security policy under supranational management should not be the excuse for regressing to intergovernmental co-operation in other policy sectors.

• *Democratic legitimacy.* Of particular import here is the agreement on: co-decision, extending the co-operation procedure, and extending the assent procedure to external relations. At present, the European Parliament's powers are rather circumscribed. However, under the SEA's small revisions to the assent procedure, the EP was able to insert itself more effectively into foreign policy issues by deploying its right to withhold assent pending the accommodation of its views. The assent procedure coupled with other treaty provisions could significantly expand the EP's role in external policy matters. The EP has, moreover, stated that it would deny assent to the EC's enlargement to Turkey pending further increases in its powers; and that its competence in respect of the trade, aid and co-operation packages with Eastern Europe should be bolstered by being brought into line with those on association agreements. In general, however, it is unusual for parliaments to have a role in formulating or implementing foreign and security policy. Their role tends to be one of general oversight, checking the executive and acting as the grand forum of debate. However, since financial powers may be exercised in such a way as to inhibit executive spending on foreign affairs and defence budgets (and the EC as yet does not have a budget line for military defence), the EP's financial powers are potentially significant. They might ultimately be used on budget lines connected with security and foreign policy objectives, including research and development, industrial and information technology policies. Indeed, the Belgian IGC delegation presented a paper in February 1991 designed to advance an EC industrial policy whose scope would inevitably impinge on defence industries, although this was not mentioned directly in the proposal.[9] However, in the past, much had been made of the inferred right of the EC to deal with defence issues through the industrial policy. In the context of the Single Market, too, repeated references were made to the possibility of saving an estimated six billion ecus through a single market in arms procurement. The potential breadth of the industrial policy, and its open encroachment into defence industry concerns, was also underlined by the Italian suggestion that a greater integration of industrial policy be accompanied by the abolition of Article 223 under which member states are allowed to refuse to disclose information on armaments.

In short, the effect of the security debate in the EC was to accentuate the broad scope of policy sectors and hence of integrative endeavour likely to be covered by security in practice. No convincing arguments for excluding foreign and security policy from democratic scrutiny have been advanced.

Implementing objectives: pressures of the Gulf emergency

By far the most problematic aspects of current EC deliberations over an EC security and foreign policy role concern not merely the distribution of authority and exercise of competence by existing EC institutions but the definition and goal operationalisation, notably when military aspects of security have to be brought into play and military resources deployed. The EC is not in a position to act in this area. For years, the Twelve have evaded dealing with this question in anything but the vaguest of terms. The international context of the 1990s, within which the EC's foreign and security debate unfurled, conditioned the different responses of the member states.

The EC was lambasted for its inability to produce an immediate, cohesive response to the Gulf crisis and especially to the war. While it has rudimentary crisis mechanisms that allow it to convene ministerial meetings within forty-eight hours, EPC's primary objectives are very modest. EPC enjoins the member states 'to endeavour jointly to formulate and implement a European foreign policy'. This translates into commitments to inform and consult on any foreign policy of general interest; to co-ordinate and promote convergence among their different positions; to take account, in national positions, of their partners' views and the desirability of adopting common EC positions; gradually to develop common principles and aims; to avoid actions or positions impairing the Twelve's effectiveness as a force in international relations; and to refrain from impeding consensus and any joint action that might flow from it. As to security *per se* the SEA sees closer co-operation as the means for promoting the kind of co-ordination on the political and economic aspects of security necessary to the projection of a European identity in external policy matters. The objectives are, therefore, ill-defined and their attainment subject to the vagaries of domestic political constraints and inadequate EC-level institutional mechanisms and legal obligations. It is therefore hardly surprising that the Gulf emergency, coupled with the immediately preceding spate of bilateral negotiations with Iraq to free hostages, resulted in shallow co-operation and co-ordination among the Twelve.

The absence of an overarching consensus on how to achieve a lasting peace in the Middle East in the short term also meant that individual member states had far greater leeway to pursue independent strategies than might otherwise have been the case. Some certainly felt that they could safely ignore their commitments under EPC. Somewhat paradoxically, however, this was matched by a simultaneous search for

EC consensus and a desire on the part of the Twelve to concert European efforts more effectively. Individual *démarches* underlined the relative weakness of each of the member states, thereby illustrating the necessity for acting in concert to preserve their collective influence. Diversity, of itself, must not be derided as weakness because it permits the Twelve to test out a range of options on a bilateral basis before homing in on a single one. The flexibility this facilitates can be extremely useful in diplomatic negotiations, providing that it is consciously deployed and third parties are not encouraged to see it as an opportunity for dividing the member states. The façade of diversity often conceals underlying consensus.

The Gulf war led the Luxembourg Presidency in January 1991 to advance security discussions. The Twelve were divided as to the purpose and ambit of such talks, so officials were charged with devising a questionnaire to ascertain views as to the precise definition and scope of foreign and security policies envisaged, their goals, means, legal instruments and timetable.

While the Twelve were divided over the details, there was broad consensus but not uniformity over expanding EC competence in foreign and security issues. Not until the December 1990 Rome European Council did Ireland feel that its neutrality had been officially accommodated (in the Presidency 'conclusions' explicitly recognising the need not to prejudice the 'traditional positions of other member states'). The United Kingdom has always had an ambiguous position on security co-operation in particular. Mrs Thatcher had keenly advocated it but such advocacy was shrouded in intergovernmental rhetoric and basically came down to requiring that EC states lend support to each other's (and notably the United Kingdom's) international *démarches* when required.[10]

By the time of the December IGCs, John Major's Government hinted that it was prepared to consider an EC security role (possibly one of a supranational nature) in restricted areas excluding 'defence'. Thus, military operations were to be excluded from EC perusal but EC action might be acceptable in a number of the areas deemed possibilities for EC 'concertation' in 1986,[11] and outlined in the first reports of the personal representatives of the Foreign Ministers as well as in the report by UK Socialist MEP David Martin for the EP, including: arms control, national controls on the export of nuclear and chemical missile components, peacekeeping issues involving the United Nations or where a need for co-ordination existed.[12] By January 1991, the United Kingdom was insisting that there could be no foreign policy without security, no security without defence, and no defence without Atlantic solidarity. Its position still fell short of what France and Germany had in mind.

Days before the opening of the IGC meeting, President François Mitterrand and Chancellor Helmut Kohl sent a joint letter to European Council President Giulio Andreotti setting out a joint position on the goals and main elements of political union. They insisted that political union should include a genuine common security policy that in time would lead to common defence. They agreed that it would be necessary to examine relations between this common defence policy, the WEU and NATO, and that foreign policy would cover all areas including development policy. Nothing could be off limits. The EC would come to play a role in the implementation of CSCE principles, disarmament negotiations, and relations with the Mediterranean basin. They seemed to obfuscate Commission President Delors' earlier suggestions that a common foreign policy need not imply a single policy by saying: 'Foreign policy will . . . be able to move towards a true common foreign policy.' Both agreed that whatever terms were employed, in the short to medium term, measures would have to be put in place to allow member states, in effect, to opt out of common policies. Thus a *single* policy would bind all the member states to a particular course of action whereas a *common* policy would be more 'flexible'. While it is easy to deride such formulae, it must be remembered that a far greater degree of commonality exists among the Twelve on international issues than is usually recognised. Their broad interests do coincide. Particular disagreements inevitably owe much to different historical traditions. Reconciling divergent, even contradictory, pressures was far from easy. The parameters of an interim solution had, however, been hinted at in the SEA.

Article 30(6.c) of the Single Act states: 'Nothing in this Title shall impede closer co-operation in the field of security between certain of the High Contracting Parties within the framework of the Western European Union or the Atlantic Alliance.' Since the Single Act already encourages the relevant member states to adopt common positions in international institutions and at international conferences, more formal measures to co-ordinate positions with the WEU seemed logical to EC actors and many in the WEU. France and Germany foresaw the WEU being organically linked to the EC, having increased operational capabilities, in the longer term becoming part of the political union and then elaborating a common security policy for the EC. In the meantime, they saw the WEU as a staging post towards the refinement of a European pillar in NATO. With the arguable exception of the United Kingdom, probably all the member states (and even some EC applicants like Austria) saw this as a means of asserting a European security identity distinct from that of NATO and the United States on the international scene.

The European Community and the Western European Union: linkage or merger?

This particular debate about an EC–WEU institutional linkage or merger is, to some extent, a prisoner of the peculiar historical conditions facing European states. It is also a product of several states' interest in trying to maintain an independent but co-ordinated European profile at the operational military level without facing the expensive and politically divisive prospect of the EC acquiring military potential with all that this would imply for the EC's budget and the idea of EC state-building. Above all, however, it is a debate about reorganising European security interests without fundamentally altering Western Europe's strategic framework. The structural deficits and lack of clarity over precise objectives make it hard to harness and harmonise divergent national positions. Moreover, the merger scenario has to be seen as a solution *faute de mieux* to the structural and political deficiencies of the EC security debate. Unwillingness to cede authority for foreign and security policies to the EC inevitably means that if certain goals are to be met (including the vague statements in favour of a common foreign and security policy), then existing security organisations cannot be overlooked. Equally, importantly, additional factors collude to make it imperative to find new rationales for maintaining existing West European defence organisations.[13] For the West, their automatic dissolution as a result of the emergence of a new European security order was never on the cards. A new European security order resting on superpower guarantees rather than reflecting superpower European interests did, however, mean that existing arrangements had to be reassessed if a European identity was to be credible. Furthermore, EC aid and assistance to Eastern Europe did not square with an offensive defence posture *vis-à-vis* Eastern Europe, nor did it correspond to reality. At the same time, EC member states were not prepared to abandon security arrangements that had served them well in the past. Rather, they had to come to terms with two accelerating pressures: that for collective security, and that for European Union. How to reconcile potentially contradictory goals was one problem. The other was how to ensure that the European Union/EC secure a role for itself in the wider security arena when its political and economic activities accentuated its interests and involvement in international affairs. All were highlighted by the dissolution of the Warsaw Pact amidst renewed interest in alternative forms of collective European security – based on force reductions, confidence-building and disarmament measures and the replacement of offensive defence by defensive defence systems – as well as the creation of nuclear-free zones and the institutionalisation of collective security in a new treaty (such as the new CSCE).[14]

Throughout the debate several themes recur in the EC camp:

- the desirability of creating a genuine European pillar of NATO;
- the need for genuine partnership with the United States;
- the need for a genuinely independent EC foreign policy, and
- the need to integrate the economic and political aspects of security.

In the spring of 1989, the European Parliament debated two key reports on security matters: one on Western Europe's security and the other on European arms exports (known as the Penders and Ford reports respectively).[15] In respect of the first, Irish spokesmen contrasted European tolerance and pluralism with the superpowers' alleged inflexibility. In respect of the second, arms trade between EC states and potential enemies in the Gulf was condemned but took second place to the imperative of EC institutional reform to enable it to deal with the military aspects of security after 1992. This was seen as a logical corollary to the creation of a single market for arms.[16]

The interest in linkage between an EC foreign and security policy and the WEU goes back a long way and derives in part from a feeling that this would provide a compromise position between advocacy of a unique, supranational EC policy (formulated and adopted according to supranational provisions) and an overt Atlantic-dependent policy in whose formulation most, but not all, EC states played a role through their adherence to NATO. The linkage partially disguised continuing fears over the implications for national sovereignty of the EC venturing into these highly sensitive areas. Moreover, there was a suspicion that unless an alternative was found to the notion of expanding the joint Franco-German brigade exercises to the rest of the EC, France and Germany would come, by default, to dominate and determine the direction of EC foreign and security policy – something none of the member states wanted.[17]

There can be little doubt that the IGC on Political Union impelled a rethink of the future of both NATO and the WEU and of the role of a more united EC, regardless of whether or not all EC members were members of the other two. Equally, given the changing constellation of threat perceptions on the European continent in the wake of East European liberalisation, NATO too was, to some extent, in search of a role. In these circumstances, it would have been unrealistic for it not to contemplate a strengthening of its European pillar and a civilianisation of its activities into the economic, political, environmental and cultural facets of security, as in the EC.[18] However, it is significant that WEU and NATO meetings occurring shortly before or after the Rome IGC European Council broadly supported linkage, when just over a year earlier modest linkage predicated on MEPs participating in the WEU Assembly proved so contentious. Following a tour of European capitals and US pressure on European governments, US Secretary of States James Baker added that the United States favoured a European security role *provided* it rested on support for the Atlantic Alliance.[19] This was a crucial qualification given suspicions that at this juncture Iraq in particular would have exploited any signs of difference between the United States and European members of NATO, especially if EC members had been prepared to go for an independent initiative.[20]

While there was a good deal of loose talk over an EC–WEU 'merger', sceptics pointed out that the role of the two organisations were only superficially complementary: the axiom was that the WEU could manage defence but not security and the EC vice versa. Such scepticism did not disguise deeper misgivings that a medium-term fudge was afoot. Neither the WEU nor the EC were competent to implement a common foreign and security policy, both had pretensions in that direction, and both had an interest in ensuring that the definition of such policies was not subordinate to NATO. Anxiety over the federal implications of a European Union, however, deterred them from taking the necessary steps to making reality out of the rhetoric.[21]

It was not always apparent from the various statements in favour of a merger between the EC and the WEU what the purposes of such a merger would be. If anything the merger scenario clouded the issues: the goals and objectives were not clearly defined. Nor were the institutional arrangements for accommodating and co-ordinating activities between the two. Instead, there were vague references to the WEU performing an ill-defined security function for the EC. Operationally, this seemed to amount to the WEU being an umbrella body for any out-of-area military operations in which EC members engaged, notably in the Gulf. Maritime co-ordination of mine-sweeping activities had taken place under the WEU. UK Defence Minister George Younger suggested in the spring of 1989 that co-operation expand to defence and security training, arms control verification and space-based surveillance. In the 1990–91 Gulf crisis, a first naval group consisting of an Italian frigate, a Spanish frigate and a French air-escort ship to ensure the protection and escort of allied ships had been supplemented by three Belgian mine-sweepers, two Spanish frigates and French ships in the Red Sea charged with monitoring the embargo against Iraq and protecting Allied supplies.[22] This co-ordination under the WEU allowed the EC states to maintain a semblance of independence from the United States and from NATO. The WEU seemed to be a useful vehicle for allowing EC states to give free expression to their individualism. It did not compromise their bilateral relations with any of the actors for it lacked a tight prescriptive role. In some senses this was also a strength for it gave the impression of flexibility and, where the belligerents were concerned, made it clear that individual states were involved in the conflict, not the EC *per se*. In the longer term and at an operational level, greater unity in EC foreign and security policy might have to sacrifice the high degree of flexibility (and the concomitant advantages) the current arrangements provide.

Rival perspectives

The EC position on a merger with the WEU has vacillated between outright rejection to sceptical acceptance in the 1990s. The idea of the EC developing a security component antedates the French initiative on reviving the WEU in 1987. The idea of giving the WEU a new role in European security was mooted by MEPs from 1981 onwards and explicitly advanced by the WEU Foreign Ministers' meeting in Rome in 1984. They foresaw the WEU adapting itself to deal with current issues of co-operation, arms control and disarmament, with NATO remaining the overarching framework within which an independent European element would be pursued.[23] The WEU was to become the proactive core, or think-tank, of a European network on security matters. In 1987, the WEU Council accepted these ideas and added a further element: the creation of a 'cohesive European defence identity'. To that end the WEU's working methods were to be refined. As to out-of-area operations, it was suggested that the WEU form the hub of an institutionalised co-operation process that would incorporate the Independent European Planning Group. These ideas were supplemented by Helmut Schmidt's proposal for an Integrated Western European Defence System based on thirty Franco-German divisions of conventional forces under supreme French command and backed by Benelux and some British and US forces. This he saw as the nucleus of a larger defence union within the WEU or beyond it.[24] Thus, by the time of the IGCs, the question of institutionalising defence and security co-operation with a view to projecting an independent or recognisably European identity had been around for several years and had gained some currency. It was, though, opposed by those who wanted the EC to be able to proceed unfettered by intervention from other organisations and states whose objectives might diverge from those of the majority in the EC.

A good deal separated the rhetoric from the reality of the situation. EC advocates of merger or closer approximation of EC–WEU activities had not thought through their position. Rather, the WEU seemed to be grasped at as a short-term political expedient. There are several reasons for this. First, defence matters have been taboo to the EC since its inception. After the third elections to the European Parliament in 1989, the EP's Political Affairs Committee introduced its 'security and disarmament subcommittee' as a device to legitimise debate and to soften up the opposition in preparation for a full-blown defence committee. Second, integrated EC defence smacks of federalism (and the failed Europe Defence Community of 1954) and a high degree of political unity which is still elusive. Third, the WEU is a means of legitimising a French role in the definition of a Community security policy given its special relationship to NATO. Fourth, the WEU has lately developed greater consultative links with Greece and Turkey and this has commended it to some in the EC, including Greece which has said it wants early membership of the WEU.

On the minus side, there is not a complete coincidence of membership between the WEU and EC. Ireland is always held out as the major stumbling bloc to an EC security policy, but in practice its positions on foreign affairs have usually coincided with those of EPC. This is not to imply that such coincidence would continue if the EC moved into the defence and security sectors more definitively. But it does underscore the degree of approximation and coherence in the Twelve's foreign policies. It would be folly to overstate this because the evidence is adduced largely from UN voting patterns and EPC successes *vis-à-vis* CSCE. However, as the last few years have shown, EPC has failed spectacularly when confronted by major international developments. Even this judgement must be qualified because its failure is spectacular only if compared to the speed with which national governments can respond to major developments, notably German reunification and the Gulf crisis. What such unfavourable comparisons highlight is the inappropriateness of the EC's existing institutional arrangements for dealing with international issues and rapidly-developing crisis situations. The absence of an appropriate legal treaty base to justify and shape EC responses, damages the EC's wider international credibility and undermines any pretensions to greater integration and unity, especially if this is predicated on the concentric rings model in which the EC forms a tightly integrated core.[25] This helps to explain too why the WEU was suddenly seen as an appropriate vehicle for moving most EC states along towards accepting the idea of greater co-operation in defence and security matters. Moreover, the WEU was far less threatening a prospect to the process of German reunification in that any suggestion of greater EC co-operation under the Euro-wing of NATO might have jeopardised and increased anxiety at a critical juncture in the negotiations to reunite Germany by a process that ultimately simply integrated East Germany into West Germany within the EC context.

The WEU Assembly was aware of the Commission's consideration of incorporating into the EC treaty Article V of the modified Brussels Treaty (establishing the Brussels Treaty Organisation and then the WEU) to render aid and assistance to treaty signatories in the event of armed aggression. The EP had already passed a resolution on CSCE matters in favour of *integrating* the WEU into the EC instead of *reviving* it. Not all endorsed the merger scenario.

The WEU Assembly President, French Socialist Robert Pontillon, argued against the official French Government position, saying that merger would contradict the goal of European Union. He felt that the WEU should be reactivated and should have representatives at the Council (parallel to arrangements with the Council of Europe and NATO). His views were not shared by all. In particular, WEU Secretary-General Wim van Eekelen had suggested in the spring of 1991 that Europe should create multinational units capable of integrating American reinforcements in military intervention around the world without assuming the role of a regional or world policeman. He favoured greater European independence via a consolidation of the EC and of a revivified WEU. In the interim, he called for bridge-building between the EC and the WEU, and for the IGC to devise new co-ordinating mechanisms between the two. He opposed expanding the WEU to Greece and Turkey pending improvement of relations between the EC, the WEU and NATO but favoured extending the information mechanism between the WEU, Greece and Turkey to non-EC NATO members.

However, there can be little doubt that WEU–EC linkage or merger was the main future scenario and that the various proposals for greater 'consultation'/'co-ordination' were designed with that in mind. The French Government argued that 'immediate' merger was not possible; the Italians spoke of 1998 as the earliest date. Therefore, it fell to the IGC to determine a specific link between the WEU and the EC, given that the merger scenario suggested a division of labour with the WEU assuming responsibility for military and operational matters and the EC for external relations and trade. The WEU had indirectly suggested such a division of labour when its Parliamentary Assembly unanimously endorsed on 6 December 1990 the Belgian recommendation that the WEU constitute a peacekeeping force (according to each state's abilities) in response to UN Security Council requests; and that the WEU Council examine the Dutch recommendation for a WEU naval force for external operations plus an air unit to make up a European rapid action force.

Prospects

Both the EC and WEU are in search of a security role in the new Europe. For some, the WEU could be a bridge between the EC and NATO pending agreement on precisely what institutions, security roles and obligations would be appropriate for an enlarged EC embracing neutrals like Austria and Sweden. Yet the WEU offers possibly more than a breathing space, as the EPC response to the Yugoslav crisis in June 1991 showed. In spite of EC divisions over the self-determination of the Slovenes and Croats, and later over economic sanctions as the Brioni Pact seemed endangered, the Twelve used their limited capabilities with some success: to move from threatening to suspend economic aid, to triggering CSCE support for a monitoring role, and ultimately to direct mediation through the EPC. More controversial was the suggestion that the EC observers be complemented by a peacekeeping force, possibly based around the WEU. The EC *per se* still adheres to its civilian power image and lacks the military and financial capacity to go beyond crisis intervention based on political and economic good offices. The EC cannot and does not wish to play the role of European policeman. It may be a bridge between NATO and the CSCE; but it seeks to evade the enormous implications of militarisation.

The new CSCE charter assists the setting up of a new security order but cannot substitute for EC reforms that would empower the EC to act effectively on the international stage and to allow member states, within the EC framework, to determine and pursue legitimate European interests without feeling that their security is jeopardised if they deviate from US priorities. This requires the EC to clarify its underlying security assumptions, goals and roles, and reform its institutional mechanisms, so as to allow it to define, finance and implement policies to maintain regional (and where possible international) peace and stability, open trade routes, arms control and disarmament and the peaceful settlement of disputes.

Notes

1 S. Nuttall, 'Where the European Commission comes in', in A. Pijpers *et al.*, *European Political Cooperation in the 1980s*, Dordrecht, Kluwer, 1988.
2 P. Tsakaloyannis, 'The EC: from civilian power to military integration', in J. Lodge (ed.), *The European Community and the Challenge of the Future*, London, Pinter, 1989, pp. 214–55.
3 D. Prag, 'International relations', ch. 5, in Lodge (ed.), *European Union: the European Community in Search of a Future*, London, Macmillan, 1986.
4 *Official Journal of the Community*, 148, 16 June 1986 and Annex 2–239.
5 *Bulletin of the European Communities*, June 1986, pt. 2.4.7ff.
6 *Ibid.*, May 1986, pt. 2.4.9.
7 *Presidency Conclusions*, 9–10 December 1990.
8 Lodge, 'Frontier problems and the single market', *Conflict Studies*, 238, 1991, pp 22–36.
9 *Europe*, no. 5431, 14 February 1991.
10 See *Bulletin of the European Communities*, May 1986, pt. 2.4.9.
11 See Reports on: *Arms Control and Disarmament and their Importance to the EC* (Vanneck) PE. doc A–2–107/86; *Political Aspects of a European Security Strategy* (Galluzzi) A–2–110/87; *The Security of Western Europe* (Boesmans), A2–425/88.
12 Interim Report on *The IGC in the Context of Parliament's Strategy for European Union* (Martin), PE. doc 13–0047/90.
13 See *The Role of the European Parliament in the Field of Foreign Policy in the Context of the Single European Act* (Planas), PE. doc B–2–960/88.
14 On Helsinki and CSCE, see PE. doc B3–1049/90 (Poettering Report); PE. doc A2–77/87 (Campinos Report). On the new CSCE, see *Europe*, no. 5375, 22 November 1990.
15 European Parliament, Political Affairs Committee, *Report on the Security of Western Europe* (Penders), PE. doc A2–410/88; *Report on European Arms Exports* (Ford), PE. doc A2–398/88.
16 *Europe*, no. 4975, 15 March 1989; T. S. Souleles, *An Industry Without Frontiers*, Athens, Hellenic Foundation for Defence and Foreign Policy Studies, 1990.
17 W. J. Feld, 'Franco-German military cooperation and European unification', *Journal of European Integration*, XII, 1989, pp. 151–64; E. Hintermann, 'European Defence: a role for the WEU', *European Affairs*, 1988, pp. 31–8.
18 Cf. the Penders Report for striking parallels.
19 *Europe*, no. 5395, 19 December 1990.
20 *Ibid.*, no. 5396, 20 December 1990.
21 Report on *The Institutional Relations between the EC and the WEU with a View to Achieving European Union* (Boesmans), PE. doc A2–425/88.
22 *Europe*, no. 5431, 14 February 1991.
23 W. Weidenfeld, *et al.*, *European Deficits: European Perspectives*, Gutersloh, Bertelsmann, 1989, pp. 160–1.
24 *Ibid.*, p. 163.
25 B. Buzan, *et al.*, *The European Security Order Recast*, London, Pinter, 1990, pp. 207ff.

5 Hans-Joachim Spanger

Germany after unity: bridge or frontier between East and West?

On 3 October 1990 the division of Germany came to an end. There was nothing deliberate about the choice of date, except that at the German Democratic Republic's fortieth anniversary celebrations a year before, on 7 October, the old guard around Erich Honecker had already openly sounded the GDR's death-knell, and the governments in Bonn and East Berlin were keen to avoid putting the citizens of the GDR through a forty-first anniversary. Far from pursuing a deliberate policy, the two states were simply stumbling towards a unity which the overwhelming majority on both sides of the border wanted but which very few wished to see arrive so quickly.

Germany on the political agenda again

There was much talk in Germany at this time of Bismarck's 'mantle of history'. The Federal Chancellor, Helmut Kohl, earned praise from all sides for having grasped that mantle with determination, though the rapid collapse of governmental authority and economic activity in the GDR scarcely left him any other option. This time, at least, the new constitution of a German nation-state did not take the form of a national awakening – despite the months of effort by that flagship of the international popular press, *Bildzeitung*, to drown its millions of readers in a sea of black, red and gold. The issue that unquestionably dominated the politics was how to tackle the multitude of everyday problems bequeathed by forty years of highly disparate development. This offered plenty of scope for grievances and misunderstandings. There were complaints in the East about a sell-out and West German colonialism; and grumblings in the West that 'that lot over there are carrying on the GDR charade with our money,' as the Chairman of the Free Democratic Party (FDP), Count Otto Lambsdorff, was pleased to remark. But the latent tensions in, and virtual opposition of, the two highly disparate parts of the country left little room for the emergence of any compensatory nationalism – which does not mean that this will continue to be the case following unification.

When the people on the streets of Gdansk, Budapest, Leipzig, Prague and Sofia brought the post-war European order tumbling down, probably the last thing on their minds was that their action would put the German question back on the political agenda. But it was inevitable. Just as the division of Germany was the cornerstone of the division of Europe into two antagonistic blocs, it was reasonable to suppose that German unification would be the first step in the resolution of the European schism. Yet such a development was inevitable only in so far as the GDR, in contrast to the Federal Republic, had been unable to justify its existence on its own account. The demise of the order to which it owed its existence therefore also meant that its own fate was sealed.

The fact that the division of Europe was abolished firstly (and for the time being only) in Germany was thus related to two prior conditions: the necessary one of the end of the cold war, and the sufficient one of the asymmetry between the two German states. It was only when the two combined that unification became inevitable, both for the Germans themselves and for their neighbours.

Whether the reordering of relations in Germany will be followed by similar reordering in Europe remains a totally open question. So far, the old, bipolar order has merely been replaced by multipolar disorder; Yalta has been succeeded, particularly in the eastern part of the continent, by much that recalls the weaknesses of Versailles. Germany is part of this disorder. Yet the agreed solution – that of replacing the external control of a divided Germany by the sovereign self-control of a united one – was by no means a foregone conclusion. Many features of the unification process – from Helmut Kohl's passing unilateralism, to François Mitterrand's attempts to play the Soviet card, and Margaret Thatcher's quest to identify the atavistic traits of the German national character – sometimes created the impression that the question of Germany's future was to be decided primarily by historians.

The danger that history might once again become a present reality cannot, indeed, be ruled out. The end of Soviet supremacy in Eastern Europe, combined with German unification, signals a renaissance, at least in the short term, of the classical nation-state. This is counterbalanced in the West by political–military and political–economic integration; these have proved their ability to function in conditions of confrontation but not in a situation of opening-up to the East. Both quasi-conflicting tendencies are brought together in Germany, which, whilst remaining a member of the European Community and

NATO, must now, following the accession of the GDR, also enter upon the inheritance of 'real, existing socialism'. To this extent Germany continues, even after the end of the cold war, to reflect the situation in Europe as a whole. At the same time, Germany has once again shifted from its position on the periphery of the two European blocs – where its containment was guaranteed – to the centre of the continent, where its scope for action is enlarged.

The idea of Germany as an influential power at the centre of Europe offers scope for ambitions and fears that are at once old and new. The attraction of a policy of oscillation between (geographic) East and West, of alternately presenting one's face to one side and one's back to the other, is an old one. A new feature, however, is that Germany is participating in Western European integration while occupying a position at the centre of Europe, the integration merely being extended eastwards. Though there may not be any dramatic changes, the cumulative effect of the small steps taken in what is virtually an area of tension between the (new) inclination to fill the Central European position and the inertial force of the (old) ties with the West can determine Germany's role in Europe and exert a major influence on the fate of the continent as a whole, on whether it pulls together or once again disintegrates.

Division and integration: the two sides of German political self-justification

When, in 1945, the German Reich collapsed under the blows of the Allied forces, the history of the German nation-state, begun scarcely seventy-five years before in the Hall of Mirrors at Versailles, seemed also to have been ended forever. The total war with which Germany had covered almost the whole of Europe had ended in total defeat. It left behind it not only a devastated country, parcelled up into zones of occupation, but also a demoralised people which had robbed itself of its state and history. Though the Germans were under compulsion to make a new start, they were scarcely in a position to do this by their own efforts.

It was only with the beginning of the cold war and the reorganisation of Europe that the Germans were allowed back into the international community. A new perspective began to open up to the Germans while the logic of the cold war fostered a need to make future allies of the erstwhile enemy. The foundation of both German states was saddled with the contradiction that it had taken place in the name of German unity. But this was viewed, particularly by Konrad Adenauer the Catholic and

Walter Ulbricht the Communist, not so much as a destiny imposed on Germany by the Allies, but rather as a chance to make a new start.

The contradiction between division and unity unfolded chiefly in a contradiction between practical politics and rhetoric. The more division was consolidated, as the two states became integrated into their respective blocs, the more excessive the two became in their claims to be committed to the prime objective of German politics, namely the recovery of national unity. This unity, however, was interpreted less and less as meaning the unity of the German people without preconditions, and more in terms of a resolution of the timeless struggle between the two social systems – as 'unity in freedom' versus 'unity in socialism'. In Germany the national and social questions therefore combined in a way that meant that East and West confrontation had a kind of cold 'civil war' added to it which was emotionally charged as well.

Mutual confrontation and the demonstrative readiness to be incorporated into the two European camps were conditions of the foundation of the two German states which did more than merely shape their political self-justification. The situation also implied a radical break with the past and made it possible for German guilt and responsibility for the division of Germany simply to be repressed. As a part of the 'free world' on the one hand, and of the 'socialist world system' on the other, the two German states saw themselves exonerated of much of the burden of history. Each camp also ranged itself on the side of the historical victors and claimed that traditional malevolence was to be found only on the other side of the inner German border. Thus the theory of totalitarianism was used to show that the Soviet Union and its 'vassals' in the eastern part of Germany embodied totalitarian domination, of which the Nazi dictatorship had been an historical variant. And on the other side, the Nazi regime was characterised as a capitalist-engendered monstrosity, albeit a particularly bloody one, the chief post-war representatives of which were US imperialism and its 'agents' in the western part of Germany. However, as provisional creations intended to be stages *en route* to either liberal or socialist unity, they remained bound up with one another, from both antagonistic and revisionist motives. This expressed itself in two ways.

Firstly, it was expressed in a time-lag: the legitimising principle for the two states was mutual delimitation from 'those who had split' the German nation. Both Germanys therefore had difficulty in throwing off the shackles of the cold war. Whilst Europe stabilised, and East and West began to seek some kind of *modus vivendi*, the German states continued unbendingly to deny each other's legitimacy – the larger of the two in a more aggressive manner, the smaller, because of its weaker position, more defensively. It was only in the late 1960s and early 1970s, with the advent of *Ostpolitik* as pursued by the social–liberal coalition in Bonn, that (in Richard Löwenthal's phrase) the 'special German conflict' was brought to an end in the face of fierce conservative opposition. Consequently, in addition to their integration into the respective blocs, both German states were truly empowered to act in the foreign arena for the first time.

Secondly, however, out of division emerged common concerns. Both states came into being as bulwarks and marshalling grounds for their two alliances, bringing the inevitable fear that the Germanys would become the prime, preferred battleground. The European dilemma – that of being able to guarantee security only at the cost of potential self-destruction – was particularly strongly felt in Germany, on the front line between the two blocs. It was for this reason that, as far back as the early 1950s, the Social Democratic Party (SPD) had opposed Adenauer's policy of integration into the West, hoping that it could keep a united Germany out of the great East–West conflict. But it needed the decade of détente and the new phase of confrontation at the start of the 1980s for the divisive influence of the East–West conflict to subside to such an extent in both states that their common dilemma became visible. The 'German national interest', so Helmut Kohl and Erich Honecker concurred in the mid-1980s, was no longer lost in a clash of particular interests, but was reflected in the overriding common interest of preventing war.

Both these aspects – the exaggerated cold war practice and rhetoric and the sensitivity to the inherent risks of the East–West conflict – were bound up in each case in a specific way with the conditions that gave rise to the emergence of the two states of one nation. They reflect a range from categoric delimitation to partial commonality of interest – without, however, implying the resolution of the fundamental antagonism between the two states. Indeed, the decision to found separate states in line with the fiction of national representation made the future of both states dependent in a very basic way on the success or failure of *their* particular system.

To this extent, Konrad Adenauer's decision to forgo German unity for the sake of integration into the West appears, with hindsight, to have been as correct as it was unavoidable. It established the conditions needed to compensate successfully for the dismemberment of the nation-state through the development of an international trading country. Current talk in the Federal Republic about 'constitutional patriotism' or 'deutschmark nationalism' indicates that, after forty years of West German history, traditional national values have at least been moderated, in both their symbolism and their content. This also applied to German unification, on 3 October 1990: in marked contrast to the opening of the Wall on 9 November 1989, and despite all the official efforts to confer greater historical solemnity on the occasion, the event radiated all the charm of a government decree.

Compared with this, GDR history was a disaster. Little survived either of Walter Ulbricht's optimistic prognosis that the GDR was willing and able to 'overtake' the Federal Republic 'without having to catch up with it', or of the forced internationalism of the Party, in both its proletarian and socialist variants. Instead, the GDR preserved a German nationalism which, although serving (like nationalism all over Eastern Europe) as a means of self-assertion against Soviet usurpation, also acted as a counterweight to the inferiority complex from which the GDR suffered as a result of its obsessive preoccupation with the Federal Republic. The euphemistically termed 'socialist integration' did little to change this either. On the contrary, it created and fostered national animosities, since in the economic conditions prevailing in the East, cross-border trade and inter-relations were at best a necessary evil, by which privation rather than prosperity was increased.

For people in the GDR, the national question therefore remained a central one, since only if this were resolved could there be any prospect of realising the right to democratic self-determination and of fulfilling the wish for a better life. This situation was in marked contrast to the virtual post-nationalism that obtained in the Federal Republic, and it played an important part in shaping the concepts with which the new political leadership of the GDR sought to exert its influence, not only in the unification process but beyond this.

Germany in transition: unification versus integration?

The parts which the unification of the two German states brought together were anything but equal. It was a highly asymmetrical process, in which the smaller state was submerged and dissolved in the larger one, as the GDR acceded to the Federal Republic. Despite the differing preconditions that obtained, the leading political forces on both sides concurred in their assessment of unification. In both German states it was carried out not so much as a recreation of the German nation-state, which had at last found its vocation. It took place rather in full awareness of the concomitant risks to the Germans themselves and the legitimate fears of their neighbours. Stress was also laid on the fact that, particularly at this time, the security of Germany must always also encompass security *from* Germany. Germany's declared readiness to pursue a policy of self-restraint was, it is true, designed not least to help avoid the imposition of a special status on the country in the form of external constraints on German sovereignty. Such a possibility had hovered a good while over the two-plus-four negotiations on unity, conducted with the victorious powers of the Second World War. A more important motive, however, was the desire and ability of the repeatedly 'delayed nation' (in Helmuth Plessner's words) to be constituted this time as part of the wider community of nations, and not, as in the past, in a process of demarcation from it.

Despite the degree of agreement in principle, there were also notable differences between the new political leadership in East Berlin and the established parties in Bonn. These differences, a product of forty years of divergent development, managed to express themselves despite the fact that the Federal Republic began, only a few months after the October revolution, to reshape the political landscape in accordance with its own conceptions. The points at issue were the management of the unification process from the point of view of foreign policy, the place and role of the new Germany in Europe, and the special contribution of the GDR to unification itself and beyond.

To begin with, the West German debate was shaped not so much by the prospect of unification with the GDR as by the new possibilities which the ending of the East–West conflict had opened up. Strategies and models for European security which, under the previous restrictive conditions, had necessarily remained limited, could now be extended and made more radical. In this process, impending German unity was assigned the role of a catalyst. It was regarded, on the one hand, as constituting the first visible step to overcoming European division, and a united Germany to be contained and thus under control was, on the other, seen as being of common interest to the whole of Europe. The original Soviet demand for a militarily neutral Germany did not at any stage meet with the assent either of the Government or of the Opposition. Both rejected the idea of a return to Germany as a nation-state without ties.

The goal was the establishment of a new European peace order. On this, also, Government and Opposition were united in principle. But the question of how such a goal was to be sought and achieved, and over what period of time, divided them. The ruling parties – the Christian Democratic Union/Christian Social Union (CDU/CSU) and FDP –

considered that, however much the details might vary, the future European order must be constructed on the solid foundation of western integration, and thus on the basis of NATO and the EC. It was not least for this reason that there was never any question, as far as they were concerned, that Germany when united would have to be a member of NATO. They conceded that the European emphasis within NATO must be strengthened – for example, in the form of the WEU 'as a European pillar of the Atlantic Alliance',[1] or else by having security and military policy integrated into the EC, so that NATO would be transformed into 'an alliance between Europe and the USA'.[2] The pan-European CSCE forum, on the other hand, could, it was claimed, play only a complementary role, in institutionalised communication and control. Given that it would not be in a position, for some time to come, to organise or guarantee collective security, the CSCE could not, it was said, take the place of joint defence. It was conceded, however, that the latter would itself have to undergo change, in order to adapt to the altered conditions and to adjust to the significant reduction in old threats and the advent of new, uncertain ones.

The social democratic opposition held a quite different view. It argued for the rapid establishment of a European security system on the basis of the CSCE. This was in the tradition of older-style proposals such as the Germany Plan of the late 1950s, which foresaw the withdrawal of both German states from their alliances and their unification within the framework of a security zone based on the 1957 Rapacki Plan. The end of the East–West conflict, the social democrats claimed, meant that both military alliances, as classic products of the cold war, were now outdated and could only continue in existence, in a modified form, if given the task of organising 'the political/military transfer of the blocs to a European security system'.[3] The emphases in this approach are quite different, but the actual arrangements for the transition remain vague. Thus it was left to individuals to demand an immediate end to NATO's military integration,[4] or the creation – between the two military alliances which would continue to exist – of a Central European 'security community established by treaty', providing a collective system of security.[5] Toning down the Western European military alliance in favour of a pan-European security system also had repercussions for the firm anchoring of a united Germany. On this point, the spectrum of social democratic views ranged from the bold and categoric observation of the candidate to the chancellorship, Oskar Lafontaine, who stated, in March 1990, that it was 'a mistake' to 'suppose that a united Germany can remain in NATO',[6] to precipitate acceptance of the 'Genscher Plan'.

The plan put forward by the West German Foreign Minister, Hans-Dietrich Genscher, proposed that, following the GDR's accession to the Federal Republic, Germany should remain in NATO but that NATO should not extend its military integration eastwards. The plan was one of a number of efforts that were tactically motivated to the extent that there was a need to offer the Soviet Union compensation for the loss of 'its Germany' to the (erstwhile) enemy alliance. In late January 1990, having given up hope of any socialist renewal and thereby any chance of continued existence for the GDR, the Soviet Union consented in principle to unification. But the conditions stipulated for unity – ranging from neutrality, via German membership of both alliances, to continued responsibility for Germany by the Four Powers after unification – were rejected on principle by the Federal Government and the Western Powers.

It was left to the bilateral negotiations between Bonn and Moscow to come up with a solution to this problem. A deal was struck in July 1990, at the meeting between the Federal German Chancellor and the Soviet President, which some western observers have sarcastically dubbed 'Stavrapallo'. The conditions could scarcely have been more favourable: along the lines of the 'Genscher Plan', a united Germany was offered a free choice of military alliance, with the prospect of an extension of NATO's military structures to former GDR territory after the ending of the Soviet military presence in three to four years' time. The price, in comparison, was small: it was fixed in terms of the Federal Republic's most powerful weapon – the deutschmark – with the additional limiting of German forces to a maximum of 370,000 men. The Federal Government had always rejected any such 'singularisation' of Germany, but the upper limit turned out markedly closer to the 400,000 figure favoured by both German defence ministries than to the 300,000 limit canvassed via tortuous channels by the two foreign ministries.

It was to the GDR Government that the Gorbachev–Kohl agreement came as the greatest surprise. Not only was the GDR, once the Soviet Union's chief ally, not involved in the negotiations over its fate; it also forfeited its role as mediator between the NATO states and the Soviet Union. As the East German Prime Minister, Lothar de Maizière, had put it in his inaugural speech on 19 April 1990, the GDR had intended to exploit that role in order to 'secure a decisive say' in the proceedings leading to unity.[7] As a member of the Warsaw Pact – the military role of which was to be reduced, but the political role of which was to be extended – the GDR sought to represent German unification as not harming the security interests of its allies, and particularly of the Soviet Union.

The East German intermediary claim, however, was not confined to this medium-term task (which soon turned out to be a short-term one), the completion of which was bound up with the existence of the GDR. It also had in its sights a united Germany which, from its central position, would bind the peoples of Europe together and – in the words of Lothar de Maizière – build a 'bridge of understanding'.[8] The GDR was concerned not just with the tactics of German unification but also with the strategy of a future Germany. It was intended that something other, something more, should result than a mere consolidation of the status quo in the form of an eastward extension of the Federal Republic. The people in the GDR might be prepared to relinquish their state, but that state should not disappear without trace; the experiences of forty years of common destiny in Eastern Europe should at least be brought into a unified Germany and anchored there. There should be a new national vocation for the Germans, one that transcended their former *raison d'être*, derived as it was from the East–West conflict.

The new GDR Government was thus obliged to consent in principle to NATO membership for a united Germany. But it stipulated that there would have to be a fundamental transformation of the Western Alliance, involving, specifically, the renunciation of the strategy of flexible response, of forward defence, and of nuclear first-use. The GDR Government also stressed its own desire to initiate and foster 'the process of replacement of the military alliances by trans-alliance structures, as the first step in establishing a pan-European security system'.[9] This clearly went beyond the intentions of the Federal Government, but it indicated agreement between the ruling CDU and SPD parties in the GDR and the social democratic opposition in Bonn.

In contrast, GDR efforts to implement the 'bridge' idea in practice, elicited no response in Bonn. The Minister for Disarmament and Defence in the GDR, Rainer Eppelmann, decreed, for example, that: 'Even after unification, there will continue to be a second German army on GDR territory; it will not be a member of any military alliance, will fulfil its own territorial security functions in this area, and must be structured, equipped, and trained accordingly.' This would ensure, Eppelmann said, that 'the two German states and their armies assume a bridging function between the military systems of the two pacts'.[10]

Nothing came of this, and the GDR's whole ambitious claim to want to act as a bridge between East and West foundered on the realities of international diplomacy shortly after the formation of the new government. 'No-one can accuse the unification process of requiring the GDR to play an independent role,' was the pertinent and rueful remark made in retrospect by one of the numerous West German advisers to the GDR Government.[11] Yet this by no means implies that Germany's future role has been decided once and for all. For although unification has taken place according, as it were, to West German terms of trade, that unification has also fundamentally altered the Federal Republic's own conditions of existence. To this extent, the GDR was merely setting out, unilaterally and in rather overstated terms, what the task of future German foreign policy will be, namely to strike a balance between Western European and pan-European integration, between the national inclination to build bridges to the East and Germany's duty as an ally to remain loyal to the West.

The ambivalence of unification

'Responsibility' is probably the most important notion to have accompanied unification, both inside and outside Germany. It is also the most puzzling: embracing obligation and inclination, expectations and fears, and signalling both trust and mistrust. It only acquires its real fascination, however, in combination with a series of illustrative or defining adjectives.

Its most obvious usage, prima facie, relates to Germany's *full responsibility* for its own fate. As a result of the negotiations with the Four Powers, Germany recovered its formal, unrestricted sovereignty – formal in the sense of being established in international law; it became a state like any other. But that is only one facet. The formative influence of the conditions in which the two former German states came into being is an equally important aspect. Both owed their creation to their ties with East or West – ties which they not only accepted but were dependent upon for their existence and the preservation of their integrity. Under the aegis of their allies, both were able to grow to be the economic giants of the two alliances, though at the cost – welcomed rather than shunned – of remaining political dwarves. All that is now past history.

It follows from this that Germany will in future have to bear a *greater responsibility*. All German politicians, in government and opposition, regard themselves equally committed to this responsibility, without, however, necessarily meaning the same thing once they move beyond their abstract declaration of belief. Increased German responsibility also has two sides to it. On the one hand, there are the continuing ties, now no longer an existential requirement. On the other, there is the increased potential that has resulted from unification and has made Germany into an influential European power – some even talk exaggeratedly of a world power. The Foreign Minister, Hans-Dietrich Genscher, never tires of breaking increased German power down into increased German responsibility.[12] But this is no more than a rhetorical declaration of intent, for whereas power has indeed increased, the art of coping with it, and thus also responsibility, has still to be mastered. The unification of the two German states is, after all, not taking place within the continuum of West German history but has created qualitatively new conditions for German politics, both internally and externally. Germany will, at any rate, no longer be able to hide behind the broad backs of its allies.

The growth in both 'full responsibility' and 'greater responsibility' therefore requires the elaboration of an 'ethics of responsibility', precisely as envisaged by Max Weber. One of the major objectives of such an ethic would be to redefine the relations between (national) autonomy and (allied) integration. Motivated more by external expectation than domestic inclination, such an ethic clearly also requires a *new responsibility*, that is to say a new role for a united Germany. A test-case in this regard is the German involvement in the Gulf crisis: in concrete terms, Germany's readiness to deploy troops there. There is broad agreement that the terms of the West German Basic Law, once tightly drawn in a spirit of prudent self-restraint, should be relaxed. This will make it possible in future for German forces to be deployed outside the territory covered by NATO, though it remains an open and hotly disputed question whether this should include out-of-area NATO operations or should be restricted to participation in UN peacekeeping forces (and possible future CSCE units).

A more difficult and far more important issue is that of defining the new German role in Europe. This leads to another type of responsibility, namely the *special responsibility* that stems from twentieth-century German history. This is a complicated story. Awareness of German guilt and knowledge of its national genealogy is undoubtedly an important yardstick and reference point for German politics. But talk of the special German responsibility has another side to it. When, in 1987, Helmut Kohl and Erich Honecker together pointed to German history and declared their commitment to a 'community of responsibility for peace', they were already thinking chiefly of the special threat under which both German states found themselves, and were therefore aiming to correct history.

This is happening again today, in a different way. On the basis of

Germany's special responsibility for peace, the end of the cold war is being used to back demands that Germany should set an example by dismantling all its armed forces and unilaterally demilitarising itself. Not only has this demand managed to rally behind it a bizarre coalition ranging from the peace movement in both German states to the Party of Democratic Socialism/Socialist Unity Party (PDS/SED) and former National People's Army (NPA) officers who evidently hope to achieve in the arena of democratic debate what they were prevented from achieving on the battlefield, namely to draw the Federal Army into the whirlpool of their own destruction. It is also based on a peculiarly Teutonic logic: who else, after all, would think that someone twice convicted of robbery was a particularly apposite and responsible choice for the task of guarding a bank?[13] Reference to a special, historically derived German responsibility also always implies – and this is the reverse side of the coin – the risk of a new, and ultimately purely morally motivated, 'special German way'.

But there are other respects in which the messages to be found in the legacy of history are equivocal. Thus unification opens up one's view to the whole of German history, in that it removes the special immunity that obtained in the two (former) German states. Lothar de Maizière already laid stress on this in his inaugural speech, when he said: 'In Germany there is a lot of history to work through, especially the history which we attributed to others and therefore related too little to ourselves.'[14] This is true for both sides. At the same time, however, there can be no doubt that the end of German division also spells the end of atonement. Not that Germany will immediately start trampling around like a bull in a china shop again. The danger is rather that, despite all the noble designs and intentions, it might feel fundamentally misunderstood, particularly where it seems that the determination to safeguard peace ends up in German unilateralism. This motif is also familiar from German history. The dual historical connotation of unification can then easily lead to a situation in which – to use another image from German ideology – after forty divided years as an 'anvil', Germany once again brandishes the 'hammer'.[15]

Of significance for the future conduct of Germany as well – a 'major asset for our future', as Chancellor Kohl put it – is the fact that unification has taken place without the country's having to mortgage itself at all externally.[16] The degree to which it is mortgaged internally, however, is enormous. Germany may have been unified politically on 3 October 1990, but economic and social unification will take many more years to realise. Unification has joined the unjoinable, with the result that the weaker elements will disintegrate and new elements will emerge only after an arduous struggle.

Since the currency union of 1 July 1990, which has steadily proved to be the most brutal and costly means to economic rehabilitation, the East German economy has been meandering on the edge of the abyss. Whole sectors of industry that were once the pearls of the SED regime are disappearing from the map. The numbers of unemployed or on short-time work is up in the millions. The social system, from pensions to sickness and unemployment benefit, can only be sustained by subsidies of tens of thousands of millions of DM from Bonn. The communes and *Länder* are drained so dry that they cannot perform even the most basic of functions. Estimates indicate that an annual transfer of at least DM130 thousand million of public money – more than one-third of the normal West German budget – is needed, and even this is only enough to assure basic provision far below western standards. It cannot come as a surprise to anyone that unification is taking the form mainly of a quarrel about distribution between a prospering West and a disintegrating East.

No doubt the free fall in which the former GDR now finds itself will sooner or later come to an end, but the end is not yet in sight. The consequences of this are all the more grave in that the SED regime has left behind it people who have been isolated from the outside world and made dependent on the care and direction supplied by the state. To be able to stand on their own two feet in a market economy, especially one which, as currently practised in the former GDR, bears all the hallmarks of Manchester School capitalism or of an invasion by western robber-barons, is simply beyond their capabilities. On top of this there is the legacy of the state security services whose tentacles penetrated so deeply into society that their poison continues to destroy relations between people even today. Finally, one must not forget the hundreds of thousands of former civil servants, now politically disorientated and socially demoted, whose prospects are extremely dim.

As a result of these developments, a potential for conflict is building up in the eastern part of Germany which harbours within it a considerable threat to the political culture and stability of the whole of unified Germany. The proportions seem to tell a straightforward story: 61 million Germans in the West versus 16 million in the East. But if one considers the political parties, the picture immediately changes. Thus the addition to the FDP of 140,000 members of the former GDR Liberal and National Democratic bloc-parties is twice the size of the FDP's membership in the Federal Republic. In the case of the CDU, the increase represented by the addition of the East German CDU and the former peasants' parties, though less, is still equal to between one-fifth and one-quarter of its total membership. Only the SPD failed to make any significant gains, winning only between 10,000 and 30,000 members.

But the PDS, the successor to the party of government, the SED, still has over 200,000 members as well, and thus still disposes of considerable potential. This is all the more critical in that the party, like an iceberg, is currently showing its reformed, social democratic tip, letting it shine out like a lighthouse under the chairmanship of Gregor Gysi. Underneath, however, lies the mass of old Stalinists and supporters of the past regime; they have been silenced by the upheavals, but not forever; and they continue to have an effect, banded together for purposes of mutual support.

In so far as it is the task of the parties to formulate and organise the political will of the populace, there are thus important platforms open for influencing politics in the Federal Republic. This is not true of the armed forces. The Federal Army took over what was left of the National People's Army unilaterally and without a fight. There is something Kafkaesque about the 1,300-strong Eastern command of the Federal Army installing itself in the former NPA holy of holies, the Ministry of Defence in Strausberg; or about former NPA soldiers serving alongside Soviet garrisons under West German command and in West German uniform. The takeover of the NPA also meant that the Federal Army acquired a squadron of MiG 29s, the Soviet wonderbird that caused such agitation in NATO and is now flying with the West German national emblem on it.

The German armed forces will probably face greater problems with their *raison d'être* in future. As is the case with NATO, their fate is crucially bound up with the East–West conflict. However, whereas NATO at least still guarantees the American presence in Europe, and guarantees an equally sought-after control on the Germans, the end of the cold war means that for the present the Federal Army has no direct justification for its existence. The attempt, in 1988, of the Defence Minister of the time, Rupert Scholz, to present ownership of one's own armed forces simply as a 'mark of sovereignty' did not, at any rate, win a particularly enthusiastic response.[17] Reference to such seemingly irrefutable laws of the nation-state is clearly disallowed by German history. This does not mean, given new and continuing threats in East and South, that the Federal Army is about to be plunged into an identity crisis. The reduction of its strength from a pan-German total of some 540,000 men to what one may suppose will be a temporary level of 370,000 is, in itself, likely to occupy all its attention for the next four years.

The problems within Germany will claim so much energy for the foreseeable future that there will be only a small proportion left to direct towards the exterior. This could lead to the paradoxical situation where Germany's foreign policy assumes much greater importance for those around it but becomes less significant for Germany itself – particularly since the country is no longer dependent on the outside or directed by it. Yet we currently find ourselves in a transitional phase, inaugurated not least by German unification, in which Germany's neighbours are also having to redefine their relationship to the new creation and change their own policy accordingly. This necessarily has a retroactive effect on Germany.

Though there may not be a 'struggle between two lines', two tendencies have become apparent. Among the British, for example, Geoffrey Howe, former Foreign Minister and deputy Prime Minister, concluded that the emergence of a stronger Germany necessitated a stronger Europe. If a stronger Germany is to remain firmly anchored in Europe, which it should and will do, he argued, it follows logically that the anchor itself must be strengthened.[18] The opposite position had an equally prominent advocate in Margaret Thatcher, in whose view the strengthened version of Germany necessitated not so much a firmer anchorage as a stronger counterweight. This is the alternative one finds throughout Europe – that between integration (the readiness to sacrifice one's own sovereignty) and coalition (the determination to defend sovereignty at any price).

Germany has followed Federal German tradition in opting for integration, in accepting 'further restrictions on sovereignty for the sake of Europe', as the German Foreign Minister, Hans-Dietrich Genscher, put it.[19] One of the reasons for this is undoubtedly that the economic interconnectedness which has now been achieved has become the basis of the Federal Republic as a trading country. But what is the correct goal in terms of broader aims should not be misconstrued as purely functional, as if there were no alternative. History has destroyed many a liberal illusion in this regard.[20] At present, however, there is indeed no alternative for Germany – however attractive the prospect may be of extending the new Central European role eastwards.

Eastern temptations

Economically, the eastern part of Europe will have to struggle so hard for at least the next ten years with the legacy of real socialism that it will largely cease operating as a partner in the international division of labour. Again, from the political point of view, the end of Soviet hegemony has left the East so fragmented that any coherent German *Ostpolitik* is impossible, and individual bilateral relations will always be accompanied by mistrust and friction. In addition there is the historical legacy, of particular significance in this area.

The most straightforward case is that of Hungary, an old ally from darker days; and those are the days Budapest seems to want to pick up on. Thus the Antall Government is openly avowing that Germany is Hungary's most important ally. The Nemeth Government was somewhat more discreet about this, out of deference to the Soviet Union and the GDR. Hungary may be rather on the periphery, yet even here there are very real possibilities of embroilment. For example, the country is currently engaged in a latent conflict of nationalities with Romania in which Germany is also involved because of the German minority – albeit now rapidly declining – in Siebenbürgen and Banat. Romania for its part enjoys the special protection of another Romance country: France. This could create openings for Franco-German influence, but it could quite possibly also lead to Franco-German misunderstandings.

Relations along the Bonn/Berlin–Warsaw–Moscow axis are much more complex. For understandable reasons, Poland is resisting the establishment of a new European frontier along the Oder. It wishes, via its co-operation with Germany, to open up the gates to Europe – but it also wishes in the process to resite the much-abused European border a little further east, along the Bug. Again, in the eyes not only of the Poles, the development of Soviet–German relations harbours the very real danger that the country in between will simply be disregarded.

Relations with Poland will continue to be difficult. All German politicians attach paramount importance to relations with their eastern neighbour, and many go as far as to equate the work that has to be done here with that involved in Franco-German reconciliation. Although the Germans' equivocation on the border question created new problems, its chief result was to expose the fundamental difficulties that obtain in this area. Polish–German relations at present also involve a confrontation between, on the one hand, an attitude of moral rigour (fuelled by Catholicism) and economic inferiority, and, on the other hand, untackled guilt and economic superiority. And finally there is a mysterious, constantly growing German minority in Poland, which has found numerous vociferous champions in Germany. Despite the fact that the border treaty will be followed up in 1991 by a comprehensive treaty on co-operation, the reality of German–Polish relations will in all probability not manage to keep pace with the declarations of intent made in such agreements.

This has already ceased to be the case for the Soviet Union. The extensive financial concessions made by the Federal Republic at unification were no doubt viewed mainly as the price to be paid for political steadfastness. But they also instituted a kind of special German custody over the progress of Soviet reforms that has quite enough momentum to carry on beyond German unification. This is all the more true in that the Soviet Union has managed to combine its own desires with attractive offers in a very effective way – not to mention its lever of more than 300,000 Soviet troops on German soil. However, as with other countries, the task of reconciliation with the survivors of the German war of extermination has yet to be dealt with. But the Germanophiles are already making their presence felt once again in Moscow. As far as they are concerned, Stavropol was clearly the turning-point that broke the ice, even though they themselves had no part in bringing it about. There is little rationality and much emotion at work here – but perhaps this is precisely what binds Germans and Russians so closely together.

Thus Nikolai Portugalov, a venerable expert on Germany from Brezhnev's time, writes that in comparison with the rosy future of German–Soviet relations, Rapallo shrinks to a mere historical footnote: 'The new conciliation between Russians and Germans means much more to the Soviet side; it means expectation of a process of osmosis that will allow us, with German help, to return to Europe. For the Soviet Union this means establishing a social market economy that merits the name; and for a united Germany it means achieving the status of a great power through this co-operation.'[21] How profound must be the Soviet Union's despair about its own situation for it to disregard all relevant yardsticks and look, of all people, to the Germans to provide, in Portugalov's words, 'salvation from the impending catastrophe'. The Moscow sirens have, at any rate, raised so much dust in Bonn that the Chancellor felt he must protest against such a 'provocation'. That provocation will be followed by others.

The main problem currently afflicting German policy towards the East – and likely to continue to do so for the foreseeable future – is not so much Germany's own ambitions but the sometimes vehement and highly disparate expectations of which it is the target. The only country to provide any relief here is Czechoslovakia which, after twenty years of 'normalised' isolation, still cogitates over a policy on Germany. The idea of building a bridge to the East in such circumstances, in order if possible to underline the 'world dimension of German politics',[22] is not just absurd, it is impossible. Germany can – and should – act as a western bridgehead to the East, but the notion of its forming a bridge between East and West is out of the question.

Notes

1 Alfred Dregger in *Die Welt*, 31 January 1990.
2 See Karl Lamers, 'Eine Europäische Lösung für Deutschland', Memorandum of 2 March 1990 and lecture at the Deutsche Gesellschaft für Auswärtige Politik, 23 April 1990.
3 SPD paper on 'Security aspects of German unification within the framework of European integration', Press Service of the SPD, Bonn, 25 April 1990.
4 See Hermann Scheer and Heidemarie Wieczorek-Zeul, 'Deutschland und die NATO', Memorandum on the question of NATO membership for a united Germany, Bonn, 5 March 1990.
5 'Ein geeintes Deutschland in einem neuen Europa. Vom Blocksystem zur Sicherheitsgemeinschaft', *Hamburger Informationen zur Friedensforschung und Sicherheitspolitik*, Institut für Friedensforschung und Sicherheitspolitik an der Universität Hamburg, April 1990, p. 6.
6 Interview on Saarland Radio, 3 March 1990.
7 Reproduced in *Neues Deutschland*, 20 April 1990, p. 5.
8 *Ibid.*, p. 6.
9 *Ibid.*
10 Speech by Rainer Eppelmann at the NPA Commanders' Conference, reproduced in *Militärreform in der DDR*, Ministerium für Abrüstung und Verteidigung, XVII, 1990, p. 2.
11 Carlchristian von Braunmühl, 'Die Herstellung der Einheit ist keine gemeinsame Sache geworden', in *Frankfurter Rundschau*, 24 August 1990, p. 14.
12 See, for example, the interview with him in *Der Spiegel*, 1 October 1990, p. 32.
13 For an instructive account, see Wolfgang Bruckmann, 'Der Berg kreisste und gebar: nichts', in *Frankfurter Rundschau*, 30 August 1990, p. 6.
14 *Neues Deutschland*, 20 April 1990, p. 5.
15 True to the motto: Be my friend or I'll strangle you!
16 Chancellor's official statement on unification, reproduced in *Frankfurter Rundschau*, 5 October 1990, p. 8.
17 Rupert Scholz, 'Schutz der Freiheit in wehrhafter Demokratie', *Europäische Wehrkunde*, XXXVII, no. 9, 1988, p. 491.
18 Speech to the British Chamber of Commerce in Germany, Frankfurt, reproduced in *Frankfurter Rundschau*, 20 September 1990, p. 16.
19 E.g., in *Der Spiegel*, 1 October 1990, p. 32.
20 The following observation dating from 1927 speaks volumes in this regard: 'But overall one can say that, in the case of the peoples of white race now inhabiting central and western Europe and America, the mode of thinking termed "militaristic" by Herbert Spencer has been superseded by that to which he has given the name "industrial".' Just six years later things turned out very differently. Ludwig Mises, *Liberalismus*, Jena, Gustav Fischer, 1927, p. 133.
21 Nikolai Portugalov, 'Der Dornenweg zur Weltmacht', in *Der Spiegel*, 8 October 1990, p. 184.
22 *Ibid.*, p. 190.

Eastern Europe: economic transition and ethnic tension

The transformation of East-Central Europe in the years towards 2000 will be an extremely complex process which cannot be understood without an appreciation of the region's economic and ethnic diversity. This chapter sets out to examine these diversities, and the relationship between them, which the collapse of communism has revealed and which threaten the stability of the whole continent.

Certainly, in the immediate aftermath of the Second World War there was a genuine concern by some western commentators to identify and address the ethnic and attendant territorial issues of Eastern Europe (mindful that these issues had been major contributory factors in the cataclysms of 1914 and 1939).[1] But the swift division of Europe into two mutually hostile blocs soon put paid to such sensitivities. Indeed, despite lip-service paid to such notions as German reunification or Baltic sovereignty, a conventional wisdom soon emerged which stressed the apparent homogeneity of the Soviet Empire in Eastern Europe, emphasising its military integration (the Warsaw Pact), its economic interdependence (through COMECON), and the twin imperatives of Marxist-Leninist ideology and the one-party totalitarian state. Marxism scorned ethnic or religious sentiment as false consciousness, elevating class conflict and the dictatorship of the proletariat instead. The Party admitted no legitimate rivals to either the ideology or to the state mechanisms that enforced it. From this perspective, the diversity of Eastern Europe seemed much diminished, leading (as Zbigniew Brzezinski has argued) to the widespread western assumption of homogeneity.[2] The assumption was seriously flawed, at best a wildly over-generalised caricature.

The persistence of national diversity

As Joseph Rothschild has shown, the reality (especially after the death of Stalin) was a series of challenges to the supposedly monolithic nature of Eastern Europe.[3] An assertion of nationalism was first apparent in

Yugoslavia's defiance of Moscow in the 1940s, followed by unrest in East Germany, Poland and Hungary in the 1950s, the Soviet Union's acceptance of 'polycentrism' (different routes to socialism) in the 1960s, the Czechoslovak Movement of the sixties (along with the distancing of Albania and Romania), and Polish trade unionism in the seventies and early eighties. At times such challenges were overtly nationalistic, opposing Soviet dominance and employing powerful symbols of national identity and unity (such as the Roman Catholic Church in Poland) to mobilise sentiment and support.[4]

In the wake of *glasnost* and *perestroika* in the Soviet Union, the process of differentiation was much accelerated by what a Soviet Foreign Affairs spokesman, Gennadi Gerasimov, dubbed 'Sinatra doctrine', by which East European countries could go their own way. The most startling consequence was the fall of the Berlin Wall and the speedy construction of a united Germany. Like the highly visible reassertions of Polish and Hungarian independence, the unification of Germany was also an expression of national identity and unity in the face of Soviet retreat; implicit was a desire to give territorial and institutional expression to the concept of German nationhood. In all the revolutions of 1989, from the basically peaceful transfer of power in Hungary to the bloody uprising in Romania, one can see 'people power' being moulded by the different experiences of countries under Soviet domination.

The return to diversity, however, was to be much more than the reassertion of the independence of nation-states. *Perestroika* heralded not only the demise of Soviet influence but also the discrediting of Marxism-Leninism and the end of one-party totalitarian rule. The resultant step towards pluralism looked at times more like a rush to fragmentation as new expectations and aspirations unleashed pent-up demands. Foremost amongst these were ethnic and attendant territorial concerns, reflected in the work of scholars who were now obliged to revise their assessment of the region. Stephen Horak, for example, catalogued the seemingly endless combinations of ethnic minorities within the states of Eastern Europe, while David Turnock explained the historical and geographical factors that accounted for the intricate patterns of population movement and settlement.[5]

It has been stated that communist rule collapsed not so much because of a triumph of civil society (a widely-shared belief in social tolerance and political participation) but because of a rotten economic system that could not satisfy even the most basic consumer expectations.[6] There is little doubt that aspirations concerning standards of living were increasingly highlighted with the opening of borders in 1989 and, in some countries, the loosening of media control. In the case of the German Democratic Republic, the proximity of a successful western economy served to highlight the failure of Stalinism. Yet this is a simplistic approach, with an inherent danger of interpreting the movement to political freedom in terms of western perceptions of sophisticated consumer desires. Initially, the real challenge to Marxism-Leninism (particularly in countries like Czechoslovakia) was the concept of human rights as enshrined in the Helsinki Charter. This provided the intellectual basis from which to attack and erode the official system, and its significance should not be underestimated.[7]

The early stages of revolution placed concepts of political freedom high on the agenda. However, as the post-revolutionary stage was reached, the diversity of experience (both political and economic) sowed the seeds of the break-up of the Eastern bloc as Westerners had known it. It was not just communist government that died; more dynamic was the demise of Eastern Europe as a conceptual entity. It now became important to take account of seven polities (at least) instead of merely one.[8] The Eastern bloc stood revealed not as a bloc at all, but as separate countries, diverse within themselves and with very different economic and political potentials. We turn, first, to the economic legacy of Stalinism.

The Stalinist legacy and economic diversity

To speak of Stalinist systems of economic management is to imply homogeneity. From such a perspective, Eastern Europe has suffered the crisis of an ideologically-driven, centralised, planned economy: unrealistic pricing policies, immobility of labour, inordinate military burdens and, above all, severe technological backwardness. The failure of technological innovation has meant that, in spite of all the efforts and promises, the Stalinist modernisation experiment failed to change the relative global position of Eastern European countries in their efforts to catch up with the West. Eastern Europe was relatively more backward in the late 1980s than it was thirty years before; technologically it had slipped to a Third World level.

This homogeneity was imposed by Soviet rule; that is, a system where all areas of political and economic decision-making were directed by a particular ideological premiss regardless of its appropriateness to the country concerned, and where individuality was sacrificed at the expense of political conformity. The dynamics of change in the international economic system were thus ignored, so that whereas the West moved away from economic planning in the late seventies, the economic structure imposed in Eastern Europe in the early post-war period remained intact. As a result, the opportunities for increasing international competitiveness diminished. Economic reality had been forced aside by strategic priorities.

Leaving aside the wider implications of this system, there existed specific debilitating features. For example, the lack of an effective pricing system produced a distortion between consumer cost and actual resource cost, resulting in either scarcity or surplus, scarcity producing an accumulation of savings. Standardisation of goods produced quantity at some levels but quality was poor. Labour mobility was restricted, training levels remained low, and lack of innovation fossilised industry at a labour-intensive level. Long-standing norms of bureaucratic procedure were perpetuated in order to maintain monopolistic practices. No income constraint was forced on manufacturers, thereby reducing competitiveness. At the same time there was an irrational use of resources, leading to environmental degradation. Thus the infrastructure of Eastern European countries remained unaffected by new technological processes. In sum, any opportunities for economic change and growth which might have resulted from enterprise and innovation were stifled.

Internal political and economic problems in Eastern Europe resulted in increasing popular discontent, the emergence of opposition movements, and splits within the ruling elite between conservatives and the reformers. This process was further complicated by the emergence of a new generation in the élite which challenged the revolutionary old guard.[9] This generation understood better the needs of a modern society and was increasingly open to reformist ideas. Beliefs in the old ideological formulae were questioned, as was the nature of the task of managing and centralising the economy.

However, to describe the economic crisis suffered by countries in Eastern Europe in these terms alone would be to ignore the differing experiences of, and reactions to, the Stalinist model. Resource availability, geopolitical considerations, cultural factors and historical experience had all contributed to a diversity of responses, reflected in the varying aspirations of the several populations and the different approaches to reform. The specific experiences of Poland and Hungary serve to illuminate this point.

Poland can be credited with having had a dominant influence in forcing the pace of change in Eastern Europe. Poland's experience of arbitrary resource allocation and her continuing dependence on labour-intensive heavy industry had produced a steadily declining standard of living. Political protest, combined with Catholicism as a focus for dissent, was fuelled by the intransigence of the regime. Indeed, the imposition of martial law in 1980 blocked any attempt at political and economic reform. Thus the parlous state of the economy brought into sharp relief the decline of the legitimacy of Soviet-backed rule.

Hungary's experience was one of 'goulash communism', involving the acceptance and implementation of a degree of economic reform.[10] Hungary's centrally-planned system was replaced in the early 1970s by a complex bargaining mechanism between enterprise managers and the government bureaucracy in which prices, credits, interest rates, subsidies and other factors were the subject of negotiation. Often the pressure of different political lobbies resulted in irrational economic decisions. Still, Hungary went much further than Poland in establishing new economic levers, like the two-level system of banking and the value added tax. However, Hungary's approach to debt-servicing undermined further attempts at reform, the government continuing to borrow heavily on the international account. But this did enable Hungary to maintain a high standard of living – unlike Romania which reduced its living standard to Draconian depths in order to repay foreign debts, effectively destroying its economy.

The process of economic transformation

Lech Walesa predicted in 1989 that the transformation of the Stalinist economic system to a western-style market economy would be complex. History demonstrated how capitalist economies (albeit backward) could be transformed to socialist economies but not how one might be moved from socialism to capitalism, a problem that was increased by the rapidly growing technological gap which made transference more problematic.

Nevertheless, the move towards markets became a fundamental goal and instrument of the anticipated changes in the economic systems in Eastern Europe. The earliest domestic debates were concerned with the notion of a socialist market economy. This concept allowed for the continuation of state control over what were considered national benefit areas (there is a close similarity here with the concepts behind the nationalisation of British industry following the financial Dunkirk of the Second World War). However, in the ideological positions of various governments and political parties, the understanding of 'the market' was by no means identical. Some saw the need to move towards a market system with the state abrogating all forms of control, while others placed emphasis on the continuing importance of state control and the establishment of a welfare state market system.[11]

Romania and Bulgaria both favoured the continuation of socialist principles, with the deregulation of areas in the economy that had suffered most under the Stalinist model. In Poland and Hungary the views and policies of the governments favoured a socialist market economy, while in Czechoslovakia more emphasis was placed on a welfare state-led market economy. But since the dismantling of the Stalinist economic system and the construction of a market economy is a parallel process, it is far from clear what kind of market system will emerge in these countries. The characteristics of their market systems will be shaped not only by economists but also by differing internal and external factors and forces, processes that under any circumstances will be difficult and full of painful problems. In particular one should not underestimate the effort in recasting the laws relating to property and economic activity, the length of the process inevitably hindering economic transformation. Throughout the region the task was made even more difficult by rising oil prices and the fall in trade as a result of the unification of Germany – though Poland and Hungary have tried to compensate for this by increasing their trade with hard currency markets, particularly the European Community.

The construction of the main institutions and the introduction of the categories of the market in themselves create significant socio-economic problems. One of the most important tasks in all the post-communist societies is the re-education of the former communist *nomenklatura* and the proletarian working class employed mainly in large state-owned factories (and desperately insecure about their future).[12] Newly-elected governments could hardly avoid the social cost of unemployment caused by the introduction of less labour-intensive working practices. The corrupt 'lubricants' by which resources were distributed under the totalitarian regime also caused severe problems of readjustment. Petr Pithart, Prime Minister of the Czech Republic, explained that 'entrepreneurship under the totalitarian system meant the black market, profit without social responsibility and parasitism'.[13] In the future, those who will get rich fastest in the new system will be those who profited under the old regime. In some countries where democracy is still fragile this could cause a swing back to more Draconian forms of government. Indeed, after the initial euphoria of the revolutions of 1989 there was a sober recognition of the difficulties ahead. The people may become increasingly dissatisfied with the bald statement of these difficulties, as in the Polish presidential elections where an outsider,

Stanislaw Tyminski, managed to achieve nearly a third of the vote. In the autumn of 1990 both Hungary and Romania suffered riots because of high prices for petrol and other commodities. In Romania, as indeed in Bulgaria, the continuing dominance of the old guard meant that tensions remained high; broken promises could lead to full-scale civil unrest in the future.

Western economic and financial institutions argue that, in the long term, change in East-Central Europe has to occur at the institutional level. Privatisation, the creation of a modern banking system and all kinds of financial institutions, the development of stock markets and the growth of new businesses, all must be confirmed if Europe is to se a real rejuvenation in the fortunes of these economies. The most pressing need at the institutional level is a drive towards privatisation. The most pertinent question is how to achieve it in countries where the wherewithal for private enterprise has been obliterated by the communist regimes. Added to this is the sheer scale of the endeavour. For example, there are 7,000 state enterprises facing privatisation in Poland alone.[14] There also exists a considerable obstacle in the chronic shortage of capital. In some cases, as in the Soviet Union and Bulgaria, this is aggravated by the population holding excess savings. However, the experiences of Yugoslavia, Poland and Hungary indicate that these reserves are quickly eroded by the inflation that tends to accompany economic decentralisation and the gradual introduction of market-orientated reforms. Finally, at the implementation stage of privatisation, another obstacle is reached: the near total absence of market forces and hence of realistic pricing mechanisms. In centrally-planned economies, the distortions in prices were compounded over the years until rational economic decisions became impossible. Labour issues are bound to make decisions harder, given that privatisation will create the formerly unheard-of phenomenon of unemployment.

Although defence spending accounts for a relatively small amount of GDP in Eastern Europe compared to that in the Soviet Union (2–4 per cent compared to 15–18 per cent), the military-industrial complex in most countries serves as another drag on much-needed resources. Czechoslovakia is renowned for production of military equipment, but Poland has the largest weapons sector, including important naval yards and a new aviation sector. Major shortfalls in arms orders due to reduced demand from the Soviet Union and the Third World has meant a drive towards efficiency, productivity and profitability. This has created pressure on the need to begin conversion and diversification, to find new markets and to develop international partnerships in order to acquire capital and expertise. However, there are significant problems in the conversion process. Specifically, there is the difficulty of securing investment to re-tool production lines, and so the financial position of these industries in the early 1990s has worsened. The best hope of dealing with this problem lies in either securing western investment through joint ventures or increasing export sales. Certainly, once the problem of technological backwardness has been overcome, the defence industries can offer a western partner a well-established infrastructure, skilled labour, some design expertise and, not least, relatively low production costs. Indeed, these industries may prove more interesting to western investment than some of the other monolithic state-owned industries.

Pace and diversity of economic change

There is little controversy, then, about the proposition that the way forward in Eastern Europe involves transformation at all levels to the sort of economic system commonly found in the European Community. Yet there is also an acceptance that this transformation cannot succeed without western help and investment, the one of course depending on the other. As to the speed of change, Jeffrey Sachs (Professor of International Relations, Harvard University), speaking at the Robbins Memorial Lecture in January 1991, pressed for rapid privatisation of all assets, lest hyperinflation and the misappropriation of resources lead to damaging waves of discontent. The risks of delay, he argued, were seen most clearly in the Soviet Union where the inability to press forward with reforms had left the power of the military-industrial complex entrenched. The failure of the reform in the Soviet Union made it even more imperative that the Eastern European countries demonstrate to the West their willingness to endure wholesale economic transition. They would have to avoid propping up loss-making enterprises, even though in the interim period living standards may decline while unemployment rises.

But whilst fiscal policy can be revolutionised overnight – for example Poland made dramatic changes in prices and exchange rates on 1 January 1990 – both western commentators and economists as well as government officials in the post-communist countries increasingly realise that structural change is going to be a slow process in which the expectations of the populations will run ahead of the practical realities involved in the move to a market-orientated economy. It is evident that macroeconomic change is one thing; changing attitudes, political language and structures is quite another.

In any case, economic change is bound to follow different paths in each of the different countries, reflecting their individual resource bases, geographical links and historical experiences. For example, the three states bordering on prosperous Austria and Germany have the best chance of attracting investment from the European Community and from American and Asian companies – drawn by low wages, a relatively skilled workforce, and proximity to EC markets. Prospects become bleaker, however, as one moves south and east. Albania, to take the extreme case, is only beginning to open its doors to the twentieth century. In Bulgaria (where a new Coalition Government replaced the Communist Party) and Romania (where the ruling National Salvation Front has links with the apparatus of the deposed Ceausescu regime), political maturity remains as elusive as economic prosperity.

Yugoslavia presents an example of how the loosening of communist authority unleashed a tide of nationalism that threatened the transition to a truly market-orientated economy. The Prime Minister, Ante Markovic, attempted to strengthen Yugoslav federalism through economic reforms. Initially he met with some success; inflation was reduced from an annual rate of 2,655 per cent in 1989 to 120 per cent in 1990.[15] However, economic issues were overtaken by political priorities in the constituent republics, allowing living standards to decline further. The republics in effect undermined the Prime Minister's economic reforms. They blocked the privatisation process and the restructuring of the banking system. The republics failed to curtail spending and continued to subsidise loss-making enterprises. As political agitation, widespread violence and clashes with the army erupted in 1991, much-needed western investment shied away from Yugoslavia.

There is, however, something of a dilemma here that may not be fully appreciated in the West. The question is, which is the more stabilising (or indeed legitimate) in East-Central Europe – the expression of ethnic identity, or the attempted creation of a carbon copy western-style market-orientated economic system? Are there dangers in the West Europeans attempting to impose a new sort of homogeneity? We now turn to the ethnic issues which have revived to destabilise states and create tensions among them.

The rise of ethnic tensions: Yugoslavia, Czechoslovakia and Bulgaria

Like the peace settlement of 1919, the considerable population movement and readjustment of borders after 1945 failed to reduce the problem of ethnic diversity within nation-states. Only Poland (where 95 per cent of its 40 million people are both ethnic Poles and Roman Catholics), Hungary (where 90 per cent of its 11 million are Magyar) and Albania approach anything like national homogeneity, and even in these three cases there are residual territorial issues based upon long-standing ethnic divisions. It was inevitable, therefore, that as the states of Eastern Europe extricated themselves from Soviet dominance, so their latent ethnic problems would re-emerge.

True, many of the new expectations and aspirations moulded by the events of the late 1980s were of an inherently economic nature. But, as argued earlier, the prospects for transformation in Eastern Europe to capitalist, market-orientated liberal democracies (though varying considerably from one country to the next) were by no means roseate, and the likelihood of early fulfilment of economic expectations was minimal. Herein lay a danger for states which were anxious to reconstruct their legitimacy in the post-communist era, for economic deprivation could mobilise disaffected ethnic groups within the state. It is relevant at this point to note that in the 1970s and 1980s, academics became more aware of diversity within *Western* European states, exploring the processes of state-formation and pointing to a series of centre–periphery relations within these states.[16] Political, economic and cultural power was concentrated in varying degrees within the centres, creating the conditions for potential conflict with relatively disadvantaged or poorly accommodated peripheries. If this was true for the West, then how much more so was it for Eastern Europe, with its legacy of centralist regimes and extraordinary ethnic diversity? Certainly, economic inequalities and disparities within states (and sometimes between them) have proved a major catalyst in the exacerbation of ethnic tension within Eastern Europe since 1989.

Yugoslavia is perhaps the most notable example. At first glance, this seems paradoxical since the Yugoslav state had successfully dissociated itself from Soviet influence and had embarked upon the process of liberalisation well before its communist neighbours. Unlike other Eastern European states, Yugoslavia had been liberated in the Second World War by internal struggle, and Titoism was subsequently a significant unifying force in defying Soviet hegemony and the Warsaw Pact in Eastern Europe. However, as the Soviet threat diminished, so the imperative for unity began to fade, especially as Tito's death in 1980 was followed by an unwieldy eight-member collective federal presidency. The demise of the Soviet threat removed the one determinant of unity in an otherwise highly disparate and perhaps artificial state. Yugoslavia (the South Slav State) had been constructed in 1918 from remnants of the old Austro-Hungarian and Ottoman Empires. The persistent influence of this dichotomy and conflicting heritage is a significant and enduring cause of cultural, religious and economic divisions within the state which emerged from the rigours of the Second World War as Tito's Communist Federal Republic – its capital in Serbian Belgrade, its constituent republics being Serbia, Croatia, Slovenia, Bosnia-Hercegovina, Montenegro and Macedonia.

From the beginning, Yugoslavia represented a curious mix of peoples. Demographically and politically dominant, the Serbs were ostensibly a similar ethnic group to the neighbouring Croats, both speaking a similar if not identical language and both of Slavonic extraction. However, Serbs and Croats were divided by historical experience: the Croats were Roman Catholic in religion and employed the Latin alphabet in their literature, the Serbs Orthodox and users of the Cyrillic script. Amongst the other ethnic groups of note were the Slovenes of North-Western Yugoslavia (still conscious of their historic links with Austria) and the large Albanian (and predominantly Muslim) component (some 90 per cent) of the Serbian province of Kosovo. To complicate matters still further, the constituent republics were by no means ethnically homogeneous – in addition to the Albanian element in Serbia there was, for example, a large Serbian contingent within Croatia.

Moreover, ethnic diversity was underscored by economic disparity, a factor that was not merely perpetuated but indeed aggravated by communist policy and action after 1945. As David Dyker has argued, a disastrous combination of corruption, bureaucratic negligence and inappropriate emphasis upon industrial projects brought Yugoslavia closer and closer to financial and political collapse.[17] Increasingly, the economically more advanced republics of the North (particularly Slovenia) were reluctant to subsidise the poorer southern republics which, it was alleged, had squandered previous aid on prestige projects of dubious worth. The southerners retorted that the prestige projects were in fact necessary structural improvements, innovations that were essential if the South was to match the performance of the North. In reality, events moved from bad to worse in the South, especially in Albanian Kosovo where increases in population (and hence growing demand for resources) were met only with increasing impoverishment, leading to riots in 1981.

Set against the already weakening legitimacy of the Yugoslav state, these ethnic–economic conflicts forced the pace of political change. Mindful of the implicit threat to Serbian territorial integrity, Serbian leaders (under the populist Slobodan Milošević, who repackaged the old communists as a new Serbian Nationalist Socialist Party) sought to assert their control over Kosovo, emphasising its place as an integral part of Serbia and seeking to remove its provincial autonomy. This provoked a series of widespread but peaceful protests amongst Kosovo's Albanian population during 1988 and 1989, protests that were repressed forcefully by the Serbian authorities. But Milošević's actions had the additional effect of antagonising the other republics, where the move to liberalisation and democratisation had already begun in earnest – most especially in westernised and sophisticated Slovenia where since 1985 there had been significant movement towards political and economic freedom, together with a growing demand (manifested in the 1991 breakaway) for secession.

In Croatia, too, similar developments were apparent, provoking a Serbian backlash in the Croatian district of Knin (where 80 per cent of the population is ethnically Serbian: in all, there are some 600,000 Serbs in Croatia – 11 per cent of the population). By 1991 Serbian nationalists had established *de facto* control of Knin, and Croatia had become the scene of bloody clashes between Serbian militias and Croatian authorities. Even moderate Bosnia, with its ethnically-mixed, predominantly Muslim government, had declared itself in favour of a much looser confederal Yugoslavia, further isolating the Serbs in their desire to preserve (or dominate) a tight federation. But Serbia itself is not immune to demands for political change, as evidenced by mass protests in Belgrade in March 1991 where anti-communist demonstrators demanded an end to Milošević's totalitarian methods.

A variant of the ethnic diversity encountered in Yugoslavia is the situation in Czechoslovakia. In addition to the existence of German and (especially) Hungarian minorities (both still viewed with suspicion as a result of wartime experiences), there is a significant ethnic (and economic) cleavage between Czechs and Slovaks, the two principal constituent nationalities of the dual state created in 1919. Broadly, this is reflected in the geographical division of the country, with more Czechs inhabiting the more economically advanced western part and more Slovaks living in the East. Despite the widespread popularity of, and respect for, President Vaclav Havel (an ethnic Czech), the period since the extrication of the state from Soviet dominance has been marked by growing tension between Czechs and Slovaks.[18]

Disagreements over land reform have added to other long-standing economic grievances, particularly the rate of unemployment which in Slovakia is almost twice as high as that in the Czech republic. In addition, the old-fashioned heavy industries constructed in Slovakia during the communist era are those least likely to survive new market conditions, while the Slovak arms industry will also contract. These grievances have informed the debate on the shape of the new federal

Czechoslovakia, a controversy which assumed particular urgency after Havel introduced a new draft constitution in March 1991. The Public Against Violence Party, a major partner in both the Slovak and Federal Coalition Governments, favoured a genuine but strictly limited level of Slovakian autonomy. Among the sixty or so political parties within Slovakia, some of them, including the extreme right-wing Slovak National Party, demanded complete independence.

To Western eyes, one of the more unusual ethnic conflicts in Eastern Europe is that between Bulgar and Turk. So redolent of ancient enmity between Christian and Muslim, and more recently of Slav struggle against Ottoman domination, Bulgaria's tensions are deeply rooted in the history of the Near East. But as elsewhere, the 'Sinatra years' saw a resurgence of conflict as Bulgaria attempted to come to terms with its new political condition. Concentrated in the south-eastern and north-eastern parts of the country, Bulgaria's 800,000 ethnic Turks were periodically subject to deliberate policies of 'Bulgarianisation' during the communist era, forced to adopt Bulgarian forms of their names, forbidden to speak Turkish in public, and discouraged from practising the Muslim religion. In 1989, in the new atmosphere of liberalisation and reform, however, the Bulgarian authorities relaxed these rules, tolerating more open expressions of Turkish ethnicity at a time when elsewhere in the world Pan-Islamicism and Pan-Turkism were enjoying new currency. Predictably, perhaps, the ethnic Bulgarian population reacted violently to this liberalism and in a wave of strikes and demonstrations forced some 300,000 ethnic Turks to flee to Turkey during the summer of 1989. Many, however, returned to take their chances amongst the uncertainties of Bulgarian economic reform when they found that for them Turkey had little to offer other than unemployment and poverty.

External implications: old enmities in new guises

The Bulgar–Turk crisis illustrates that ethnicity not only destabilises the internal cohesion of states but exacerbates relations between them. Under Soviet hegemony such irritants were kept under firm control. Not surprisingly, Yugoslavia's internal ethnic problems have had direct external consequences. Bulgaria expressed an interest in the future of Macedonia, and the newly emergent Albania, having abandoned at last its long self-imposed isolation, continued to view with alarm the fate of the Albanian population of Kosovo. Furthermore, in the spring of 1991, the Hungarian Prime Minister, Jozsef Antall, forged closer relations with Croatia in order to exert pressure on Serbia to treat the large Hungarian minority in Vojvodina with respect.[19] Ethnic conflicts in Eastern Europe have thus acquired extra-state dimensions, placing potentially explosive inter-state territorial disputes upon the regional political agenda. A significant feature of these disputes is often economic disparity.

Perhaps the most notable case is the relationship between Poland and the new united Germany. Quite apart from the dismay in Poland that West German economic resources which might otherwise have been spread more evenly across Eastern Europe (and Poland in particular) are now concentrated and focused more directly upon the need to assimilate East Germany, there are residual Polish fears about the status of the Oder-Neisse border. At the end of the Second World War, Poland was moved westwards, shedding territory to the Soviet Union in the East and gaining land (Silesia, Pomerania and East Prussia) from Germany in the West – the border adjustments being matched by a consequential movement of populations, especially ethnic Germans fleeing to the West. Despite the high degree of ethnic and religious homogeneity which characterised the new Poland, the state continued to ponder its territorial integrity, doubts which came to the fore suddenly in 1989 and 1990 with the surprise prospect of a united Germany on the horizon.

Put simply, Polish fears were that a newly unified Germany might cast its eyes eastwards to the lost lands in Poland, a concern exacerbated by Chancellor Helmut Kohl's unhelpful remarks that the Oder-Neisse line had never been ratified formally and would have to form part of the agenda for the German unification process. To alleviate these fears, Poland was a direct member of the two-plus-four negotiations which set the ground rules for unification.

But uncertainties were perpetuated when the hitherto invisible German minority in Western Poland began to voice demands for cultural and political accommodation. In practice, however, German nationalism within Poland proved more an economic than political demand, hitherto 'Policised' families searching suddenly for Germanic credentials which might afford German passports and hence unrestricted entrée to the affluent West. This, in turn, reflected expectations of economic disparity between the unifying Germanys and Poland, expectations which would encourage Polish workers to take advantage of new freedoms to move across the border in search of work but which would also precipitate anti-Polish outbursts in a frustrated Eastern Germany yet unable to match the affluence of the West.[20]

The German ideological commitment to ethnic Germans beyond the state meant that elsewhere in Eastern Europe German minorities would also be able to claim passports and the right to emigrate to

Germany. Again, many ethnic Germans welcomed this opportunity with enthusiasm, for it represented the chance to escape perceived cultural or political discrimination as well as the prospect of enjoying a higher standard of living in the foremost European economy. In the aftermath of the fall of Ceausescu in Romania, for example, some 80 per cent of the Romanian ethnic German community of 210,000 souls indicated their collective desire to emigrate to the Fatherland they had never seen. To deal with the issue, the West German Foreign Minister, Hans-Dietrich Genscher, met Romanian President Ion Iliescu in January 1990, and indicated that Germany would indeed absorb those wishing to migrate but would also provide economic assistance for those ethnic Germans who chose to remain in Romania, insisting at the same time that they should be afforded full cultural rights.

From the Romanian perspective, however, the ethnic Germans were comparatively small fry, the major concern being the aspirations of the vocal two-million-strong Hungarian (Magyar) minority in Transylvania. Enforced 'Romanisation' had continued apace since as long ago as 1918 (when Romania had acquired the province) but linguistic, religious and other cultural distinctions had endured intact to the extent that the Hungarian minority was able to precipitate and offer a distinctive contribution to the anti-Ceausescu revolution at the end of 1989. Early attempts at the cultural accommodation of the Hungarians by the post-revolutionary National Salvation Front Government appeared to fall by the wayside, however, a source of major irritation to the Hungarians who looked across with envy to the relative success of Hungary proper, with its superior record of movement towards political freedom and economic reform. Not surprisingly, Hungary looked anxiously at the lot of the minority in Romania (and elsewhere in Eastern Europe), though unlike Germany, Hungary does not have the economic clout to mitigate the potential sources of conflict.

For Romania, a further complication to its ethnic tensions is the territorial issue prompted by Moldavian nationalism within the Soviet Union. Annexed from Romania as a Union Republic by the Soviet Union after the war, Moldavia has – despite considerable ethnic Russian immigration – maintained its separate identity. Dreams of Romanian reunification seemed unattainable until *perestroika* offered the possibility of loosening ties with Moscow and, equally, the fall of Ceausescu made the aspiration more desirable. Needless to say, the Romanian government was not inclined to press claims against a Soviet Union already concerned for its territorial integrity, but within Moldavia the Romanian language achieved official recognition and status. Ironically, as Michael Kirkwood has noted, at a time when ethnic tensions were heightened by economic crisis, this linguistic change (with the need to convert from the Cyrillic to the Latin alphabet) was itself 'an expensive drain on economic resources which could have been allocated elsewhere'.[21]

Conclusions

Taken together, the economic stresses and the myriad ethnic tensions within Eastern Europe pose a bewildering series of threats to the stability and security of the region, challenging the integrity (and even *raison d'être*) of certain states, and provoking mistrust and hostility between others. Economic concerns are aggravating, and in some cases causal, factors in inter-ethnic antagonisms. In the difficult and uncertain period of economic transition – with all its imponderables, false starts and unmet expectations – the potential for further conflict and dislocation in the next decade is enormous. Inexperienced and often inarticulate practitioners of democracy that they are, politicians in Eastern Europe find it difficult to explain to their restive peoples why full employment or fixed prices are impossible to maintain, pushing many critics towards the panacea of nationalism. Of course, the picture is by no means a homogeneous one, and there is a distinction to be drawn between Central Europe (Poland, Hungary and Czechoslovakia), with its genuine progress of reform, and the chaos of the Balkans.[22] It is also a mistake to accept too rigidly any geographical definition of Eastern Europe which insists upon the total exclusion of the Soviet Union. To be sure, the Baltic states of Lithuania, Latvia and Estonia – for all the difficulties of their constitutional entanglement in the Union – prefer to see themselves as part of the search for autonomy, participating fully in the transition of Eastern Europe.

In reshaping the conceptual framework within which nationalism will be tackled, the perceptions formed in Eastern Europe about the whole of Europe's future, and the level of interest shown and assistance offered by the wider European polity, will have vital functions.

Assessing the future of the region, Havel has commented that it would be almost impossible to imagine an ideal system of borders in Eastern Europe in which every ethnic group would be allocated a satisfactory territorial and constitutional identity.[23] But the successful accommodation of ethnic demands is an important component of reform within Eastern Europe. Optimists such as Roman Szporluk see the possibility of such accommodation within new constructs such as a reestablishment of the old 'Polish Lithuanian Commonwealth', a platform for mutual understanding and co-operation which might stretch from Germany to Russia.[24] More sober estimates such as that of Marcin Król, however, see ethnic tensions as a serious obstacle to economic and political reform, with the constant threat of civil wars and even wars between states.[25] As Brzezinski has added, there is no equivalent of the Marshall Plan to aid the recovery of Eastern Europe, no European Steel and Coal Community, no Common Market, so that 'the de-Sovietization of Eastern Europe is not likely to be automatically tantamount to the peaceful expansion of all-European co-operation'.[26] The key, perhaps, lies in Gwyn Prins' observation that: 'Like tamed, harnessed capitalism, tamed, harnessed nationalism is essential to pull the chariot of the new Europe'.[27]

Notes

1 See Oscar I. Janowsky, *Nationalities and National Minorities*, New York, Macmillan, 1945.
2 Zbigniew Brzezinski, 'Post communist nationalism', *Foreign Affairs*, Winter 1989–90, pp.1–25.
3 Joseph Rothschild, *Return to Diversity: A Political History of East-Central Europe since World War Two*, Oxford, Oxford University Press, 1989.
4 Patrick Michel, *Politics and Religion in Eastern Europe: Catholicism in Hungary, Poland and Czechoslovakia*, Cambridge, Polity Press, 1991.
5 Stephen M. Horak, *Eastern European National Minorities 1919–1980: A Handbook*, Lyttelton, Libraries Unlimited, 1985; David Turnock, *Eastern Europe: An Historical Geography 1815–1945*, London, Routledge, 1989.
6 R. Boyes, 'Nations avid for capitalism, but where is the capital?', *The Times*, 23 October 1990, p. 14.
7 Geörge Schöpflin, 'The end of communism in Eastern Europe', *International Affairs*, LXVI, no. 1, 1990, pp. 3–16.
8 J. M. C. Rollo and B. Granville, in J. M. C. Rollo (ed.), *The New Eastern Europe: Western Responses*, London, Pinter Press, 1990, p. 40.
9 Mihaly Simai, 'The emerging new market economies and the evolving new democracies', Paper at International Studies Association Convention, Vancouver, 20–22 March 1991.
10 Xavier Richet, 'Hungary: reform and transition towards a market economy', *Communist Economies and Economic Transformation*, III, no. 1, 1991, p. 509.
11 Branlo Milanovic, 'Privatisation in post communist societies', *Communist Economies and Economic Transformation*, III, no. 1, 1991, p. 41.
12 'Eastern Europe in transition: a survey', *Financial Times*, 4 February 1991, p. 11.
13 *Ibid.*
14 Ernst and Young International Ltd., *Viewpoint: The Free Market Revolution in Eastern Europe*, London, 1991.
15 'Eastern Europe', *Financial Times*, 4 February 1991, p. 12.
16 See Yves Meny and Vincent Wright, *Centre–Periphery Relations in Western Europe*, London, Allen & Unwin, 1985.

17 David Dyker, *Yugoslavia: Socialism, Development and Debt*, London, Routledge, 1990.
18 Niels Barfoed, 'Havel's Universe', *Regional Contact*, 1990–91, pp. 5–9.
19 Jonathan Eyal, 'Neighbours start planning for life after Yugoslavia', *Guardian*, 8 April 1991, p. 6.
20 'Neo-Nazis in border clash with Poles', *Guardian*, 9 April 1991, p. 7.
21 Michael Kirkwood, 'The national question and Soviet language policy', *Soviet Studies*, XLIII, no. 1, 1991, p. 76.
22 Europe's lost cousins, *Financial Times*, 5 December 1990.
23 Lidove Noviny, 'The helpless rage', *Guardian*, 7 September 1990, p. 27.
24 Roman Szporluk, 'The burden of history – made lighter by geography', *Problems of Communism*, XXXIX, July–August 1990, pp. 45–8.
25 Marcin Król, 'A Europe of nations or a universalistic Europe?', *International Affairs*, LXVI, no. 2, April 1990, pp. 285–90.
26 Brzezinski, p. 5.
27 Gwyn Prins, 'Home is where the heart is: reflections on social democracy and nationalism in the Common European Home', *Political Quarterly*, LXII, no. 1, January–March 1991, p. 15.

7 Manfred Efinger and Volker Rittberger

The CSBM regime in and for Europe: confidence building and peaceful conflict management[1]

Since the Second World War, Europe from the Atlantic to the Urals (the ATTU zone) has become the area with the largest peacetime concentration of armed forces in the world, and even in history. Two opposing alliances, NATO and the WTO, have deployed almost six million active ground forces, more than 70,000 main battle tanks, 70,000 armoured combat vehicles, 70,000 artillery pieces, 11,000 combat aircraft and 3,000 armed helicopters in this part of the Northern Hemisphere.[2] The concentration of conventional and nuclear forces in Europe was mainly a consequence of the rivalry which existed between East and West since the beginning of the cold war in the late 1940s.

Since this concentration of military forces and troops poses, even in peacetime, serious security threats to all European states, measures have been proposed, and eventually agreed upon, to assist in the interpretation of an adversary's defensive intentions, thereby reducing uncertainties and tensions, as well as to limit the opportunities for surprise attack, by imposing constraints on 'normal' military activities. Such measures are generally called confidence- and security-building measures (CSBMs).

Whereas for over forty years, until 1990, the United States and the Soviet Union failed to agree on reduction of conventional forces in the ATTU zone, they did establish another security arrangement in and for Europe which included CSBMs. The project of confidence building in and for Europe was originally launched at the Helsinki Conference on Security and Co-operation in Europe (CSCE) in 1975 and significantly expanded at the Stockholm Conference on Confidence-Building Measures and Disarmament in Europe (CDE) in 1986. This project of East–West security co-operation in Europe can be said to have evolved into a specific international security *regime*. At the Vienna negotiations on CSBMs (1989–90) a new set of mutually complementary CSBMs were agreed upon, which will lead to a further evolution of the CSBM regime.[3]

This chapter aims to demonstrate that the issue of military confidence and security building in Europe is regulated since the

Stockholm Accord of 1986 by an international regime – the *CSBM regime*. After introducing and defining the concept of international regime, the principles, norms, rules and decision-making procedures of the CSBM regime will be elaborated. Moreover, it will be asked whether, and to what extent, the behaviour of the CSCE states has actually been governed by these norms and rules. Next, special attention will be given to different hypotheses about the formation of international regimes in general, and the CSBM regime in particular. Thereafter, the consequences of the CSBM regime concerning military security in Europe will be assessed. This will be followed by analysis of the evolution of the CSBM regime since the Stockholm negotiations and the future role of CSBMs in and for Europe. Finally, the CSBM regime will be discussed in the light of a vanishing 'East–West conflict'.

The concept of international regime

The concept of international regime was introduced in the mid-1970s and gained wide acceptance in the study of international governance during the 1980s.[4] It has become an important, though not easily applied, analytical tool. Some contemporary surveys have amply demonstrated the difficulties involved in arriving at a satisfactory definition which is capable of delimiting and differentiating this domain of scientific inquiry.[5] Stephen Krasner's definition, which involves four terms (principles, norms, rules and decision-making procedures), became most influential. But since Krasner allows for both the explicitness and implicitness of normative regulation, he faces practical difficulties in deciding whether norms produce less or more stable behaviour patterns – or whether behaviour patterns are to be explained by other factors. A narrower definition of international regime may therefore be desirable. It is defined here as:

> one form of regulated conflict management, the distinctive feature of which is its institutionalisation. Institutionalisation implies that principles, norms and rules of the regime have been internalised by its members, that is, that the behaviour mandated by them is taken for granted by all members of the regime and that every member's behaviour is based on the expectation that all others will abide by the norms and rules of the regime too.[6]

Besides the principles, norms, rules and decision-making procedures which constitute the core of an international regime, we stipulate that its injunctions be effective. This means that the behaviour of actors is actually guided by the constraints, i.e., that the norms and rules are implemented.[7]

The Helsinki CSBMs

During the CSCE negotiations, from November 1972 to August 1975, CSBMs were formally put on the multilateral European security agenda. Since the reduction of the conventional military forces was to be dealt with in the negotiations about Mutual and Balanced Force Reductions (MBFR), and since both superpowers preferred to exclude arms limitation issues from the CSCE negotiations,[8] only CSBMs were left for discussion in the all-European forum.

In the 'Document on Confidence-Building Measures and Certain Aspects of Security and Disarmament', contained in the Helsinki Final Act as part of Basket I, three *principles* of European military security can be identified. According to the first principle, states will:

> refrain in their mutual relations, as well as in their international relations in general, from the threat or use of force against the territorial integrity or political independence of any state, or in any other manner inconsistent with the purposes of the United Nations and with the Declaration on Principles Guiding Relations between participating States as adopted in the Final Act.[9]

This is not only a general restatement of the prohibition of the use or threat of force according to Art. 2, §4 of the UN Charter. It also includes the acceptance of the territorial status quo in Europe and the renunciation of unilateral military attempts to change this status quo. However, as a second principle, it follows from the sovereign equality of states which is recognised in the Final Act (§24 and 25), and Art. 51 of the UN Charter that states are still allowed to defend themselves against aggression by military means either individually or collectively. Obviously, there is a tense relationship between the prohibition of the use or threat of force and the right of self-defence. In order to reduce this tension a third principle was agreed upon which directs states to strengthen confidence among them and thus to contribute to reducing the danger of war in Europe.

In the Helsinki Final Act of 1975, the last mentioned principle, in particular, has been translated into more specific *norms*. Thus states shall notify major military movements in advance; they shall exchange observers at military manoeuvres by invitation, and they shall use 'other ways' to strengthen confidence, e.g., through the exchange of military personnel.

In accordance with these principles and norms five *rules*, that is, concrete CSBMs, have been laid down in Basket I of the Final Act. These rules are: (a) prior notification of major military manoeuvres with a notification threshold of 25,000 troops and an advance period of twenty-one days; (b) prior notification of other military manoeuvres of less than 25,000 troops; (c) invitation of observers on a voluntary, bilateral basis and in a spirit of reciprocity; (d) prior notification of major military movements on a voluntary basis; (e) other CSBMs such as the exchange of military personnel.

Although the CSBMs agreed upon in Helsinki barely scratched the surface of what could be undertaken to reduce the risk of accidental or inadvertent war in Europe, the Helsinki Final Act represented an important step forward in the process of establishing mutually accepted principles, norms, rules and decision-making procedures in this sphere. The Helsinki Final Act enjoins the participating states to 'also recognise that the experience gained by the implementation of the provisions set forth above, together with further efforts, could lead to developing and enlarging measures aimed at strengthening confidence' (§129).

In general, the Helsinki CSBMs were modest, mostly voluntary, militarily insignificant and only binding in a political, not legalistic, sense. Moreover, the few rules laid down in the Helsinki Final Act were not thoroughly complied with by all parties. As far as prior notification of large and small military manoeuvres is concerned, compliance with these rules was weak for some states, especially during the early 1980s. Whereas the NATO and Neutral and Non-Aligned states (NNAs) announced all major and most minor military manoeuvres, the WTO countries did not notify major manoeuvres (*Zapad-81*, *Sojuz-81*, *Shield-82*) as required.[10] Moreover, they notified only a very small number of minor military exercises.

Concerning the exchange of observers at military manoeuvres by invitation, the behaviour of NATO and NNA countries also differed from that of the Eastern bloc states. Whereas the former invited observers from all CSCE states to 89 per cent and 70 per cent of their large military exercises respectively, the latter invited observers to only 30 per cent of these activities, and those observers who were invited mostly came from neighbouring countries. Between 1979 and 1985, for instance, no western observers were invited to notified manoeuvres in the Soviet Union.[11]

In view of the low rule density and the weak compliance with the rules, the conclusion seems inescapable that the Helsinki CSBMs did not yet satisfy the criteria of an international regime. Although the compliance problems were discussed at the CSCE follow-up meetings in Belgrade (October 1977–September 1978) and Madrid (November 1980–September 1983), and several more substantial CSBMs were proposed, a major improvement did not come about until the CDE negotiations.

The Stockholm CSBMs – formation of an international security regime

At the second CSCE follow-up meeting in Madrid the participating states agreed upon a mandate for the CDE. According to this mandate all state signatories of the Helsinki Final Act will: 'undertake, in stages, new effective and concrete actions designed to make progress in strengthening confidence and security and in achieving disarmament, so as to give effect and expression to the duty of states to refrain from the threat or use of force in their mutual relations.'[12] The first stage of the CDE was devoted to negotiations about, and the adoption of, a set of CSBMs which are both militarily significant and politically binding and which are accompanied by adequate forms of verification. These CSBMs should cover the whole of Europe, that is, from the Atlantic to the Urals, as well as the adjoining sea area and air space.

The CDE, which began as scheduled on 17 January 1984, finished its work after two-and-a-half years of negotiations on 22 September 1986 with a substantive agreement on CSBMs. The negotiations, which cannot be described in detail here,[13] had to find a compromise between different proposals made by the NATO countries, Romania, the NNA countries, the Soviet Union and Malta. The basic clash during the negotiations was one between countries which favoured 'declaratory' CSBMs (e.g. no first use of nuclear weapons, non-use of military force, freeze and reduction of military spending, a ban on chemical weapons, and nuclear weapon-free zones) and countries that supported 'concrete' CSBMs (e.g., increased exchange of military information, more stringent prior notification rules, obligatory observations and verification measures). Whereas the former type of CSBM was supported by the Soviet Union, the latter type was favoured by the NATO countries. Romania as well as the NNAs favoured a combination of both types emphasising, however, 'concrete' CSBMs.

The Stockholm Accord includes, to a large extent, the measures originally proposed by the NATO group which has led to a substantial improvement and broadening of the CSBMs as compared to those of the Helsinki Final Act. The Stockholm Agreement expanded the number of norms and rules and spelt out some of the already existing rules. Therefore, it is assumed that a CSBM regime in and for Europe has since come into existence. The Stockholm Document[14] restates and confirms the three *principles* which have been already agreed upon by the CSCE states in the Helsinki Final Act in 1975.

At the level of *norms* the CSBM regime incorporates the following rights and duties of the CDE states: (a) states shall notify military activities which may have threatening effects on other states; (b) states shall exchange observers to military activities by invitation; (c) states shall agree to on-site inspections; and (d) states shall not engage in large military activities close to borders. These norms are intended to enhance the transparency and calculability of the overall military situation in Europe and thus to strengthen confidence and reduce threat perceptions among the CDE states.

For every norm a set of explicit *rules* has been established. Compared with the provisions of the Helsinki Final Act on CSBMs the Stockholm rules are more numerous and specific and cover a much broader range of military activities (see Table 7.1).

Finally, the CSBM regime encompasses *decision-making procedures* which are part of the overall CSCE policy-making system. Since the CDE is an outgrowth of the CSCE process each participating state has the right, in the words of Annex III to the Stockholm Accord, to 'raise any question consistent with the mandate of the Conference on Confidence- and Security-Building Measures and Disarmament in Europe at any stage subsequent to the Vienna CSCE Follow-up Meeting'.

As far as the *effectiveness* of the Stockholm rules is concerned, the record shows that all participating states have satisfactorily implemented the new provisions. Since the entry into force of the Stockholm Accord on 1 January 1987 no serious violations have been reported regarding the annual calendars, prior notification and exchange of observers by invitation. Moreover, some states voluntarily notified military activities even below the 13,000-troops threshold (e.g. Hungary, the Soviet Union, the United States, West Germany) or, like Finland, have voluntarily invited observers (see Table 7.2).

The inspection rules, too, have been implemented without major problems. Between January 1987 and December 1990, forty-four inspections were carried out (see Table 7.3). Since January 1987 the Soviet Union has carried out fifteen inspections, the United States eight, followed by Great Britain (five), West and East Germany (four each), Italy (two) and six other states with one inspection each. States which have been inspected most often are the Soviet Union (ten times), West

Table 7.1 *Norms and rules of the Helsinki and Stockholm agreements*

	Helsinki	*Stockholm*
Norms	a) prior notification b) invitation of observers (optional) c) other CSBMs e.g. exchange of military personnel (optional)	a) prior notification b) exchange of observers by invitation c) verification and on-site inspections d) constraining measures
Rules		
Types of forces:	manoeuvres and movements	military activities include ground forces, amphibious and airborne forces, transfers, concentrations, alert exercises
Threshold of notification:	25,000 ground troops	13,000 ground forces, 3,000 amphibious or airborne troops
Advance warning:	21 days	42 days
Area of notification:	European territory, extending 250 km, into the USSR and Turkey	Europe from the Atlantic to the Urals (ATTU zone)
Form and contents:	not standardised	standardised
Annual calendar:	not required	exchange (as of 15 November) of forecasts of notifiable military activities, standardised form
Threshold of observation:	not specified	17,000 troops (ground) or 5,000 (amphibious, airborne)
Programme of observation:	not standardised	standardised
Verification:	no provision	a) use of national technical means b) on-site inspections: compulsory, short notice (24 hours) and duration (48 hours), inspections on the ground, from the air or both, by a maximum of four inspectors, passive quota (three per year), access, entry and unobstructed survey except for restricted areas whose number and extent should be 'as limited as possible'
Constraining measures:	no provision	two years of advance notice for any notifiable military activity beyond 40,000 troops; prohibition of military activities beyond 40,000 troops and under 75,000 unless notified one year in advance; prohibition of military activities beyond 75,000 troops unless notified two years in advance

Table 7.2 *Stockholm CSBMs – the record 1987–1990*

	NATO	*NNA*	*WTO*	*Totals*
Notifications				
1987	17	5	25	47
1988	13	3	22	38
1989	10	3	12	25
1990	7	3	3	13
Totals	47	14	62	123
Invitations of observers (obligatory)				
1987	9	0	9	18
1988	8	3	7	18
1989	6	2	5	13
1990	4	0	1	5
Totals	27	5	22	54

Source: SIPRI, *Yearbooks*, 1987–90; Foreign Office, Federal Republic of Germany (personal communication, 28 August 1989 and 25 October 1990).

and East Germany (eight times each), followed by Italy (three times). NNA states have neither inspected other nations nor been inspected themselves. No questionable practices or outright breaches of agreed CSBM provisions were discovered by any party as a result of these inspections.[15]

The principles and norms established in the Stockholm Accord have obviously been accepted by the participating states. Moreover, compliance with the Stockholm rules is much higher than was the case with those established by the Helsinki Final Act. Since 1987 no significant breach of the rules of the regime has been publicly reported. Even the inspection rules have been adhered to by states which have received requests for on-site inspections. The norms and rules of the CSBM regime must therefore be judged as rather effective.

Explaining the CSBM regime

Research on international regimes has always aspired to theory building. It turned out very quickly, however, that the task of accounting for

Table 7.3 *Inspections under the Stockholm Accord, 1987–1990*

	NATO	*NNA*	*WTO*	*Totals*
1987	2	0	3	5
1988	7	0	6	13
1989	9	0	7	16
1990	5	0	5	10
Totals	23	0	21	44

Source: Foreign Office, Federal Republic of Germany (personal communication, 28 August 1989 and 25 October 1990).

international regimes could not escape theoretical eclecticism. The following attempt at explaining the CSBM regime draws on four categories of independent variables: issue-area characteristics; structural causes; normative-institutional factors; and subsystemic variables.

First, in terms of issue-area characteristics, there is nothing novel in the effort to explain the nature and outcome of policy-making processes. Functionalists distinguished long ago between 'high politics' and 'low politics' and used this distinction to account for international integration in 'technical' spheres. In a more generalised version, Theodore Lowi argued that 'policy determines politics' – implying that political processes and their outcomes vary across issue areas depending, *inter alia*, on their characteristic features.[16] Indeed, the task of identifying and explaining international regimes is facilitated by turning to hypotheses which suggest that certain *qualities* of an issue or object of contention induce the participants to select one mode of conflict management rather than another.

For analysing the conditions under which the formation of security regimes in East–West relations can be expected to occur, Efinger, Rittberger and Michael Zürn have developed a typology of conflict. The hypotheses derived from it are that the potential for establishing regimes for four kinds of conflict vary as follows:

- very low for conflicts about values, such as human rights;
- low for conflicts of interest about relatively assessed goods which gain their value only if one has more than others, such as military power;
- medium for conflicts about means, such as economic co-operation;
- high for conflicts about absolutely assessed goods which are valued independently of what others possess, such as food.[17]

A quantitative test of the hypotheses reveals that they seem to hold up against empirical evidence from East–West relations.[18] The crucial point here, however, is to ask how such a typology can help account for the formation of the CSBM regime. We expect security issues to fall within the categories of either disputes about relatively assessed goods or disputes about means. Both the typology developed from theory and the quantitative test suggest that security issues which take the form of conflicts about means are more conducive to building a regime than other security issues.

We now have to examine what kinds of conflicts are being dealt with by the CSBM regime. In general, the CSBM regime can be viewed as primarily addressing a conflict about means but also touching on other dimensions of the conflict typology. More specifically, it is based on the premise that all participating states agree on the value of confidence building as a stepping-stone to improved security. Its 'regulatory function', however, consists of mediating between widely divergent conceptions of what 'confidence' actually is supposed to mean as well as between strongly opposed preferences for ways and means to build confidence.

On the western side, especially among NATO countries, confidence building is identified with removing the mistrust and fear which arises from uncertainty about the intentions of a heavily armed adversary. To reduce this uncertainty and, thus, to build confidence in the 'defensive' intentions of the adversary, CSBMs are conceived in such a way as to increase the disincentives for using military power for aggression, intervention or hostile pressures. Western countries, therefore, emphasise transparency, 'concrete' restraints and verification. Until the mid-1980s, member states of the WTO, particularly the Soviet Union, linked confidence building to the halting of the arms race and to disarmament, on the one hand, and to confirming the political–territorial status quo, on the other. Besides expressing a strong preference for declaratory measures, WTO countries put forward proposals which aimed at denying NATO military postures which form part and parcel of the strategy of 'flexible response' but which WTO countries considered a threat to their security.

Despite these differences between NATO and WTO countries (leaving aside the special concerns of the NNAs) a CSBM regime proved feasible because, eventually, disagreement revolved around means. The CSBM regime would thus seem to corroborate the proposition derived from the above conflict typology that conflicts about means are amenable to regulation by institutionalised co-operation. However, since we could not possibly claim to have presented an exhaustive causal explanation of the CSBM regime, we have to take into account other hypotheses about the likely formation of security regimes in Europe.

The second kind of explanation is based on structural causes. The 'theory of hegemonic stability', the most prominent example of a power-structural hypothesis for explaining international regimes, proves to be of little, if any, explanatory value when applied to security regimes in East–West relations.[19] In Europe, with the constellation of two 'hegemonic' powers, this 'theory' cannot account for the co-operative management of security issues such as CSBMs. Another structural hypothesis holds that the likelihood of regime formation increases as the *difference in overall power* between West and East, or between the United States and the Soviet Union, decreases in relative terms.[20] This theory might prove more valuable. In the mid-1950s, the difference, in terms of power, between eastern and western countries was rather high. This difference even increased slightly from the 1956–60 period to the 1961–5 period. Thereafter, it decreased steadily until the 1981–5 period, after which the CSBM regime was finally created.[21] Therefore the hypothesis about the relationship between the relative difference in overall power and the likelihood of regime formation holds up in the case of CSBMs.

The third set of explanations concerns the normative-institutional factors which played a role in the creation of the CSBM regime. The CSBMs agreed upon between the superpowers such as the Hot Line agreements (1963, 1971, 1984), the Accidents agreement (1971), and the Incident at Sea accord (1972) have apparently worked well.[22] In the sense that these agreements proved that CSBMs can reduce tension and increase confidence between the superpowers, they can be regarded as a 'model' for European CSBMs. The first special session of the United Nations General Assembly on disarmament in 1978 also contributed to raising the general awareness of CSBMs as an important means toward enhancing international security. It recommended that an in-depth study of CSBMs be undertaken which was launched in the same year and completed in 1981. In this study, an effort was made to reconcile eastern and western conceptions of CSBMs. Moreover, in a series of resolutions, the General Assembly expressed its support for regional CSBMs and requested the United Nations Disarmament Commission to elaborate concrete proposals to be submitted to the General Assembly for consideration and approval.[23]

In addition, the CSCE as an international, multilateral 'policy-making system' deserves special credit for facilitating agreement on CSBMs. Although the superpowers play an important role in the CSCE process, including the CDE, they are influenced by the 'bloc-transcending multilateralism' of the smaller countries and 'middle powers' in Europe.[24] To some extent, this reflects the CSCE's consensus principle in reaching decisions. The CSCE allowed the smaller countries and the 'middle powers' to put CSBMs on the multilateral security agenda. Once introduced, the demand for CSBMs could not be suppressed by any state or group of states and the negotiations about them generated their own momentum. Finally, the timing of both the Stockholm Conference and the CSCE follow-up meeting in Vienna, which was scheduled to begin in November 1986, reinforced the institutional pressures for reaching agreement on confidence building. When the participating states finally agreed, on 13 December 1985, to bring the Stockholm Conference to a close on 19 September 1986, the negotiations for the first time faced a definite deadline.[25]

So far we have noted that issue-related hypotheses, structural factors and normative-institutional explanations contribute to our understanding of the formation of the CSBM regime. There seems to exist a gap, however, in explaining more fully the reaching of a CSBM agreement, by the superpowers in particular, as the outcome of the CDE. For a more complex explanation we must turn to variables at the subsystemic level of analysis.

The United States modified her approach toward the Stockholm Conference on CSBMs in the course of 1984. Playing down the previously emphasised 'linkage' between CSBMs and human rights, the Reagan Administration began to show greater interest in reaching at least some kind of modest agreement on East–West security issues to satisfy domestic concerns, heightened during the presidential election campaign, about a spiralling arms race, and to accommodate those alliance members which had implemented the NATO double-track decision against massive internal opposition. Prompted, too, by the concessions which the new Gorbachev leadership offered at the negotiating table, the Reagan Administration concluded in 1985/6 that NATO countries did not give away much of what constitutes their defence posture in exchange for making Soviet and Warsaw Pact military activities in Europe less secretive.

Change in Soviet policy toward concrete CSBMs also contributed significantly to generating the Stockholm Accord. The major shift in the Soviet approach in 1985/6 facilitated agreement. This shift found its most spectacular expression in the acceptance of on-site inspections which the then Foreign Minister Andrei Gromyko had rejected at the opening session of the CDE negotiations. Moreover, the Soviet Union accepted many of the 'concrete' measures proposed by the other participants in the CDE without insisting on having most of her own proposals for 'declaratory' measures incorporated in the Final Document.[26]

The willingness to compromise and to agree to the formation of a security regime may be interpreted in the broader context of the Gorbachev leadership's groping for a redefined Soviet strategy and international role. CSBMs are clearly compatible with the 'new political thinking' about foreign policy and international relations, since they can be seen to implement, in a small way, the meaning of 'common' or 'equal' security – a concept which was originally developed in the Palme Commission – and to give expression to the notion of Europe as a 'common home'. In addition, agreeing to the CSBM regime made good sense, in the new Soviet view, as a means to promote a long-term accommodation with the United States in the field of security.

Summing up this section we conclude that all of the aforementioned variables help shed some light on the conditions of reaching agreement at Stockholm. Although none of them can account fully for the establishment of this regime, some variables seem to have greater explanatory power than others: notably issue-related hypotheses and subsystemic explanations.

Consequences of the CSBM regime

The CSBM regime as outlined above basically fulfils two major functions: it produces information otherwise not available, or only at high cost, and it stabilises mutual expectations.

Firstly, the CSBM regime includes a number of norms and rules which, if implemented, increase the exchange of information about planned and ongoing military activities in Europe from the Atlantic to the Urals. In particular, the on-site inspections decrease uncertainty between the parties. They give insight into basic guidelines for the military training of ground forces. The quality and quantity of information gained would not be available to the participating states without this regime. To obtain similar information, legally or illegally through national means, would certainly be much more costly. For smaller countries especially it would be impossible to receive this kind of militarily relevant information without the regime.

Secondly, the CSBM regime stabilises the still highly militarised security situation in Europe. It defines a consensus about what the participating states are not permitted to do for their own defence and security. Compared to the Helsinki CSBMs, the Stockholm CSBMs satisfy more strongly the criteria of military significance and adequate verification. More specifically, the CSBM regime contains a set of rules about permissible activities of military forces in peacetime. These seek to reassure the participating states about the 'defensive' character of military activities and, thus, forestall exaggerated perceptions of military threat. In addition, standards of international behaviour enhance convergent expectations of mutual self-restraint. The convergence of expectations has already become obvious through the numerous official assessments of the Stockholm Agreement. The political leaders in the West and, to a lesser extent, in the NNAs and even in the eastern countries, expressed their overall satisfaction with the Stockholm results. Moreover, these assessments very often include the hope that if the Stockholm CSBMs are fully implemented they will not only contribute to the reduction of the risk of military confrontation in Europe and to the improvement of the European security situation, but also to the improvement of overall East–West relations.

Summing up this brief discussion about the importance of the CSBM regime to security in Europe, CSBMs can be said to stabilise the convergent expectations that there is no imminent danger of war. The regime indicates that alarmist perceptions of military threat are not only unjustified but are themselves a source of destabilising influence on the overall security situation. Furthermore, the evolution of the CSBM regime provides a lesson for the usefulness of 'disjointed incrementalism' by moving ahead in one track (confidence building) without losing sight of the risks of immobility in the other (arms control).

Regime evolution and the future role of CSBMs in and for Europe

Since the CSBM regime was positively assessed by all CSCE states during the Vienna CSCE follow-up meeting (November 1986–January 1989) all participating states agreed that CSBM negotiations would continue. These negotiations were aimed at improving on the results already obtained at the Stockholm Conference and at elaborating and adopting a 'new set of mutually complementary' measures designed to reduce the risk of military confrontation in Europe.[27]

The negotiations on a new set of measures began in Vienna on 9 March 1989 between the thirty-five CSCE states.[28] In the first rounds of negotiations comprehensive but diverging proposals were submitted to the conference by NATO, the WTO and NNA countries. The main difference between the participating states concerned CSBMs for air and naval activities. NATO rejected demands by the WTO states that naval and air force activities be put on the agenda. The more modest NNA proposal of 12 July 1989 suggested that air and naval forces be included in the information exchange on active mobile units and that stricter provisions for the notification of airborne and amphibious activities be laid down.

This major disagreement notwithstanding, on 17 November 1990 the participants agreed not only to improve the Stockholm Accord but also to introduce some additional CSBMs. As far as the Stockholm provisions were concerned, the CSCE states strengthened the rules for notification of military activities and the exchange of observers by invitation. According to the new Vienna Accord, observers will have more opportunities to observe military activities and will get more information about observed military activities. Some minor improvements were made in the area of military constraints. According to the Vienna Document military activities beyond 40,000 troops are prohibited unless they are not notified one year in advance. More important are the additional *norms* agreed upon as follows:

- states shall exchange information annually on military equipment and forces, planned deployment of weapon systems and military budgets;
- states shall notify unusual and hazardous military activities;
- states shall allow visits of military airfields, and
- states shall increase contacts between high level military personnel.

For every norm, several explicit *rules* were established. These rules are relatively specific and cover a wide range of military activities. In order to verify the information on military equipment and manpower to be provided annually, states are allowed to carry out a restricted number of visits per year to foreign territories. The duration of such visits may not exceed one working day of twelve hours and the visiting team may consist of no more than two persons.

The Vienna Accord also strengthened the *procedures* of the CSBM regime. The CSCE states will establish a Conflict Prevention Centre (CPC) and a communications network. The task of the former will be, *inter alia*, the explanation of any unusual and hazardous military activity. The annual assessment of the implementation of the norms and rules of the regime, which will take place for the first time in 1991, will be held in the CPC. Any relevant information on military activities and other related issues will be transmitted to the CSCE states through a communications network, the technical details of which are elaborated in Annex II of the Vienna document.

The new set of measures became possible for various reasons. As a consequence of the revolutionary changes which occurred in Eastern Europe and the Soviet Union in the late 1980s, many states concluded that large-scale military exercises and movements were no longer needed. The number of notifiable military activities in Europe decreased from forty-seven cases in 1987 to thirteen in 1990, a reduction of more than 70 per cent. Similarly, the number of observers invited decreased from eighteen in 1987 to only five in 1990, a reduction of almost 70 per cent. The general trend is clearly toward fewer and smaller military activities.

Secondly, there are neither divergent conceptions of what confidence actually is supposed to mean nor are there strong differences about ways and means to build it. Apart from as yet unresolved positional differences about extending CSBMs to cover independent air and naval activities, there is no basic conflict about means between East and West in the issue area of military confidence building in Europe. The western concept of 'concrete', militarily significant and verifiable measures is now accepted by all CSCE states.

Thirdly, the evolution of the CSBM regime in Europe can be explained with reference to normative-institutional factors. Since it was agreed that the negotiations on conventional forces in Europe (CFE) between the NATO and WTO states should come to an end before the Paris CSCE meeting in November 1990 some states, such as France, Italy and West Germany as well as the NNA states, argued very strongly in favour of a first agreement on a new set of CSBMs at the same date. Without such an agreement the relevance of the CSBM negotiations in comparison with the CFE negotiations would have decreased even more. In addition, the positive learning of the CSCE states which became possible because of the very successful implementation of the Stockholm Accord helped to overcome differences between the negotiating parties.

While CSBMs in and for Europe were particularly important as long as NATO and the WTO disagreed about the level of conventional (and nuclear) forces in Europe, the relevance of CSBMs may decline in a period of reduced conventional forces in Europe. For more than forty years such reductions seemed impossible. Since the early 1970s the primary approach to reducing security threats was the formation of a CSBM regime. In the late 1980s, however, NATO and WTO countries shifted their emphasis to negotiations for reducing conventional armaments and ground forces with a view to establishing common ceilings at substantially lower levels. In November 1990 an agreement was signed by the sixteen NATO allies and the six remaining members of the Warsaw Treaty Organisation. It provided for disarmament measures affecting tanks, artillery, armoured combat vehicles, combat aircraft and helicopters.[29] In addition, the United States, the Soviet Union and unified Germany agreed to reduce their ground forces in Central Europe.

Even after the reduction of conventional forces in the ATTU zone, Europe will still be the area with the largest peacetime concentration of armed forces in the world. By no means therefore will CSBMs become superfluous. On the contrary, such a reduction of conventional forces in Europe will increase their importance in terms of reassuring states, now entering a period of cutting their armaments, that serious threats to their security have ceased to exist.

Conclusion

The purpose of this chapter has been twofold. On the one hand, it has sought to explore the applicability of regime analysis to the collective management of international security relations, especially in Europe.This also included some consideration of how international regimes come into being. On the other hand, and more specifically, it has attempted to determine whether the agreement on, and implementation of, CSBMs can be understood as a security regime in Europe.

Our analysis has shown, first of all, that international security regimes in the CSCE region are possible, and that CSBMs actually do work. Secondly, the discussion of several approaches for explaining the formation of a CSBM regime in Europe has confirmed the expectation that issue-area-related hypotheses and subsystemic explanations are superior to systemic variables in accounting for the emergence of security regimes in the CSCE region.

The special character of an international CSBM regime does not lie in the creation of a legal framework comparable to national law, but in the provision of a 'quasi-law' in the form of mutually agreed 'rules of the game' or a 'code of conduct'. This allows for a certain degree of trust that the rules generally will be complied with, and contributes to the convergence of actors' expectations. CSBMs are collective arrangements about the function and use of military power in peacetime. They are designed to confirm the non-aggressive intentions of all states and therefore to build stable expectations concerning their military activities. However, CSBMs do not substantially restrict the autonomy of states in choosing their own national defence policy. Therefore they can be classified as a pragmatic contribution to peacefully managing the classical 'security dilemma' based on both the proscription of the threat or use of force and the right of military self-defence.

CSBMs provide for some central prerequisites of international security regimes which exceed the norms of a merely declaratory no-use-of-force convention. They are capable of strengthening at least a few aspects of 'negative peace'; that is, they lessen the likelihood of a conventional surprise attack as well as of intra-bloc intervention, and they enhance crisis stability. International regimes are relevant in that they increase the exchange of information between the participants simply because they generate regular interactions. Moreover, they involve the creation of a network used to gather and exchange special information. Over time this builds up a considerable measure of peace-promoting 'routine behaviour' which, in the view of the political élites on both sides, is obviously different from purely unilateral actions. As manifested by the Stockholm Accord of 1986 and, in a more sophisticated way, by the Vienna Agreement of November 1990, the European CSBM arrangement is an important example of the pacifying potential of international regimes.

In the long-range perspective of a true peace structure in Europe based on 'non-offensive defence' and conventional stability, CSBMs are nothing more than a first, admittedly small step. The Stockholm and Vienna Agreements, at least, have shown that CSBMs are an important item on the agenda of European security policy and that, under certain circumstances, the persistence and expansion of this security regime seem possible. Since the Vienna negotiations on CSBMs will continue until the next CSCE follow-up meeting in Helsinki in 1992, it is very likely that a further improvement of the Stockholm CSBMs as well as an agreement on additional norms and rules may come about.

Notes

1 This chapter is based on and updates Volker Rittberger, Manfred Efinger and Martin Mendler, 'Toward an East–West security regime: the case of confidence- and security-building measures', *Journal of Peace Research*, XXVII, Spring 1990, pp. 55–74 and Efinger, 'Preventing war in Europe through confidence- and security-building measures', in Rittberger (ed.), *International Regimes in East–West Politics*, London and New York, Pinter, 1990, pp. 117–50.

2 See International Institute for Strategic Studies, *The Military Balance 1990–1991*, London, Pergamon-Brassey's, 1990, pp. 232–3.

3 The Vienna Document on CSBMs of 1990 is reprinted in Austrian Committee for European Security and Co-operation (ed.), *Focus on Vienna*, no. 21, December 1990, Vienna, pp. 9–15.

4 Stephen D. Krasner (ed.), *International Regimes*, Ithaca and London, Cornell University Press, 1983; Robert O. Keohane, *After Hegemony, Cooperation and Discord in the World Political Economy*, Princeton, NJ, Princeton University Press, 1984; Efinger, Rittberger and Michael Zürn, *Internationale Regime in den Ost-West-Beziehungen*, Frankfurt/M., Haag & Herchen, 1988; Beate Kohler-Koch (ed.), *Regime in den Internationalen Beziehungen*, Baden-Baden, Nomos, 1989; Oran R. Young, *International Cooperation, Building Regimes for Natural Resources and the Environment*, Ithaca and London, Cornell University Press, 1989; Rittberger (ed.), *International Regimes in East–West Politics*, London and New York, Pinter, 1990.

5 Stephen Haggard and Beth A. Simmons, 'Theories of international regimes', *International Organization*, XLI, Summer 1987, pp. 491–517; Friedrich Kratochwil and John Gerard Ruggie, 'International organization: a state of the art on an art of the state', *International Organization*, XL, Autumn 1986, pp. 753–75; Young, 'International regimes: toward a new theory of institutions', *World Politics*, XXXIX, October 1986, pp. 105–22.

6 Rittberger and Zürn, 'Towards regulated anarchy in East–West relations: causes and consequences of East–West regimes', in Rittberger (ed.), *International Regimes in East–West Politics*, London and New York, Pinter, 1990, p. 16.

7 See Klaus Dieter Wolf and Michael Zürn ' "International regimes" und Theorien der internationalen politik', *Politische Vierteljahresschrift*, XXVII, 1986, pp. 201–21; Efinger, Rittberger, Wolf and Zürn, 'Internationale Regime', in Rittberger (ed.), *Theorien der Internationalen Beziehungen*, Opladen, Westdeutscher Verlag, 1990, pp. 263–85.

8 John Maresca, 'Helsinki Accord, 1975', in Alexander L. George, Philip J. Farley and Alexander Dallin (eds.), *US–Soviet Security Cooperation: Achievements, Failures, Lessons*, Oxford and New York, Oxford University Press, 1988, p. 114.

9 Paragraph 97. The Helsinki Final Act is reprinted in John J. Maresca, *To Helsinki: The Conference on Security and Cooperation in Europe 1973–1975*, Durham, NC, Duke University Press, 1987, pp. 249–306 (Appendix II).

10 See Lynn Hansen, 'Confidence and security building at Madrid and beyond', in Stephen F. Larrabee and Dietrich Stobbe (eds.), *Confidence-Building Measures in Europe*, New York, Institute for East–West Security Studies, 1983, pp. 134–64; John Borawski, Stan Weeks and Charlotte E. Thompson, 'The Stockholm Agreement of September 1986', *Orbis*, XXX, 1987, pp. 642–62; and Borawski, *From the Atlantic to the Urals: Negotiating Arms Control at the Stockholm Conference*, Washington, DC, Pergamon-Brassey's, 1988, p. 29.

11 Dieter Mahncke, *Vertrauensbildende Maßnahmen als Instrument der Sicherheitspolitik: Ursprung-Entwicklung-Perspektiven*, Melle, Knoth, 1987, pp. 42–3.

12 'Concluding Document of the Madrid Meeting 1980 of Representatives of the Participating States of the Conference on Security and Cooperation in Europe, held on the Basis of the Provisions of the Final Act Relating to the Follow-up to the Conference', cited in Borawski, *From the Atlantic to the Urals*, p. 164.

13 See Wolfgang Loibl, 'Die Konferenz über vertrauens- und sicherheitsbildende maßnahmen und Abrüstung in Europa (KVAE)', *Österreichisches Jahrbuch für Internationale Politik*, Wien, Böhlau, 1986, pp. 89–111 and Borawski, *From the Atlantic to the Urals*, pp. 35–101.

14 The complete text of the 'Document of the Stockholm Conference on Confidence- and Security-Building Measures and Disarmament in Europe convened in Accordance with the Relevant Provisions of the Concluding Document of the Madrid Meeting of the Conference on Security and Cooperation in Europe' is reprinted in Borawski, *From the Atlantic to the Urals*, pp. 221–37.

15 See Bernd A. Goetze, 'Verification of confidence- and security-building measures:

evolution and future prospects', in Jürgen Altmann and Joseph Rotblat (eds.), *Verification of Arms Reductions, Nuclear, Conventional and Chemical*, Berlin, Springer, 1989, p. 148; SIPRI, *Yearbook: World Armaments and Disarmament*, Oxford, Oxford University Press, 1987–90.

16 Theodore J. Lowi, 'American business, public policy, case studies and political theory', *World Politics*, XVI, July 1964, pp. 677–715.

17 Efinger, Rittberger and Zürn, *Internationale Regime in den Ost-West-Beziehungen. Ein Beitrag zur Erforschung der friedlichen Behandlung internationaler Konflikte*, Frankfurt/M., Haag & Herchen, pp. 93ff.

18 For the results, see Efinger and Zürn, 'Explaining conflict management in East–West relations: a quantitative test of problem-structural typologies', in Rittberger (ed.), *International Regimes in East–West Politics*, pp. 78ff.

19 Joseph Nye, 'Nuclear learning and US–Soviet security regimes', *International Organization*, XLI, 1987, p. 374; Duncan Snidal, 'The limits of hegemonic stability theory', *International Organization*, XXXIX, 1985, pp. 579–614; Robert Jervis, 'Security regimes' in Krasner (ed.), *International Regimes*, pp. 173–94; Janice G. Stein, 'Detection and defection: security regimes and the management of international conflict', *International Journal*, XL, 1985, pp. 599–627; Harald Müller, 'Regime-analyse und Sicherheitspolitik: das Beispiel Nonproliferation', in Kohler-Koch (ed.), *Regime in den internationalen Beziehungen*, pp. 277–313.

20 Daniel Frei and Dieter Ruloff, 'Reassessing East–West relations: a macroquantitative analysis of trends, premises and consequences of East–West cooperation and conflict', *International Interactions*, XV, 1988, pp. 9–10.

21 See Rittberger and Zürn, 'Towards regulated anarchy in East–West relations: causes and consequences of East–West regimes', in Rittberger (ed.), *International Regimes in East–West Politics*, pp. 35–7.

22 Barry M. Blechman, *Preventing Nuclear War*, Bloomington, Ind., Indiana University Press, 1985.

23 Falk Bomsdorf, 'The confidence-building offensive in the United Nations', *Aussenpolitik*, XXXIII, 1982, pp. 370–90.

24 Berthold Meyer, Norbert Ropers and Peter Schlotter, 'Der KSZE-Prozeß', in Gert Krell, Egon Bahr and Klaus von Schubert (eds.), *Friedensgutachten 1987*, Frankfurt/M., Hessische Stiftung Friedens- und Konfliktforschung, 1987, p. 140.

25 Borawski, *From the Atlantic to the Urals*, p. 77. Klaus Citron, Chief delegate of the Federal Republic of Germany at the CDE, makes the same point; see his 'Experiences of a Negotiator at the Stockholm Conference', in Frances Mautner-Markhof (ed.), *Processes of International Negotiations*, Boulder, Colo., Westview, 1989, pp. 79–84.

26 James E. Goodby, 'The Stockholm Conference: negotiating a cooperative security system for Europe', in George, Farley and Dallin (eds.), *US–Soviet Security Cooperation*, pp. 155ff.

27 'Concluding Document of the Vienna Meeting', in SIPRI, *Yearbook 1989*, pp. 416–26.

28 For a detailed description of the Vienna negotiations, see Austrian Committee for European Security and Co-operation (ed.), *Focus on Vienna*, Vienna, 1989–90.

29 *Ibid.*, no. 21, December 1990, pp. 2–8.

Alternative security systems for Europe

As the nature of the security agenda facing the Europeans in the 1990s changes, the security structures of the continent will change too. The post-war security system – based on the bipolar arrangements of the cold war era – is no longer appropriate for a Europe in which there is no credible Soviet threat; in which Germany is united; and in which communism is a spent force. The Western Allies are now having to reconsider the nature of their security policies in a Europe 'beyond containment'. Europe is currently in an uncertain and fluid period of transitional instability, in which many of the old verities are open to question. Will NATO remain relevant to the security needs of its sixteen members? What long-term effect will the 1989 revolutions in Eastern Europe have on the process of West European integration? What sort of relations should the West develop with a fragmenting Soviet Union? Should the European Community (EC) develop common foreign and defence policies? What should be the role of the Conference on Co-operation and Security in Europe (CSCE) in the new Europe? Will the passing of the cold war mean that Europe reverts to pre-war patterns of multipolar instability and nationalist rivalry?[1]

A wide-ranging debate is currently under way in Europe which revolves around these and other questions. Although it is impossible to predict with any certainty the precise nature of Europe's post-cold war security arrangement, a number of broad alternatives are emerging. To begin with, it is apparent that the new European security system will be structured around three key institutions – NATO, the European Community and the CSCE. The precise nature of Europe's future security system will depend on what sort of relationship develops between these three crucial bodies.

This suggests that there are four broad alternative security systems for Europe: an 'Atlanticist' security framework centred on a reformed NATO, a 'Europeanist' structure based on what I shall call a 'West European Defence Community' (WEDC); a CSCE-based system of pan-

European collective security; and a more polycentric bloc-free *Europe des Etats*. They are derived from current proposals for future security structures, and encapsulate the views of significant schools of thought within the contemporary debate on European security. These four alternative security systems should be seen as 'ideal types' or 'models'. Although there are a number of methodological problems inherent in this sort of model-building, I hope that by extrapolating current trends, it is possible to see some of the longer-term consequences of current proposals on Europe's future security 'architecture'.[2]

Model 1: a NATO-based Atlanticist security system

This first scenario of European security in 2000 assumes that NATO can successfully adapt to a post-cold war environment, and that the Alliance becomes the central element of a transformed security regime. It also assumes, firstly, that despite its considerable economic importance, the European Community will fail to develop a common foreign and defence policy by the turn of the century, and secondly, that whilst the CSCE will emerge as a vital forum for pan-European dialogue and co-operation, it will not provide an effective and credible mechanism for collective security amongst its thirty-four members (or thirty-five when, in June 1991, Albania joins the CSCE).

If NATO were to become the central institutional support of a new European security system, it would need to change in three crucial respects. First, it would have to develop into a more 'European' organisation. Despite its formally democratic decision-making processes, the Alliance from the start has been dominated by the Americans. In his 1962 Independence Day speech in Philadelphia, President Kennedy outlined his vision of a NATO Alliance resting on two pillars, an American and a European one. However, given the nature of extended nuclear deterrence and the substantial US military commitment to Europe, the United States has remained *primus inter pares*. With the reduced reliance on nuclear weapons (especially theatre nuclear forces), and a reduction in the size of US forces stationed in Europe, this is already beginning to change. A more 'European' Alliance could be further developed by giving more senior command positions to Europeans (perhaps even a European Supreme Allied Commander Europe – SACEUR); by expanding the competence and remit of the Eurogroup; or associating the Western European Union (WEU) more closely with NATO. This in turn might make it possible for the French and Spanish to associate themselves more closely with the military command structures of the Alliance.

Second, NATO would have to demonstrate that it is willing to develop a more co-operative relationship with the Soviet Union and the countries of Eastern Europe. A start has already been made to do this. In November 1990 at the Paris CSCE Summit, NATO and Warsaw Pact members agreed to a declaration stating that they no longer saw each other as enemies, and that they wanted to 'extend the hand of friendship' to each other. At its summit meeting in July 1990, NATO also suggested the establishment of a series of formal diplomatic links between the Alliance and individual Warsaw Pact countries. In this respect, NATO has been building on the recommendations of the 1967 Harmel Report, which called for the Alliance not only to provide deterence for its members, but also to take responsibility for developing détente and managing the co-operative aspects of the East–West relationship. If NATO could effectively develop diplomatic and political links with the Soviets as well as East Europeans, then it could begin to function as a focus for broad-ranging discussions and consultations on security issues affecting the continent.

Third, if it were to remain relevant to the security concerns of its sixteen members, the Alliance would need to develop an out-of-area competence. The collective defence provisions of the 1949 Washington Treaty (which established NATO) do not apply for conflicts involving its signatory states outside of the North Atlantic Area. This has prevented the Alliance from becoming embroiled in regions like South-West or South-East Asia. However, the Gulf crisis led to renewed calls for NATO's logistical infrastructure – if not its integrated command – to be put at the disposal of member countries involved in conflicts outside the NATO area. There are also NATO projects for the creation of a multinational Rapid Reaction Corps which could then be deployed out of area if required. Such proposals are extremely controversial, and were strongly opposed by the French.[3] Nevertheless, it is difficult to see how the Alliance can remain relevant to its members' security needs following the demise of the Soviet threat and the Warsaw Pact if it does not develop an out-of-area competence.

This vision of a NATO-based European security regime enjoys considerable support in the Anglo-Saxon countries. It also has supporters in Christian Democratic and conservative circles on the continent. Proponents of such an Atlanticist security system argue that it would provide a sound and proven recipe for maintaining peace and stability in the continent, for a number of reasons.

First, they argue that NATO has successfully kept the peace in Europe for over forty years, and that a security system built around the

Alliance would be one founded on a tried and tested organisation of collective defence. Moreover, as an alliance of sixteen democratic nations, they suggest, NATO has an inbuilt 'structural incapacity for aggression'. The Alliance would thus not present a threat to any peaceful state in Europe. Second, giving NATO an expanded security role would cement the US commitment to Europe. The United States, it is argued, provides a strategic counterweight to the Soviet Union, and reinforces stability by acting as 'Europe's American "Pacifier" '.[4] Third, NATO provides a framework for integrating German power into broader European and Atlanticist frameworks. This helps prevent the re-nationalisation of German defence policy, thereby addressing one of the central security concerns of Germany's neighbours and former enemies. Fourth, NATO's existing military structures and integrated command could provide a valuable mechanism for co-ordinating Allied responses to out-of-area crises, should this be felt desirable. Fifth, NATO provides an invaluable insurance policy in case of a recidivist blacklash in the Soviet Union. It also makes it possible for the Allies to co-ordinate their defence cuts and military restructuring, thereby preserving a balanced military structure at lower levels (based perhaps on multinational force integration and a degree of task specialisation within the Alliance). Finally, there is some evidence to suggest that at least some of the East-Central Europeans would welcome a substantial role for NATO, because it provides a major element of stability in an otherwise fluid and turbulent strategic environment.[5]

On the other hand, critics of an Atlanticist security regime argue that in post-cold war Europe, there is no place for an organisation designed – in the words of NATO's first Secretary-General, Lord Ismay – to 'keep the Russians out of Europe, the Americans in, and the Germans down'. NATO, its detractors suggest, is a product of the cold war, created for the express purpose of providing a deterrence against a perceived Soviet threat. Despite the Harmel Report's call for NATO to combine deterrence with détente, it has never been very effective in managing the co-operative aspects of East–West relations. Such a body, it is alleged, is thus no longer relevant to Europe's changed security agenda.

To begin with, opponents of a NATO-based Atlanticist regime point out that security in Europe is increasingly economic and political in nature. Yet NATO, they argue, is a military alliance which is not suited to tackling non-military security concerns. Second, it is argued, the Alliance would not be a legitimate international actor in regional crises outside the North Atlantic area. Its involvement in regional crises (such as that in the Gulf in 1990–91) would only risk alienating the Soviet Union, and would be perceived by many Third World countries as a form of Western neo-imperialism. Third, NATO itself does not provide any solution to the specific security concerns of the East Europeans. For the Alliance to give former Warsaw Pact members security guarantees would seriously antagonise the Soviet Union, and anyway would be difficult to make operational in military terms. A NATO-based security system would therefore not provide an effective mechanism for tackling minority nationalism, disputed borders or ethnic conflicts, problems which have already generated violence between rival nationalist forces in Yugoslavia. Finally, an Atlanticist security system would preserve US hegemony over West European affairs, and impede the development of a more autonomous and self-reliant Western Europe. Given the degree of supranational integration already achieved by the EC, it is argued, Europe no longer needs its American 'pacifier'. Indeed, amongst critics of a NATO-based security regime, the most popular alternative is a security system centred around some form of West European defence entity, linked to a more politically integrated European Community. This takes us on to our second model of European security.

Model 2: a West European Defence Community (WEDC)

In the 1980s, 'Eurosclerosis' was replaced by 'Europhoria' as the pace of integration in the European Community perceptibly quickened. This was accompanied by the development of new forms of West European security co-operation – notably the reactivation of the West European Union (WEU), and the creation of a Franco-German joint brigade and Defence Council.[6] For some, however, these modest developments should be but the prelude to a much bolder leap forward in the integration process in Europe. There is now a growing constituency – which is particularly strong in France, Spain and Italy, and amongst proponents of closer Community integration – in favour of some form of West European Defence Community (similar in some respects to the failed EDC of the early 1950s). Such an organisation could be created by fusing the WEU with the EPC (European Political Co-operation), as proposed by the Italian Foreign Minister, Gianni De Michelis, in the Autumn of 1990.[7]

The West European defence entity envisaged in this model would consist of two main elements: multinational conventional forces with an integrated command structure on the one hand,[8] and a West European nuclear deterrence on the other (based on Anglo-French nuclear co-operation, and some form of WEDC Nuclear Planning Group). This scenario clearly assumes that NATO will decline as an effective military–political alliance. But it does not preclude a looser form of strategic alliance developing between a politically integrated EC and the United States. However, America's direct military commitment to Europe would be much more limited than it is today (certainly in terms of stationed forces).[9]

Proponents of this 'Europeanist' alternative argue that it provides the only reliable long-term basis for a durable and robust security regime in Europe.[10] NATO, they argue, was a product of the cold war. With the demise of the Soviet threat, the relative decline of American power and the rise of a more cohesive Western Europe, the Alliance has lost its *raison d'être*. A pan-European collective security system based on the CSCE is not a feasible proposition, given the widespread unwillingness to abandon the unanimity principle upon which it is based. Thus, they argue, it is essential to construct a robust West European defence entity. This body would then provide a central element of stability within a Europe of concentric circles.[11]

A West European Defence Community, linked to a federated inner grouping of EC members, would provide the solid core of this proposed Europe of concentric circles. Around this core would be a broader group of those Community members unwilling to pool their national sovereignty in such a supranational federation. Beyond this would be a 'European Economic Space', consisting of the European Free Trade Association (EFTA) and East Central European countries. Finally, the CSCE – which includes the North Americans and the Soviet Union – would provide the institutional framework for wider pan-European dialogue and co-operation.

For advocates of a stronger and more integrated West European security entity, this arrangement would have a number of additional advantages. First, it would crown the process of post-war integration in Western Europe, and would give the European Community an international political influence commensurate with its prodigious economic strength. Second, it would provide a framework for harnessing the potential of a united Germany to broader European purposes. Third, West European security interests are not necessarily identical with those of the United States. Consequently, it is argued, the Europeans need to develop an independent capability for collective power projection. This requires the creation of an integrated military structure which alone can give substance to a common defence and foreign policy. Finally, a West European Defence Community could emerge as a strong force for peace within a new international order. The Europeans, it is claimed, have tended to be less ready to resort to military solutions to international problems than the Americans, and in the post-war period have shown a greater propensity to diplomatic and political initiatives.[12] Having a capability for co-ordinated military policy might therefore give the West Europeans added diplomatic clout and political influence.

This vision of a West European Defence Community as the bulwark of a Europe of concentric circles is criticised on a number of counts. First, convinced Atlanticists point out that the transatlantic partnership has provided a solid security guarantee for four decades, and sacrificing that in pursuit of the elusive goal of a West European security entity would be folly – especially given the uncertainties surrounding the Soviet reform programme. Second, other critics allege that this *Kleineuropa* solution to Europe's post-cold war security problems risks recreating a new division of Europe. The notion of concentric circles already implies elements of hierarchy and exclusivity. Creating a nuclear-armed West European superpower – especially one with a prominent German role – would probably strengthen the hand of conservative forces in the Soviet Union, and this would impede the process of wider pan-European integration. Third, this security model provides no solution to the security problems of Eastern Europe and the Balkans, except in an indirect, 'existential' way. In other words, although it might provide an element of stability in the European security system, it would not provide a mechanism to address the specific security concerns of Eastern and South-Eastern Europe (such as rising nationalism, economic dislocation and political instability). Finally, some on the political left and in the peace movement worry that West European security co-operation will engender new forms of imperialist and neo-colonialist aggression. This they believe, would be neither in the interests of the Third World nor of the Europeans themselves.[13]

The Gulf crisis gave a further twist to the debate on a common Community defence and foreign policy. 'Eurosceptics' argue that the Gulf war revealed the continuing deep national divisions between the Europeans on security issues. The crisis, they maintain, was the first real test of the Community's willingness to act as a cohesive international actor, and the Community failed dismally. On the other hand, proponents of European political union and security co-operation argue that the Gulf crisis highlights the need for a common security policy, and that the current divisions between the Twelve on strategic and political questions is symptomatic of the lack of institutional mechanisms for foreign and defence policy co-ordination.[14]

Model 3: a CSCE-based pan-European collective security system

This projected security system enjoys considerable support in East-Central Europe, and amongst those on the political left and in the peace movements. It envisages the development of a pan-European system of collective security, based on the CSCE process. This collective security system would gradually absorb the functions and responsibilities of the old alliances such as NATO, the Warsaw Pact and the WEU, and would guarantee the security of all participating states.

With the Paris CSCE Summit meeting in November 1990, the CSCE acquired a permanent institutional structure. Regular meetings of heads of state are to take place every two years, whilst foreign ministers are to meet annually. An 'Assembly for Europe' consisting of parliamentarians from CSCE countries is to be convened, and a permanent CSCE secretariat is to created. Furthermore, two specialist agencies have been established: an Office for Free Elections in Warsaw, and a Conflict Prevention Centre (to encourage greater military transparency and to monitor unusual military activity) in Vienna.

If the CSCE were to develop into a framework for collective security, it would need to acquire an institutional mechanism for conflict prevention and crisis management. This could take the form of a 'European Security Council' modelled on the UN Security Council, with the authority to insist on a mandatory arbitration and conciliation process in the event of a serious inter-state conflict in Europe. In order to enforce its decisions, the CSCE would also need to create peacekeeping – or perhaps even interventionary – forces. In this way, the CSCE would seek to act as a regional branch of the United Nations Organisation, operating within the broader framework of the UN Charter.

Such a pan-European collective security system would depend upon the following prerequisites being met. First, there would have to be a continuation of reform trends in the Soviet Union, and a Soviet leadership committed to developing a more co-operative relationship with its European neighbours. Second, it would need a continued spirit of co-operation and broad consensus amongst the major powers in the European security area – the United States, the Soviet Union, Germany, Britain, France and Italy. Third, further progress would be necessary in arms reductions (including a robust verification regime), defensive military restructuring and the development of a comprehensive system of confidence- and security-building measures.[15] And finally, it would require the definition of common security interests and human rights acceptable to all the CSCE participating countries, and their co-ordination in joint institutions within the CSCE's institutional ensemble.

There are a number of advantages claimed for such a pan-European collective security arrangement. First, it would provide a framework for addressing many of the specific security concerns of the East Europeans, such as national and ethnic conflicts, minority rights and border disputes. Second, the CSCE embraces thirty-five countries, including the Soviet Union and the United States (see Table 1.1, pp. 4–5). Its comprehensive membership is seen by some as one of its major advantages over competitors like NATO or a West European security entity. Third, the CSCE has acquired a high standing and considerable political legitimacy as a result of the role it played in facilitating East–West dialogue and co-operation in the 1970s and 1980s.[16] It is therefore well placed, it is suggested, to assume responsibility for collective security on the continent in the wake of the cold war. Finally, the CSCE provides a significant framework for anchoring Germany into broader security structures. Within the Federal Republic, many Germans are hoping that the passing of the cold war will allow the emergence of a security system which transcends NATO (with its commitment to nuclear deterrence and its notions of containment). The commitment of a united Germany to a collective security system based on the CSCE could be a very important factor in its ultimate success.

A pan-European collective security system, in which all states receive the same guarantee of security and free self-determination, is an eminently desirable goal. It seems appropriate for a time in which the 'iron curtain' has been dismantled, and in which East and West are now increasingly co-operating together to tackle common problems. Indeed, for the first time in its long and troubled history it seems less than fanciful to imagine a Europe 'whole and free'. Europe, many hope, may finally be in a position to develop a durable peace order, based on common standards of human rights, thickening ties of economic interdependence and a common commitment to collective security.

Criticisms of this model focus on its feasibility, rather than its desirability. The *Economist*, for example, dismissed what it dubbed 'the dream of Europax' as being completely untried and untested.[17] The criticisms of a CSCE-based security regime are the same as for any system of collective security, namely, how can it be made to work? How can unprovoked aggression be prevented or reversed, without thereby generating a wider and more destructive conflict? There are two specific problems facing any plans to develop the CSCE into a forum for collective security. First, there is the unanimity principle of the CSCE. At the moment, all actions and decisions of the CSCE have to be approved unanimously by all participating countries. But it is impossible to conceive of a collective security system operating effectively on the basis of unanimity. Although there are proposals to introduce some form of qualified majority voting, it is hard to imagine how any such scheme could win the approval of all thirty-five states. Second, the CSCE lacks any mechanism for enforcing its decisions. Without an effective enforcement mechanism (ranging from diplomatic ostracism through economic sanctions to military force), no collective security arrangement can command credibility.

One further problem facing a collective security system in Europe is that its political foundations are not of uniform strength; they are firm in Western and Central Europe, and unsound in much of Eastern Europe, the Soviet Union and the Balkans. Constructing such a comprehensive and unitary structure of collective security in Europe on such uneven foundations would therefore be extremely difficult. Finally, it should be noted that the historical and contemporary precedents for a pan-European collective security system are not very reassuring. Historically, neither the League of Nations nor the Concert of Europe succeeded in developing a durable security regime. The United Nations has a patchy record in this regard, whilst regional bodies such as the Organisation of African Unity or the Organisation of American States have a fairly dismal record.[18] Despite the optimism generated by the ending of the cold war, therefore, the immediate prospects for a pan-European collective security regime are not encouraging.

Model 4: a *Europe des Etats*

The preceding three models all share one common assumption. They assume that European security will be constructed around a solid institutional structure – either NATO, a West European security entity or the CSCE. The nation-state model, however, is fundamentally different. It envisages a more fluid security arrangement, without cohesive military alliances or institutionalised multilateral security structures. In this Europe, the continued vitality of the nation-state in Western Europe would be complemented by the assertion of national identity in Eastern Europe and the Balkans, and perhaps too by the fragmentation of the Soviet Union into its constituent republics. It would be a Europe, in other words, of nation-states, free from the bipolar hegemony of the superpowers and from supranational structures.

This security system assumes firstly, that NATO will wither and die. Thus it would entail the withdrawal of American troops from Western Europe, German neutrality and the disintegration of the integrated military command. Secondly, it assumes that although the EC will remain important for economic integration, it will not develop significant forms of political co-operation, and certainly not a common foreign and defence policy. Instead, the Community will concentrate on widening its membership, rather than deepening its supranational forms of integration. Thirdly, that the CSCE will provide a valuable forum for pan-European discussion and consultation, but will not develop into an institutional basis for a collective security system.

This vision of Europe derives from Charles de Gaulle's notion of a *L'Europe de l'Atlantique à l'Oural*, in which the bipolar hegemony of the superpowers was to be replaced by a new political and security arrangement based on nation-states.[19] In this model, co-operation between nation-states will take the form of inter-governmental co-operation, rather than supranational integration. A Europe of nation-states would be increasingly polycentric, pluralistic and diverse. With the passing of the East–West divide, this model assumes that the European security system will become more and more fragmented. Regional and sub-regional forms of co-operation will emerge. For example, in 1990 the *Pentagonale* was formed amongst the nations of the former Austro-Hungarian Empire. It comprises Italy, Austria, Hungary, Czechoslovakia and Yugoslavia, and aims to foster regional economic, diplomatic and cultural links between them. Other sub-regional groupings or forms of security co-operation are likely to emerge around the Baltic Sea, around the Black Sea or between those Southern European countries bordering the Mediterranean.

At the same time, a network of shifting, diverse alliances is likely to reappear across the continent, as the old balance of power logic reasserts itself in a *Europe des Etats*. The security structures in this scenario will rely on a mixture of national military capabilities (as deterrence and defence becomes an issue for individual nation-states rather than military alliances) and a new system of limited multilateral defence agreements and bilateral non-aggression pacts. This will take the form of a new set of 'Locarno Treaties' between Germany and its eastern neighbours,[20] and a series of bilateral non-aggression pacts (modelled on that signed between Germany and the Soviet Union in November 1990). France will no doubt seek to re-establish its traditional alliances with Poland, Romania and the Soviet Union, in order to 'contain' Germany. A new version of the Entente Cordiale of 1904 is also likely, given France and Britain's common concern with out-of-area issues, their possession of nuclear weapons, and their membership of the UN Security Council.[21] Germany and the Soviet Union may also seek to evolve a more co-operative relationship, which will in turn revive fears (especially in France and Poland) of a 'new Rapallo'.[22] Italy, on the other hand, is likely to expand its political and economic ties with countries in South-Central Europe and the Balkans, as a potential counterweight to the German-dominated *Mitteleuropa*.

From this it can be seen that a neutral Germany would play a pivotal role in this bloc-free Europe. Germany will once again be the focus of the security concerns of the continent, given its prodigious economic strength, its size and its geographical centrality. Germany would have enormous political influence in Europe by virtue of its economic might, but would not be strong enough to control its external security environment. The country would also be faced with the unenviable diplomatic task of seeking to balance the competing demands emanating from its neighbours in both East and West. Once again, then, Europe's old security problem would reappear: how to accommodate, if not contain, a country with the economic size and energy of Germany, situated as it is at the very heart of a loosely-knit and polycentric Europe.

This security system is one currently favoured by latter-day Gaullists, such as the French *Rassemblement pour la République*, and by critics of 'Euro-federalism', such as the British Conservative Party's Bruges Group (named after the anti-integration speech by Margaret Thatcher in Bruges in September 1988). A bloc-free Europe – without divisive military alliances – has also been the long-standing goal of many in the peace movement. They tend to assume that once Europe was freed from the hegemonic conspiracy of 'Soviet Stalinism and Atlanticist Imperialism', a new, more peaceful equilibrium between European states would emerge.[23] The advantages claimed for this model of Europe are fivefold.

First, it is argued that this security system takes into account the diversity and pluralism of the European peoples, and builds on the continued vitality of the nation-state. Second, it would reflect the more diverse security agenda in a post-cold war Europe. The emerging security problems specific to the Eastern Mediterranean, for example, are of limited concern to the Scandinavians, and therefore unitary security systems like the CSCE or multilateral alliances like NATO are, it is suggested, of limited utility. Third, such a loosely-knit security system would facilitate regional and sub-regional forms of inter-governmental co-operation between neighbours. Fourth, trying to contain Germany by deepening the supranational integration of the European Community, some suggest, could be counter-productive, because Germany could well end up dominating such an integrated body. Instead, Germany's economic and political power can best be contained through a balance-of-power arrangement within a loosely-knit *Europe des Etats*.[24] Finally, it is claimed, this security arrangement would not mean a return to the multipolar instabilities of the pre-war years. Europe is characterised by a much higher degree of interdependence than in the pre-1939 period; the European Community already provides an important forum of intergovernmental co-operation; Europe's political energies have been channelled into more peaceful and democratic directions than in the 1920s and 1930s; and the existence of nuclear weapons makes war in Europe unthinkable.

On the other hand, critics of this model argue that a Europe of nation-states would generate more security problems than it would solve. To begin with, they argue that the military disengagement of the United States from Europe would leave the Soviet Union – or even the Russian Federation on its own – as the leading military power on the Eurasian continent, and that this would destabilise the delicate European equilibrium. Second, a neutral Germany no longer integrated into NATO or into a deeply integrated EC would be a major security concern to its neighbours. Germany, it is suggested, would begin to act as a 'wanderer' between East and West, destabilising the European balance of power. Furthermore, no German government would be free of the dangers of nationalist pride and assertiveness – especially within a balance of power framework. Third, Europe is strewn with unresolved national and ethnic conflicts, and a bloc-free *Europe des Etats* would tend to lead to the 'Balkanisation' of European security, with a return to the multipolar instabilities of the 1930s. Fifth, it would be much more difficult to negotiate and implement a comprehensive arms control and verification regime. Sixth, it would leave Europe diplomatically weak and incoherent, and therefore unable to exert a political influence in the international system commensurate with its collective economic potential. Finally, it is pointed out that the historical precedents of this sort of security system – like that of a system of pan-European collective security – are not encouraging; balance of power arrangements are notoriously unstable and risky, and both the Locarno Treaties and Bismarck's system of defensive multipolar alliances failed to prevent the slide towards war.[25]

Conclusion

European security is currently in a period of great fluidity and change.

With the ending of the cold war, a new security agenda is taking shape. This will stimulate the gradual evolution towards a new European security system – one more appropriate to the changed strategic and political realities in the continent.

However, it is important to understand the nature of the dynamics of change within the European security system. A new security framework will not emerge as the result of a conscious plan – either in the form of Gorbachev's 'Common European Home', Mitterrand's 'European Confederation' or Bush's Europe 'whole and free'. Indeed, the words of Thomas Schelling are even more apposite today than when they were first penned twenty-five years ago: 'The time for the Grand Schemes is over. We are moving out of our architectural period in Europe into the age of manoeuvre.'[26]

In this 'age of manoeuvre' – with its uncertainty and fluidity – the shape of the new European security order will evolve in response to specific crises and problems. If, for example, the Soviet crack-down in the Baltic republics in January 1991 proves to be a prelude to a more general conservative retrenchment in the Soviet Union, then NATO's relative importance within the European security system will be strengthened. However, if economic and social issues dominate the security agenda of the 1990s, then the role of the European Community is likely to grow. Similarly, if the reform process in the Soviet Union continues and a spirit of co-operation and consensus pertains amongst the leading powers in the European security area, then it is possible that the CSCE could begin to develop into a framework for collective security. On the other hand, if a rising tide of nationalism weakens both NATO and the European Community, whilst at the same time the CSCE fails to develop as an effective forum for pan-European collective security, then Europe could find itself with a fluid balance-of-power security arrangement. As the debate on Europe's post-cold war security system unfolded in the course of 1991, the main alternatives being considered were either a security system based on a reformed NATO (with an expanded out-of-area role and a new, more co-operative relationship with the Soviet Union and Eastern Europe), or one based on a more autonomous West European defence entity. A central question in this debate concerned the WEU: should it be more closely associated with NATO, or with the EC? However, the political and strategic situation in the continent is likely to remain fluid for many years to come, and a CSCE-based system of collective security or a *Europe des Etats* – although at present unlikely – should not be excluded as possible models of a future European security system. Europe's post-cold war security system will thus evolve organically on a piecemeal and incremental basis, as the result of *ad hoc* and largely pragmatic responses to specific security challenges.

Notes

1 These questions are addressed in greater depth in Adrian Hyde-Price, *European Security Beyond the Cold War: Four Scenarios for the Year 2010*, London, Sage, 1991.
2 There are a number of classic examples in strategic studies of this sort of model building: see, for example, Alastair Buchan, *Europe's Futures, Europe's Choices: Models of Western Europe in the 1970s*, London, Chatto & Windus/Institute of Strategic Studies, 1969; Pierre Hassner, *Change and Stability in Europe*, Adelphi Papers 45 and 49, London, ISS, 1968; and Lincoln Bloomfield, *Western Europe to the Mid-Seventies: Five Scenarios*, Cambridge, Mass., Center for International Studies, Massachusetts Institute of Technology, 1968.
3 'NATO raises the project of joint action "out of area" ', *Financial Times*, 19 December 1990.
4 The phrase was coined by Joseph Joffe: see his article of the same name in *Foreign Policy*, no. 54, Spring 1984.
5 Expressed, for example, in the speech by the Polish Foreign Minister, Krzysztof Skubiszewski, to the Royal Institute of International Affairs on 8 January 1991, in which he spoke of NATO's crucial role as an element of stability in the European security system.
6 See Ian Gambles, *Prospects for West European Security Cooperation*, Adelphi Paper 244, London, Brassey's/IISS, 1989.
7 'Italy says EC should consider forming its own "army for defence" ', *Independent*, 19 September 1990, p. 11.
8 As proposed by Edward Heath, 'Now we need a new army for Europe', *Sunday Correspondent*, 7 October 1990.
9 See, for example, Stanley Hoffmann, 'A plan for the new Europe', *New York Review of Books*, 18 January 1990, pp. 18–21.
10 'Western Europe,' Robert Rudney has argued, 'can no longer function as an economic superpower, a political schizophrenic, and a military vassal.' See Robert Rudney and Luc Reychler (eds.), *European Security Beyond the Year 2000*, New York, Praeger, 1988, p. 2.
11 The notion of a Europe of 'concentric circles' has been developed by, amongst others, Michael Mertes and Norbert Prill, 'Eine Vision für Europa', *Frankfurter Allgemeine Zeitung*, 19 July 1989, p. 8.
12 David Allen and Michael Smith, 'Western Europe's presence in the contemporary international system', *Review of International Studies*, XXVI, no. 1, January 1990, pp. 19–37.
13 For example, see Dan Smith, 'The changing strategic context', in Smith (ed.), *European Security in the 1990s*, London, Pluto, 1989, p. 23.
14 See 'Looking to the day when 12 will meet the world as one', *Independent*, 6 December 1990, and 'EC "needs a common policy on security" ', *Financial Times*, 24 January 1991.
15 Jürgen Nötzold and Reinhardt Rummel, 'On the way to a new European order', *Aussenpolitik*, XLI, no. 3, 1990, pp. 212–24.
16 Karl Birnbaum and Ingo Peters, 'The CSCE: a reassessment of its role in the 1980s', *Review of International Studies*, XVI, no. 4, October 1990, pp. 305–19.

17 'The dream of Europax', *The Economist*, 7 April 1990, pp. 14–15.
18 'CSCE, OAU, OAS, etc.', *The Economist*, 1 September 1990, p. 21.
19 Jolyon Howorth, 'Atlanticism, Gaullism and the Community: the debate between security and history in the post war world', *Foreign Policy*, no. 65, Winter 1986–7.
20 The Locarno Treaties were signed in 1925 by Germany, France, Great Britain, Italy, Belgium, Poland and Czechoslovakia, and consisted of guarantees of existing borders and provided for the peaceful resolution of disputes between the signatory states.
21 On Franco-British relations, see Yves Boyers, Pierre Lellouche and John Roper (eds.), *Franco-British Defence Cooperation: A New Entente Cordiale?*, London, Routledge/RIIA, 1989, and Françoise de la Serre, Jacques Leruez and Helen Wallace, *French and British Foreign Policies in Transition: The Challenge of Adjustment*, Oxford, Berg/RIIA, 1990.
22 This refers to the 1922 Treaty of Rapallo signed between Soviet Russia and Weimer Germany, which included clauses on joint military co-operation.
23 See, for example, Mary Kaldor, 'Beyond the blocs: defending Europe the political way', *World Policy*, I, no. 1, Fall 1983, pp. 1–21, and E. P. Thompson, 'Beyond the blocs', *END Journal*, no. 12, October/November 1984, pp. 12–15.
24 Frédéric Bozo and Jérôme Paolini 'Trois Allemagnes, deux Europes et la France', *Politique Entrangère*, no. 1, Spring 1990, pp. 119–38.
25 Thomas J. Christensen and Jack Snyder, 'Chain gangs and passed bucks: predicting alliance patterns in multipolarity', *International Organization*, XLIV, no. 2, Spring 1990, pp. 137–68.
26 Stanley Hoffman, *Gulliver's Troubles*, New York, Prager, 1968, p. 495.

9 Owen Greene

Transnational processes and European security

The traditional view that security is almost exclusively about military power and the maintenance of order amongst states was increasingly questioned during the 1980s. However, the 'cold war' bipolar division of Europe helped to sustain its dominance, and debates about European security tended to focus on military policy and the balance of power. The irreversible change in the security order in Europe in 1989–90 gave rise to concerns that the European state system might fragment into a multipolar structure or a 'Balkanised' Eastern Europe, resulting in intensified 'security dilemmas', tension and instability. It is in this context that attention has focused on building a new European security regime, which would aim to establish accepted regulations, norms and procedures to promote peaceful processes between states.

Towards a security community

The transition from a bipolar security system is not, however, the only fundamental change in European security affairs. Over the last few decades the nature of European society has been changing profoundly, as the development of international institutions, transnational organisations and movements, and integrative processes have undermined the power and autonomy of states. Arguably, the 'realist' perspective on international relations, focusing on sovereign states in search of power and military security, provides an unreliable guide to the dynamics of European security affairs as the year 2000 approaches.[1] The rival perspective of 'complex interdependence' is less blind to the importance of transnational economic, social, environmental and migration issues and concerns about human rights, terrorism or ethnic conflict. It also points to the possibility of moving beyond a new security regime to establish a European 'security community', in which the use or threat of military force between European states never arises as a possibility. This does not appear to be an unrealistic goal for the early twenty-first century. Already the use of force between states in Western Europe is not an issue.[2]

Such a security community not only rejects the use or threat of force among its members, but also requires a shared set of basic political values and well-tried peaceful ways of settling disputes. It is greatly strengthened by the development of supranational organisations and a multiplicity of international and transnational links of every type (economic, political, social, cultural) and on every level (individual, social and governmental), becoming so dense that state borders, state sovereignty, and autonomous state action in international affairs become increasingly notional.

Central and Eastern Europe are clearly some distance from meeting these conditions. After the withdrawal of Soviet domination, the region demonstrates much of the fragmentation and instability characteristic of decolonisation. The borders of the newly-independent states have been determined by the dynamics and priorities of old empires (Ottoman, Austro-Hungarian, Nazi and Soviet in this case), rather than by local conditions. The 'divide-and-rule' policies of the old hegemonic power leave a legacy of fragmentation, with relatively few transnational connections and international institutions linking the newly-independent countries in the region. It is now widely accepted that tackling non-military problems, such as economic and environmental crises or the promotion of social justice, human rights and democracy, may be of greater immediate significance to the military security and stability of East-Central Europe than attention to the military balance and arms control. Moreover, if the concept of security is broadened, these non-military issues can be seen as important security problems in their own right.

This chapter aims to outline some of the major non-military, transnational issues associated with European security in the 1990s, and with the possible development of a security community across Europe. The next section outlines the development of people power and non-violent civil resistance as a factor in European politics, and discusses its potential for reducing the role of military power in European security affairs. Next, the establishment of democratic institutions and respect for human rights is discussed in relation to European security. In the same context, the significance of emerging patterns of migration, economic development, and environmental co-operation are discussed in the following sections.

Non-violence, people power and social defence

Analyses of European security can no longer marginalise the importance of popular movements or the values and transnational links they promote. The 1989 revolutions in Eastern Europe had profound implications for European security and provide a dramatic illustration of the potential of 'people power'. They demonstrate the weakness of any European government ruling without popular legitimacy and also the potential power of non-violent civil resistance.

Similarly the rise of new social movements in Europe, such as the peace, Green, and women's movements, while not transforming the political order, have been undeniably important in setting agendas and promoting reform. Throughout Europe, popular movements have had an important influence on national security debates and on the values of élite groups and the population at large. Moreover, such movements have helped in creating and developing links and shared values across national boundaries. As such, they not only constrain and influence their individual governments but also build the fabric of social relations necessary to build a security community.

The increasing respect for both the ethics and effectiveness of non-violent approaches to achieving political change may be of enduring significance for European security. Apart from Romania, the 1989 revolutions in Eastern Europe were achieved with virtually no violence. The non-violent strategy of the opposition groups in much of Eastern Europe almost certainly enhanced their national and international support, and increased the political inhibitions on the state's use of violence against them. If the democratic oppositions had used violence, many of their supporters might have demobilised and the state would almost certainly have been able to respond with overwhelming force. The understanding and discipline amongst the leaders of the East-Central European opposition groups and their supporters – necessary for effective non-violent resistance – did not emerge suddenly and spontaneously. It drew upon their past experiences, influenced greatly by their links with the churches and the new social movements in Western Europe.

The churches played an important role in the development of opposition groups in much of Eastern Europe, both as refuges and as rallying points. The ruling communist parties typically allowed them considerable autonomy, in order to reduce popular alienation and to some extent to broaden the governments' base of support. In Poland, for example, the Catholic Church was not only an important symbol of national identity and culture, but also a source of considerable practical and moral support for Solidarity activists and other opposition groups. Pacifism, or at least peaceful approaches to problems, have been strong elements of the Christian tradition, and the churches helped to promote non-violent approaches to social change amongst opposition groups. For example, some evangelical churches in the GDR made striking efforts to guide demonstrators towards effective non-violence, even to the point, in November 1989, of protecting the lives of Stasi secret policemen from angry crowds.[3]

Being organisations with strong transnational connections, the churches had long provided channels of communication with the outside world. The development of transational links between political groups was also important. Prior to the late 1970s, there was little dialogue between the western peace movements and opposition groups in Eastern Europe. Indeed, East European opposition groups often regarded the peace movement with suspicion, seeing it as being either sympathetic to, or manipulated by, the communist authorities in the Soviet bloc. However, the mass anti-nuclear demonstrations in Western Europe in the early 1980s were given wide coverage throughout the Soviet bloc, and ironically helped to stimulate the growth of independent peace movements there. Media coverage of the protests against western governments influenced the forms that protests took in Eastern Europe and the Baltic republics in the late 1980s. Examples include techniques of civil disobedience or the formation of human chains to enclose or link sites of symbolic significance.

Furthermore, at the end of the 1970s a dialogue developed between opposition and dissident groups in different Eastern European countries, and then between these groups and leading figures in the western peace movement. In 1978 the first of a series of meetings took place between key Polish and Czech dissident groups, KOR (Committee for Defence of Workers) and Charter 77. Eventually, links between the European Nuclear Disarmament (END) campaign, Charter 77, KOR, the GDR 'ploughshares' movement and Hungarian groups flourished. In 1980, Solidarity accepted the arguments of KOR leaders, such as Jacek Kuron, in favour of non-violence, and adjusted its tactics in order to reduce the risk of violent confrontations with the authorities.[4] From 1982, the annual END conventions became an important forum where transnational links within the Soviet bloc and between East and West were forged. In 1984, a European Network for East–West Dialogue was established to work out common positions. The process resulted in a series of joint declarations and publications, linking the priorities and values of the peace movements with human rights and democracy.[5]

During the same period, environmental groups in the East were increasingly co-ordinating their activities and forming new networks. They also established contacts with the western Green movement, with its broader value system linking environmentalism with non-violence, decentralised democracy and human rights.

These links and shared values may have seemed marginal in the mid-1980s. However, by the 1990s many of the personalities and groups involved in the process were in positions of influence in Central and Eastern Europe, and the agendas developed then occupy a key place in the ideologies and programmes in many of the main political parties and movements in the region. The transnational links formed in opposition provide an important basis for developing a sense of solidarity and interdependence in the new Europe. Moreover, many of the agendas promoted by the new social movements in Western Europe have now entered the political mainstream.

There are also signs that popular support for the military and military values is in decline. In much of Southern Europe, memories of military involvement in sustaining unpopular dictatorships are slow to fade. Similarly, in Poland, Hungary, Czechoslovakia and the (ex-)GDR, the military were very much identified as part of the old regimes and likely to be regarded with suspicion for some time to come.[6] In much of Yugoslavia, the national army is seen as an unwelcome representative of central (and Serbian) power, and a threat to aspirations for increased autonomy. Likewise, the prestige of the Red Army amongst the Soviet people declined rapidly after 1987, as it became involved in internal policing and its flaws, such as the ill-treatment of conscripts, became widely disseminated. Throughout these societies, the military is also widely seen as consuming a disproportionate share of resources.

In Western Europe, too, support for the military and military spending has declined. In Germany and the Low Countries, resentment against military conscription has been growing and the numbers of young men registering as conscientious objectors has increased.[7] Indeed, although the Gulf war revealed continuing support in France and the United Kingdom for military action in certain circumstances, throughout the rest of Europe popular attitudes remained much more ambiguous and critical. In the early 1990s, military status and values are under strong challenge in most East-Central European states, and nowhere in Europe is there a country in which militarist values predominate.

The capacity for self-defence is nevertheless still widely perceived as a necessary precaution and deterrent. In this context, proposals have been made that a 'social defence' policy should also be considered.[8] Social defence refers to non-violent civil resistance to defend a country and/or its institutions against external aggression or an internal military coup. As with military defence, social defence would aim both to deter and to resist aggression. However, scepticism about its effectiveness on both counts has been such that few states have so far tried to incorporate it into their defence policies.[9]

The enhanced prestige of 'people power' after its successes in the 1980s may greatly increase the credibility of social defence in the 1990s. Indeed, experience of civil resistance in Eastern Europe and the Soviet republics is probably a greater deterrent to an attempted Soviet invasion of one of the East European states than the capability of these states' armed forces. Initially, social defence could be incorporated into a state's defence preparations as a fallback strategy in the event of military defeat. As confidence in the policy increased, or the threat of military coercion seemed increasingly remote, greater reliance could be placed on the social defence component of security policy.

Democracy, human rights and security

It is often noted that war has not yet occurred between two liberal democracies. Many argue that this is a fundamental characteristic of relations between such states.[10] The theory is that democracies tend to respect the democratic rights of other peoples and therefore do not use armed force against each other. Even if this is not an absolute rule, regular elections, democratic institutions and a degree of openness in decision-making almost certainly impose severe constraints on any government tempted to engage in military intervention, particularly against another democracy. To the extent that this argument is valid, the democratic reforms in Eastern Europe and the Soviet Union are of profound significance for European security.

By the 1980s, the liberal capitalist democracies of the EC and Council of Europe had come to represent models for 'modern' political and economic systems for many people in East-Central Europe, and for 'radical' reformers in the Soviet Union and the Balkans. Even cautious Communist Party members and conservative technocrats came to regard free elections as the only way for a government to gain sufficient legitimacy to take tough economic decisions without provoking massive popular upheavals. The revolutions in Eastern Europe were largely carried out in the name of democracy, human rights and the rule of law, and these values, commonly regarded as the hallmark of 'Europeanness', now command widespread popular support. The question is whether they can be firmly established.

The elections held throughout East-Central Europe in 1990 were typically carried out efficiently and peacefully, and resulted in remarkably smooth transfers of power. Dozens of new political parties were formed in early 1990. Yet the elections established reasonably stable governments based on 'umbrella' groups (such as Solidarity in Poland and Civic Forum–Public Against Violence in Czechoslovakia) or coalitions (such as the Democratic Forum and its allies in Hungary, and the Christian Democrats and allies in the GDR). However, united primarily by their opposition to the old regime, divisions were bound to emerge in these ruling coalitions as they tried to develop policies to tackle the great problems their countries faced. Uniquely, the GDR was rapidly absorbed into the FRG, and its incorporation seems to guarantee the establishment of democratic institutions in its territories. There are no such guarantees elsewhere in the region.

By the spring of 1991 there had been splits in the Solidarity movement in Poland and a division in Civic Forum in Czechoslovakia. Such splits were inevitable, and also welcome in that they may provide the basis for stable multi-party democracy. Throughout East-Central Europe, there is a prospect that democratic politics will be established around competing social democratic and centre-right parties, forming coalition governments with smaller centre, Green, peasant, (ex-)communist or right-wing parties. Such a pattern is characteristic in most Western European continental politics.

However, constitutions were still under review in early 1991 with, for example, constitutional guarantees undefined. Moreover, the instruments of communist party domination, such as the *nomenklatura* system, penetrated deep into these societies and it will take years before the judiciary, police, civil service, army and many other state and social bodies are relatively depoliticised and trusted. In the context of ethnic divisions and economic and social crisis, there remains the possibility that authoritarian regimes may emerge in one or more of these countries during the 1990s. This possibility presents a problem for European security, in that authoritarian regimes may be more prone to military adventures and also more vulnerable themselves to foreign intervention.

Democratic institutions are even more fragile in the Balkan countries. By the end of 1990 Romania seemed to be governed by a small group of reform communists and technocrats led by President Iliescu. The 'historic' opposition parties were weak and the new opposition groups were fragmented. Worryingly, the most potent popular movements seemed to be based upon tensions between the Romanian majority and the Hungarian community. Similarly, the ex-communist Bulgarian Socialist Party formed a government after the Bulgarian elections in May 1990, though by the end of the year it had been joined by the opposition coalition, the Union of Democratic Forces, whose leader, Zhelyu Zhelev, became President of Bulgaria. Moreover, the anti-Turkish 'Bulgarianisation' campaigns had been reversed, and some progress was being made in reconciling the Turkish minority and the majority community. Nevertheless Bulgaria remained some way behind East-Central Europe in the establishment of democratic institutions. Democratic reforms were at an even earlier stage in Albania. A mass exodus of Albanians in the second half of 1990 was followed by large demonstrations and the election of a communist government which fell, after strikes, in June 1991.

Finally, the establishment of democratic institutions is even more complex in the Soviet Union and Yugoslavia, since nationalist fragmentation has accompanied democratic elections. The threat of secession, combined with a tendency to authoritarianism, led the central authorities to try to rein back democratic and economic reforms. The Soviet situation is discussed in the next chapter. In Yugoslavia in early 1991, there was irascible confrontation between the Slovenian and Croatian authorities and the federal army (dominated by Serbs). By the summer, declarations of independence by Slovenia and Croatia had hastened a drift into civil war and dissolution. It seems certain that progress towards establishing stable democratic institutions in these countries will be halting and difficult, prone to violence, and closely linked to the politics of regional autonomy.

International organisations and transnational links will play an important role in determining whether the transition to democracy in Eastern Europe is achieved successfully. For example, western states, the European Community and international financial and trading organisations can link progress towards democracy with the granting of much-needed economic concessions and aid to Eastern European countries.

Such linkage was used to some effect throughout the 1980s and 1990. The prospect of receiving further western loans was an important factor in the Polish Communist Party's search for accommodation with opposition groups in the 1980s, and also in the Hungarian Government's critical decision to allow GDR citizens to escape to the West across its borders in the summer of 1989. The EC made it clear to Albanian President Ramez Alia in late 1990 that no western aid would be forthcoming unless there was progress towards democratic elections in Albania, and also suspended aid to the Soviet Union after military action in the Baltic republics in January–February 1991. In most cases, the western policy of linking economic concessions and aid to progress on democracy and human rights issues seemed to have an effect.

Several Eastern European states aim to join the EC and are therefore anxious to demonstrate progress towards a stable, democratic society and market-based economy. But even Czechoslovakia and Hungary acknowledge that there is little prospect of joining before the mid-1990s. However, to operate as a real political constraint against authoritarianism, there needs to be manifest progress towards achieving this goal at an early stage. The threat that membership of the EC might be denied has little potency if people doubt that the goal can be achieved in any circumstances in the foreseeable future. For this reason, the early granting of associate membership of (or privileged arrangements with) the EC is of more than economic importance.

The West's use of its economic power to promote democracy needs to be done on the basis of generally agreed principles. Otherwise it may lead to intense resentment and suspicions of neo-colonialism. Fortunately, the CSCE process has established official consensus across Europe about both the desirability and the meaning of establishing democracy and the rule of law, and the protection of human rights. Agreed 'democratic practices' include holding regular, free, multi-party elections involving a secret ballot, honest counting and the publication of results. Every citizen should be able to seek public office, or establish a political party which would be permitted to campaign with unimpeded access to the media (unless it engaged in, or refused to renounce, terrorism or violence). All seats in at least one chamber of the national legislature should be freely contested in a popular vote. Achieving agreement on these principles in the 1989 Concluding Document of the Vienna Review Conference and the 'Charter of Paris' of the CSCE summit in November 1990 was an enormous advance, and lays the basis for pan-European institutions to promote democracy.

The Charter of Paris established an Office for Free Elections in Warsaw to promote democratic practices. An important element of its work is to facilitate the presence of observers, both foreign and domestic, in order to monitor the electoral process in CSCE states, at national, regional and local levels. The presence of foreign observers during the 1990 elections in most of Eastern Europe contributed greatly to the smooth transfer of power. In an atmosphere of suspicion and confusion, accusations of malpractice could have undermined the legitimacy of the new governments. The seal of approval from respected outside observers helped to avoid this.

In this way, transnational links to promote democracy are being facilitated by norms and institutions established through the CSCE process, effectively extending the work of the Council of Europe. The Council is restricted to democratic states that have adopted conventions such as the European Convention for the Protection of Human Rights and Fundamental Freedoms. Through its Committee of Ministers and Parliamentary Assembly, the Council of Europe has helped to develop shared norms and values in Western Europe since 1949. Spain and Portugal were not permitted to join until they became democratic in the late 1970s, and Greece and Turkey had their membership suspended during their periods of military rule. Thus, the Council of Europe can directly increase the political costs of authoritarian rule. By early 1991, Poland, Czechoslovakia and Hungary had joined the organisation, with the expectation that other Eastern European states would follow in due course (see Table 1.1, pp. 4–5).

Another important transnational process in reinforcing constraints against authoritarianism is the development of links between European political parties. In 1989–90, many emerging parties in Eastern Europe were advised and supported by 'sister' parties in the West. For example, the West German Social Democrats, Christian Democrats, Greens, and Free Democrats provided resources to, and formed links with, groups with similar ideologies in Czechoslovakia, Hungary and Poland, as well as in the GDR. As this process develops, such transnational political associations should promote democratic practices across Europe, and also help to overcome the fragmentation of European society.

The establishment of a pan-European CSCE regime for the protection of human rights is equally important for reducing the likelihood of international conflict. Respect for human rights tends to be associated with the establishment of democracy and respect for non-violence. The CSCE process has made great progress in establishing accepted norms and procedures for protecting individual practice. Although there are still many occasions where people are denied such rights, the political costs to a state for abusing human rights is growing, as is the likelihood of exposure. Moreover, as the membership of the Council of Europe expands, so will the jurisdiction of the European Court of Human Rights, to which individuals as well as states can appeal to obtain redress in respect of violations of the European Convention on Human Rights.

However, while much attention has been devoted to establishing a regime for the protection of individual human rights, no coherent framework for the protection of minority rights had been developed by early 1991. No international treaty regulated the inherent conflict between individual and group rights and there had been little sustained attempt to build a consensus on this issue. Yet most scenarios for violent conflict during the 1990s relate to possible disputes about the maltreatment of minority or oppressed groups. For example, violent oppression of ethnic Hungarians in Romania could start a chain of events leading to confrontation and conflict between Hungary and Romania. Similar scenarios for conflict within the Soviet Union and Yugoslavia are disconcertingly easy to devise. Thus, progress on minority rights is a key issue for European security.

Belatedly recognising this, the CSCE states declared in the Charter of Paris that the rights of national minorities must not only be respected as part of universal human rights, but also that friendly relations among peoples require that 'the ethnic, cultural, linguistic and religious identity of national minorities be protected and conditions for the promotion of that identity be created'. To begin the process of developing a minority rights regime, a CSCE 'meeting of experts' was convened in Geneva in July 1991. The outlines of such a regime have been readily identified.[11] In addition to having equal individual rights and equal access to political and economic participation in society, members of minority groups should be free to use their own language and practice their faith. In regions where they comprise more than a certain proportion of the population, they should also be able to educate their children, and to plead before courts, in their own language, and special funds should be available for the construction and maintenance of appropriate cultural institutions.

A difficult balance has to be struck between minority autonomy and integration with the majority community. Any effective pan-European minority rights regime would have to be sufficiently flexible to accommodate different local circumstances. However, the principles would have to be clear. Preferably minority groups should, in the last resort, be able to take their case to an international court for adjudication. Accepting such a regime will be uncomfortable for many states in Western as well as Eastern Europe, but the task is of central importance for European security.

Population movements

From the beginning of the CSCE process, the West criticised the Soviet Union and its allies for their severe restrictions on emigration and travel.

Although these criticisms were made in the context of cold war politics, their rationale was substantial. Freedom of movement is not only an important human right *per se*, but can also promote international security. Migration, tourism, and exchanges between social, economic and political groups all help to develop a transnational social fabric on which long-lasting co-operative political relations can be built. The dramatic increase in population movements in Western and Southern Europe since the early 1950s has been a key factor in the development of a security community throughout much of this region.[12] The end of the bipolar division of Europe has substantially removed the barriers to travel between East and West Europe. Yet western celebrations of this development have been mixed with mounting anxiety. The prospect of large-scale migration from the poor East to the prosperous West is now widely accepted to be a major non-military security issue.

Migration has long been a major feature of European society.[13] Since the mid-1970s, the labour-importing states in Western Europe have stopped the large-scale and deliberate recruitment of foreign workers and introduced increasingly restrictive immigration controls. However, legal immigration continued as the fixed-term hiring of workers gave way to family regrouping, and 'migrant workers' became permanently settled as 'ethnic minorities'.[14] Moreover, as immigration restrictions grew tighter, illegal immigration increased. In the late 1980s, for example, estimates indicated that between 300,000 and 500,000 illegal immigrants were in France and almost one million were in Italy. The number of refugees and asylum seekers arriving in Western Europe also increased rapidly, from 70,000 per year in Council of Europe countries in 1983 to 350,000 in 1989 (excluding the migration of ethnic Germans).

In 1989, a large new source of migrants opened up. Whereas formerly the outflow from Warsaw Pact states to the West amounted to no more than about 100,000 people annually, a total of 1·2 million left these states in 1989. The number of internal refugees also increased. In the Soviet Union, for example, there were about half a million internal refugees following events in Armenia, Azerbaijan and Central Asia, and increasing numbers in Yugoslavia and elsewhere. Large-scale migration continued in 1990. Almost an additional one million ethnic Germans moved to Germany and 600,000 people emigrated from the Soviet Union. The number of people attempting to migrate to Western Europe is unlikely to diminish in the near future. After the Soviet Union adopts a law of free emigration there is the prospect of two to three million Soviet citizens wishing to leave their country. There are large numbers of potential migrants from the Balkans and parts of Eastern Europe. At the same time, poverty and population increases in North Africa mean that migration (legal or illegal) from the Mahgreb will continue on a large scale.

Furthermore, as West European border controls are reduced or eliminated as part of the '1992 process', it will be harder for individual states to monitor or restrict population movements, and also to combat international crime and terrorism.[15] These developments have raised much debate throughout Western Europe, amidst increasing fears that immigration will lead to social tension.

The way in which Western Europe responds to this issue will be of great significance for European security. It is clear that immigration policy will have to be co-ordinated across Western Europe. Since 1986, the EC Ministers of Justice and the Interior have been developing common policies. In the 1990 Dublin Convention, which most European Free Trade Association (EFTA) states are also willing to ratify, they provided a framework for managing requests for asylum and in combating terrorism and international crime. The 'Schengen Group' (France, Germany, Benelux and Italy) signed an agreement in June 1990 to remove all border controls between them and adopt common policies on immigration and co-ordination of internal policing. This development is almost certain to be widened and deepened in the early 1990s.

However, there is a great temptation for Western Europe to respond to the new 'threat from the East and South' in a unilateral manner by imposing tough immigration restrictions. For example, in September 1990, after many years of offering a safe haven for East European political refugees, Austria deployed much of its army to restrict the number of economic refugees (especially Romanians) crossing its border from Eastern Europe.

It is doubtful that such a policy could be successful for all of Western Europe. It would fail to tackle the poverty and instability that leads to migration, and would probably fail to prevent large-scale illegal immigration. Further, the restrictions and internal policing associated with such a policy would have political and social costs within Western Europe. Above all, such an approach could also be detrimental to European security. It would block the development of transnational links across Europe and across the Mediterranean, and thus obstruct the development of a security community throughout the region. Unilateral policies that make the Oder-Niesse line and the Mediterranean into Western Europe's 'Rio Grande' would symbolise a new division of Europe, promoting resentment and political fragmentation.

An alternative approach would be to place moderate limits on immigration into Western Europe. This would probably cause little resentment if limits were formulated with some sensitivity to the concerns of East European states; if they respected humanitarian and human rights requirements; and if they were associated with co-operative policies to tackle the underlying causes of migration. Poverty is typically the foremost cause, and so western economic aid and investment would be an important part of such an approach. However, oppression and political insecurity are also important incentives to migrate, and thus sustained support for democracy and respect for universal and minority rights would reinforce a limited entry policy. But immigration restrictions which seemed designed to permit entry only to highly-skilled workers, much needed in Eastern Europe, would appear merely self-interested.

The Council of Europe could facilitate the development of co-operative approaches to migration problems. It has long played a role in this area, but the membership is dominated by destination states. If regional co-operation on this issue is to develop, the CSCE probably provides the most appropriate framework. Not only does it include all European states and North America (another potential immigration point), but it has also begun to facilitate co-operation between all Mediterranean countries. At the 1989 Vienna Review Conference it was agreed to hold a series of conferences on Mediterranean co-operation. Representatives from *all* littoral states were invited, together with representatives from interested international agencies, to one of the first conferences, at Palma de Mallorca in September and October 1990. Italy, Spain and France proposed that this should lead to a Conference on Security and Co-operation in the Mediterranean, modelled on (and perhaps linked to) the CSCE, and providing a forum for discussion of migration policies in relation to economic and environmental co-operation.

Economic relations

Economic developments are of great importance for European security in a number of ways. Most fundamentally, perhaps, market reforms in Eastern and Central Europe permit the development of complex economic interdependence across the continent. In early 1991 the Soviet Union, Albania and Serbia were less advanced than other areas in this reform process, but had nevertheless made significant changes. Transnational webs of trade, production and investment can now extend throughout much of Europe, and become less subordinate to states' foreign policies.

As long as the Soviet-bloc countries maintained 'state-socialist' centrally-planned economic systems, East–West economic relations were inevitably limited. Although trade expanded after the early 1970s, it remained under state control and was hindered by the non-convertability of currencies. Direct investment in enterprises across the 'Iron Curtain' was minimal. Furthermore, the COMECON trading system tended to fragment the economies of East-Central Europe, so that they focused on bilateral economic relations with the Soviet Union rather than encouraging regional interdependence.[16] The structural differences between the western and Soviet bloc economies hampered the development of the dense international and transnational links necessary to build a security community. The cold war confrontation further exacerbated this situation. For example, trade in high technology goods was severely restricted by the western COCOM export restrictions designed to prevent Soviet access to militarily-useful technologies.[17]

The political and economic reforms in Eastern Europe since 1989 mean that the old economic division of Europe could be overcome in the 1990s. However, in most states the reforms or popular revolutions occurred in the context of deep economic crisis, and market reform programmes pursued by the new governments have further increased disruption and economic hardship. Many industries in Eastern Europe are uncompetitive, and unlikely to survive the reform process. The disruption of established trade with the Soviet Union and the increase in oil prices during 1990 hit already-ailing economies hard. Standards of living dropped and unemployment increased substantially throughout Eastern Europe, leading to increased social tensions. Few economists anticipate rapid economic improvements in the early 1990s. Several of these states are also deeply in debt, particularly Poland, Hungary and Yugoslavia, with little prospect of ever being able to repay the debts or even keep up with their interest repayments.

In this context, there is a risk that a new division of Europe will become established, in which Eastern Europe remains poor, indebted and unstable – dominated economically by the wealthy and stable western states. This would increase the risks of political instability and violent confrontations. Awareness of economic dependence and disparities of wealth between East and West can only increase migration, breed resentment and obstruct the development of a European security community. Addressing effectively the security issues associated with these economic problems means not only improving the economic outlook for each country in Central and Eastern Europe, but doing it in a way that reduces fragmentation in the region and integrates it into the West European and international economy.

Large amounts of emergency aid were provided by the West in 1990, particularly to Poland, Hungary and Romania, in the form of food and emergency goods and also to support currency reform. Similarly, the EC provided about $1 billion in emergency aid to the Soviet Union in early 1991. However, proposals for a new 'Marshall Plan' to tackle the economic problems of Central and Eastern Europe gained little support amongst western governments. It was widely argued that many of Eastern Europe's economic problems are structural, and large-scale aid would be ineffective without market reforms and privatisation. But some western governments and commentators initially regarded such reforms as panaceas for the economic problems of Eastern and Central Europe, and they relied primarily on private western investors to provide the resources for economic regeneration. In practice, private investment in Eastern Europe during 1990 occurred on a much smaller scale than governments had hoped. Political and economic instability, combined with uncertainties about ownership rights and other economic regulations, proved a deterrent to investors. Moreover, the economic rewards of investing heavily in Eastern Europe remained uncertain.

This experience reinforces the case for medium- or long-term assistance from western governments through credits and grants. Whereas grants constituted 80–90 per cent of the Marshall Plan in the 1940s, western governments have limited their grants to Eastern Europe to only 25 per cent of the total assistance offered. The rest (which is co-ordinated through the EC) is devoted to underwriting western business investments, 'soft' loans and new credits, debt relief and 'know-how' funds for training. The sources of such assistance include some twenty-four western governments, about seven multilateral agencies (such as the IMF and the EC) and countless private institutions, so it is hard to monitor, let alone co-ordinate, these activities. Overall, in 1990 financial assistance probably amounted to $10–15 billion, which was mostly given to Hungary and Poland. In addition, tens of billions of Deutschmarks were distributed to ex-GDR territories, mostly by the German government. These sums seem large, but not when compared to the scale of the problem. By contrast, Marshall aid amounted (in 1990 terms) to over $800 billion.

The particular needs of each Central and Eastern European state vary. As mentioned, debt relief is of particular importance to Poland and Hungary. Poland paid only about 15 per cent of the amount due in 1989, and its total debt increased by over $2 billion even before new loans were taken into account. But a deal to write off some of Poland's debts posed problems of justice and consistency and caused resentment among other Eastern European and Third World states which had to continue repayments.[18] For this reason, general debt reduction schemes were considered, in which the European Bank for Reconstruction and Development (EBRD) would play a major role.

The EBRD was established by OECD states in the spring of 1991 to promote market reforms and economic development in Central and Eastern Europe. About 60 per cent of its funds are to be directed at private firms, with the remainder earmarked for joint ventures in the public sector to promote reform. It has been provided with $12 billion to be lent on commercial terms. Its resources are thus too small and restricted to replace government aid programmes, and there are concerns that its remit could preclude adequate support for infrastructure projects relating to transport, education and communications.

By early 1991, therefore, it seemed clear that the overall scale of economic western assistance would be relatively modest: of the order of $5–20 billion a year, mostly in the form of credits and investment guarantees. This means that economic development and security in Central and Eastern Europe will probably only be achieved slowly and with greater social and political tensions than might have been hoped. It is vital for regional stability that the peoples of Eastern Europe feel that they will be able to join the economic 'mainstream' of Europe soon. This can be partially achieved by actively linking the countries of Eastern and Central Europe into the institutions of the western economic system.

Membership of the International Monetary Fund (IMF) has been a critical factor in the relative success of Poland and Hungary in obtaining credits for economic stabilisation. Helping other Eastern European states and the Soviet Union to join may therefore be an important step. This almost certainly would involve assurances that the conditions attached to IMF loans would be flexibly applied. Similarly, a gradual integration of Central and Eastern states into the General Agreement on Tariffs and Trade would be advisable.

However, for both political and economic reasons, the goal of most reforming states is membership of the European Community. EC governments have reacted to these intentions cautiously, to say the least, concerned that any widening of the EC would disrupt the integration process in Western Europe, and the development of a common security policy. Moreover, states such as Austria, Sweden, Finland and Norway are likely to have prior claims to membership.

As an interim measure, in April 1990 the EC offered negotiations on 'association' to Poland, Hungary and Czechoslovakia, which were due to be completed in late 1991. These would involve a full customs union and other measures to integrate the East-Central European economies with those of Western Europe. However, EC Commissioners emphasised that such agreements do not imply a promise of ultimate EC membership – they continue to be embarrassed by similar promises made to Turkey in the 1970s.[19] This has exasperated the Polish, Hungarian and Czechoslovakian governments, which have stressed that they intend to apply for membership in the early 1990s. Romania, Bulgaria and the Soviet Union also wish to embark upon the process. East European governments need to show that their countries are progressing towards full membership. Thus there is a strong case for the EC explicitly to identify the various stages along the way in order to increase confidence within states embarked on the journey, and thereby to promote democratic and political stability and economic investment, which in turn will reduce incentives for migration.

One of the reasons why the EC governments are reluctant to do this may be that they want to distinguish between the states of the former Austro-Hungarian Empire which have close historical and social links with the West, and the rest of Eastern Europe. Germany has an interest in promoting stability among its immediate neighbours. Similarly, Italy and Austria have a strong interest in developing relations, through the *Pentagonale* process, with Hungary, Czechoslovakia and western parts of Yugoslavia. In contrast, the Balkan states, Turkey and the Soviet Union (except the Baltic republics), seem to many Western and Central Europeans to be of peripheral significance. The process by which East-Central Europe is being preferentially integrated into western institutions can be seen in other areas. Consider, for example, the 1990 reforms in the COCOM regime regulating western high-technology exports. In response to the relaxation of East–West tensions and reforms in Eastern Europe, restrictions were substantially reduced on exports of 'dual-use' technologies (i.e. civilian technologies that could be used for military programmes). However, tight restrictions on certain sensitive technologies were retained for the Soviet Union, Romania, Bulgaria and other socialist states, whereas a more liberal approach was applied to Czechoslovakia, Hungary and Poland, with a promise that all COCOM restrictions against them would be lifted if they cut intelligence links with the Soviet Union.[20]

Whilst some distinction between the Soviet Union and East-Central Europe is understandable, the denial of equivalent privileges to

Romania seems to be symptomatic of the general approach to the Balkans. Powerful states such as Germany were prepared to champion the interests of their neighbours, whereas Romania's interests were of peripheral concern. There is the prospect, then, that by the end of the century, Poland, Czechoslovakia and Hungary will be integrated into the West European network, albeit as a relatively poor area. This would lay the basis for a security community extended to include East-Central Europe. But the Balkan states, Turkey and the Soviet Union could remain on the economic periphery: dependent on aid and trade with an extended EC, but without representation within the organisation or the substantial regional aid and investment that would follow from membership. Their slower economic development would increase the risks of instability or conflict in South-Eastern Europe, and thus pose a continuing security problem.

Thus economic processes may not on their own lead to the desirable patterns of European integration. The development of the economic basis for a European security community including South-Eastern Europe and the western Soviet Union will probably require sustained and deliberate acts of government policy in the West.

Environmental issues

Environmental problems present a transnational threat to well-being and security throughout Europe: air and water pollution does not respect state borders. For example, radioactive material released as a result of the 1986 Chernobyl disaster spread right across Northern Europe. Disputes about transnational pollution and degradation are an increasing feature of international relations. Yet environmental problems remind the international community of its interdependence. They characteristically arise as an unintentional by-product of economic activities, rather than as a deliberate act directed against neighbours. However, only through international co-operation can many environmental threats to states and communities be tackled.

Since the late 1960s, measures have been taken in Western Europe to reduce and regulate environmental problems. This has not been the case in Eastern Europe. Although official standards for air and water quality were frequently much more stringent in the East than in the West, they were largely ignored or unenforced. Priority was given to meeting economic production targets. Combined with a rigid and highly inefficient economic system, an emphasis on heavy, energy-intensive industry, and outdated equipment, this led to environmental disaster.

The problems are particularly acute in East-Central Europe. The former GDR and Czechoslovakia have relied heavily on burning lignite for energy. Poland has mined hard coal, but exported the higher quality grades to earn foreign currency, leaving lower grades for domestic consumption. Combined with very poor energy efficiency, this led to massive emissions of dust and smoke, and a range of toxic gases. High levels of atmospheric pollution substantially reduced life expectancy and increased illness throughout large parts of the region.[21] Acid rain devastated forests and damaged agriculture and other ecosystems. About 83 per cent of the forest in the GDR is reportedly damaged or dying as a result, and over half of the forests in Poland and Czechoslovakia are similarly affected.

Water pollution is a similarly serious problem. Heavy industry, refineries and mining operations have polluted rivers with chemical effluent, heavy metals and toxic wastes. Heavy use of fertilisers, liquid manure and pesticides in agriculture have further polluted water resources. Finally, untreated sewage is dispersed into rivers in much of Eastern Europe. Some 95 per cent of surface water in Poland was estimated in 1990 to be polluted and unfit for human consumption.[22] In addition, there has been widespread soil degradation through poor agricultural practices and mining. Huge quantities of toxic waste have been buried without adequate safeguards.

The new governments in Central and Eastern Europe understandably blame these environmental disasters on the former communist authorities which governed the region. Indeed, environmental concerns were an important element in opposition platforms during the 1980s.[23] Although the extent and depth of the environmental problems remain uncertain, much more information on environmental problems has become openly available since 1989. However, the costs of cleaning up pollution are likely to be immense. In the former GDR alone, German authorities estimate that over $100 billion will be required. In Poland and Czechoslovakia the estimates are $70 billion and $30 billion respectively.[24]

There is no prospect of these countries spending such amounts on the environment. Significant progress will only be achieved with the help of resources from the West, which has a major incentive to respond in that it is directly affected by pollution from Eastern and Central Europe. Sweden, Germany and Austria are now finding that, in order to protect themselves, it is often more cost effective to invest in curbing emissions from power stations in Poland or Czechoslovakia than in further improvements at home. The Bavarian state authorities have lent desulphurisation equipment to a Czech power station, and other German *länder* have contributed to various East European energy and environment programmes.[25] Although it seems likely that Germany will continue to play a leading role in the 1990s, the costs would have to be shared amongst a large number of countries and multilateral organisations. All European countries would benefit from reductions in transboundary pollution, but improving the quality of life in Central and Eastern Europe, in particular, must also be an important component of any approach in order to reduce migration and increase political stability.

In June 1990, East European and EC Environment Ministers agreed that international collaboration on safety at nuclear power plants, radioactive waste disposal, atmospheric pollution and contamination of water supplies would be given priority. The mechanisms for such co-operation remain unclear. However, the UN Economic Commission for Europe, as well as the EC, will play a significant co-ordinating role, having sponsored the Convention on Long-Range Transboundary Air Pollution of 1979 and several protocols during the 1980s which limited sulphur and nitrogen oxide emissions. Co-operation to tackle environmental problems in Central and Eastern Europe must be closely integrated with economic development programmes, for in many cases the most appropriate approach to reducing pollution from a particular factory will be to close it down.

However, market forces will tend to push Eastern Europe into emulating western production and consumption patterns which could incur some *new* environmental costs. For example, there is substantial demand for private cars throughout Eastern Europe, and western car manufacturers such as Fiat and Volkswagon have been a major source of investment in the region. By the same token, investment in energy-efficient public transport systems has a low priority for multilateral development institutions such as the new European Bank for Reconstruction and Development (EBRD). It would be tragic if Central and Eastern European states copied patterns of development which are currently being reassessed in the West.

A further consequence of the inter-relationship between economic aid and environmental co-operation is that most western resources are likely to be focused on the East-Central European states, where problems are particularly severe. However, once again patterns of co-operation may leave the Soviet Union and Balkans on the periphery of European integration.

Conclusion

It is possible that a set of basic political and economic values may soon be shared across European society. However, the development of a European security community is not inevitable. Just as the establishment of the EC and associated institutions have encouraged integrative processes and shaped security expectations in Western Europe since the late 1950s, transnational links in Central and East Europe will be shaped by the way in which international and supranational institutions develop. Without the reassurance provided by the rapid establishment of a new European security regime, insecure states and communities could limit the development of cross-border connections and impose unjust policies in the declared interests of national security.

Actions taken in the early 1990s could determine whether a complex interdependence develops across the continent, or whether a multipolar state structure emerges in which traditional military concerns continue to dominate European security debates. From the trends examined in this chapter there is reason to expect that the West European community will be extended to include East-Central Europe by the beginning of the next century, though the process will be difficult in the mid-1990s. However, unless deliberate policies are adopted to include them, there is a risk that much of the Balkans and the Soviet Union will be left on the margins, to the detriment of European security.

Notes

1 For an application of the realist model to the new Europe, see J. Mearsheimer, 'Back to the future: instability in Europe after the cold war', *International Security*, XV, no. 1, Summer 1990, pp. 5–56. For criticisms of this article, see 'Correspondence', *International Security*, XV, nos 2 and 3, Summer 1990.
2 See, e.g., W. Wallace (ed.), *The Dynamics of European Integration*, London, Pinter/RIIA, 1990.
3 M. Randle, *People Power: the Building of a New European Home*, Social Defence Project, Stroud, Hawthorn Press, 1991.
4 *Ibid.*
5 See, e.g., J. Kavan and Z. Tomin (eds.), *Voices from Prague*, Prague, Palach press/END, 1983; 'Charter 77 – the Prague Appeal', *East European Reporter*, I, no. 1, Spring 1985, pp. 27–8; European Network for East–West Dialogue, 'Memorandum on giving real life to the Helsinki Accords', in *From Below*, Helsinki Watch Report, October 1987, pp. 239–58.
6 Karen Dawisha, *Eastern Europe, Gorbachev and Reform*, Cambridge, Cambridge University Press (2nd edn), 1990.
7 David Gow, 'A child among the bully-boys', *Guardian*, 15 February 1991, p. 23.
8 See Randle, *People Power.*

9 Sweden decided in principle in the 1980s to include social defence as a fallback strategy in the event of military defeat. See generally, Gene Sharp, *Making Europe Unconquerable*, London, Taylor & Francis, 1986.
10 See, e.g., Michael Howard, *War and the Liberal Conscience*, New York, Rutgers University Press, 1978; Bruce Russett, *Controlling the Sword: the Democratic Governance of National Security*, Cambridge, Mass., Harvard University Press, 1990.
11 See Jonathan Eyal, 'Eastern Europe: what about the minorities?', *The World Today*, December 1989, pp. 205–8.
12 For a discussion of such population movements, see F. Romero, 'Cross-border population movements', in Wallace (ed.), *European Integration*, pp. 171–91.
13 J. Widgren, 'International migration and regional security', *International Affairs*, LXVI, no. 4, 1990, pp. 749–66.
14 *Ibid.*; see also François Heisbourg, 'Population movements in post-cold war Europe', *Survival*, XXXIII, no. 1, January/February, 1991, pp. 31–43.
15 Richard Clutterbuck, *Terrorism: Drugs and Crime After 1922*, London, Routledge, 1990.
16 See, e.g., Dawisha, *Eastern Europe*, ch.4.
17 S. MacDonald, *Technology and the Tyranny of Export Controls: Whisper Who Dares*, London, Macmillan, 1990.
18 Simon Fidler, 'Poland's debt deal will irritate others', *Financial Times*, 14 March 1991, p. 1; Maciej Percyzynski, 'Security threats from economic instability in the East', in Paul Eavis (ed.), *European Security: The New Agenda*, Bristol, Safer World Foundation, 1990, pp. 37–9.
19 John Palmer, 'EC takes stock of Eastern promise', *Guardian*, 6 March 1991, p. 14.
20 Owen Greene, 'Reforming the CoCom regime', in J. Poole (ed.), *Verification Report 1991*, London, Apex Press/Vertic, 1991.
21 J. Russell, *Environmental Issues in Eastern Europe: Setting an Agenda*, London, RIIA, 1991.
22 Helmut Schreiber, 'Security threats from environmental degradation in the East', in Eavis (ed.), *European Security*, p. 46.
23 See, e.g., M. Waller, 'The ecology issue in Eastern Europe: protests and movements', *Journal of Communist Studies*, V, no. 3, September 1989, pp. 303–38.
24 Schreiber, 'Security threats from environmental degradation', p.46.
25 Ibid., pp. 49–50.

10 Michael C. Pugh

Conclusion: from cold war to cold peace?

At the beginning of the 1990s the prospects for a new European peace order were jeopardised by the war in the Gulf and the deepening crisis in the Soviet Union. The two crises were interrelated in several ways. Preoccupation with domestic affairs weakened the Soviet leadership's ability to play other than a diplomatic role in the Middle East. Its self-appointed function as peacemaker in the Gulf whilst concurrently breaching the Helsinki Accord in the Baltic republics made the Americans, and to a lesser extent the Europeans, wary about the trustworthiness of the Gorbachev regime in foreign policy generally. Furthermore, the increase in military assertiveness in the Soviet Union was deeply worrying for the rest of Europe, particularly as the military lessons of the Gulf war could lead to Soviet demands for new equipment and herald a new arms race. Connections between the two crises – and between national, European and global security – were illustrated by the circumstances of Eduard Shevardnadze's resignation as Soviet Foreign Minister on 22 December 1990. Shevardnadze despaired at enforced centralisation in the Soviet Union, earlier exemplified by the brutal actions of troops in Tbilisi in April 1989. He appreciated that using military force to curb independence movements would invite foreign condemnation and endanger Soviet integration and co-operation with the West, including collaboration over the Gulf. His opponents attacked the terms of integration with the West and argued that the level of collaboration with the anti-Iraq Coalition compromised Soviet interests.[1]

This concluding chapter examines the extent to which each of these upheavals affected developments in European security. It then offers general conclusions about the factors which will shape European security in the future. It considers whether the Europeans can hope for little more than a 'cold peace' in which the impulses for integration and disintegration are more or less balanced out.

The Soviet crisis – Marshall aid or martial law?

In its scale, depth and significance for European security, the Soviet crisis was strategically more destabilising than the Middle East conflict. The prospect of the Soviet Union collapsing into civil war in the absence of any consensus about what constitutes the state, casts a long shadow over the next few years.

It can be argued that a golden opportunity to foster a new European security environment, through a Soviet 'Marshall Plan', was missed in the 1980s and early 1990s. In the summer of 1990, Chancellor Helmut Kohl proposed a $20 billion aid programme, derived largely from defence savings, to facilitate the transition to democratic politics and market economics in the Soviet Union. Actual German support, including payment for housing and relocating Soviet troops, was about $10 billion over four years, and EC aid, announced in December 1990, was to be $1·6 billion. The United States offered $1 billion in recognition of Soviet support in the United Nations against Iraq. The West's caution reflected, in part, its inability to provide aid on the generous scale of the original Marshall Plan. But another factor was the policy of using aid as leverage. The EC made it clear that large-scale aid would be conditional on IMF approval of Soviet economic policies. When *perestroika* faltered, from mid-1990, capitalist interests then contended that aid was pointless because the Soviet system would not use it efficiently to create a full-blown market economy. Furthermore, it was argued, Gorbachev and his disintegrating Union was neither worth rescuing nor safe for investments.[2] To some extent, it seems, western caution became self-justifying. *Perestroika* was supposed to mark the Soviet Union's integration with the world community after years of 'unnatural isolation'. The West's caution did little to ease Gorbachev's burden. To Gorbachev, even winning the 1990 Nobel Peace Prize must have seemed like the Kiss of Caiaphas.

However, the 'too little, too late' argument overlooks the fact that Gorbachev and the reformers also erred. Gorbachev loosened the old political and economic system but failed to impose a new one, prevaricating particularly over land reform. He can also be criticised for failing to devote attention to wooing Japanese support for industrial reform. If Gorbachev was always an opportunist without a plan, then radical liberals initially relied too heavily on his leadership. For their part, radicals failed to create alternative party structures to the Communist Party of the Soviet Union (CPSU). One can only speculate whether Gorbachev would have transferred his allegiance to another party, but in the spring of 1990 he probably missed an opportunity to acquire legitimacy by seeking a direct mandate from the voters at large. Historians will judge whether Gorbachev was a great 'reforming Tsar' or a failed power-broker. In the autumn of 1990 he appeared to make a Faustian pact with the hardline wing of the CPSU and the forces of law and order, but behind this ploy he remained firmly wedded to reform.

The economy entered the 1990s plagued by dislocation of production, an unstable currency, and an absence of technical, entrepreneurial and commercial expertise. Official statistics revealed that in 1990 GNP had shrunk by 2 per cent and productivity by 3 per cent compared to 1989. Far worse was predicted for 1991. A record harvest in 1990 failed to obviate the need for grain imports, partly because priority was given to military movements over crop distribution. The Soviet people endured the winter of 1990–91 amidst rumours of sabotage and famine, and Leningrad introduced food rationing for the first time since the Nazi blockade.

However, the Soviet Prime Minister, Nikolai Ryzhkov, rejected the plan for a rapid switch to a market economy proposed by the economist Stanislav Shatalin. Shatalin and other radical reformers, notably Alexander Yakovlev, the father of *glasnost*, Vadim Bakatin, Minister of the Interior and Nikolai Petrakov, an economic adviser, were eased out of power because they opposed the decision to apply brakes. Eduard Shevardnadze, a champion of domestic as well as foreign policy reform, alleged that reformers 'had slunk into the bushes'. *Perestroika*, it was argued, was dead.[3]

It might be more accurate to characterise changes in the autumn of 1990 as a rejection of *headlong perestroika* in favour of *incremental perestroika*. Gorbachev and Valentin Pavlov, Ryzhkov's successor as Prime Minister, criticised Shatalin's nineteenth-century-shopkeeper mentality, and instead sought 'market socialism'. Thus they shied away from private ownership of land, but agreed to lease 19,000 square miles for private production. Price reforms announced in mid-February 1991 allowed 30 per cent of products to be sold at unrestricted prices, whilst protecting vulnerable social groups from the full effects. To curb inflation and the black economy, a fifth of the currency was taken out of circulation and bank withdrawals limited. Pavlov claimed that western banks were plotting to flood the Soviet Union with the millions of roubles held abroad in order to create hyperinflation. This was scarcely credible given the profligate printing of notes by the Soviet Government itself. With more reason, perhaps, Pavlov also attacked foreign companies which treated the Soviet Union like a colony, exploiting Soviet resources at knock-down prices, or producing little of social value.[4]

In theory the Soviet economy has considerable growth potential. Scrapping the many inefficiencies would lead to a recovery based on a more capital-intensive system. But would incremental *perestroika* work? In the view of radicals like Shatalin, tinkering with the system would do nothing to stop a slide to economic catastrophe. Nor did gradualism win support from the increasingly impoverished population. Yet the freeing of prices and the anti-inflationary currency reform deserved some plaudits from capitalists quarters. In view of the economic 'betrayals' which followed the revolutions in Eastern Europe, it was also politically prudent, perhaps, to take gradual steps towards a market system. Boris Kagarlitsky, a member of the Supreme Soviet, pointed out that each step toward the market threatened greater chaos; relative passivity benefited people by postponing unemployment and huge price increases.[5] But apart from arthritis in the system, what made this an intractable crisis of international significance was the extent to which the economic and sovereignty issues were interlocked.

The sovereignty crisis

As a direct consequence of the repeal of Article 6 of the Soviet Constitution in February 1990, ending the communist monopoly of power, nationalists gained control in five out of the fifteen republics. Economic power was wrested from the central government. The Ukraine introduced its own 'currency' in the form of ration coupons. The Russian Federation (RSFSR) claimed sovereignty over its raw materials and severely reduced the revenues normally forwarded to the Kremlin for central functions. A budget compromise was reached in January 1991. But the RSFSR, the Ukraine, Byelorussia and Kazakhstan, between them controlling 85 per cent of Soviet output, forged closer relations in a deliberate challenge to Union economic control.

Constitutional control was challenged in November 1988 when the Estonian Supreme Soviet initiated a 'war of laws' between the republics and the centre by claiming the right to veto all-Union legislation. The Lithuanian Government's declaration of independence from the Union in March 1990 began a new phase in the sovereignty crisis. An economic blockade, followed by negotiations, failed to shift the Lithuanians. Gorbachev's response had the makings of an *18 brumaire*. Partly to preserve the Union and partly to direct the economy, he was granted additional constitutional powers in the autumn of 1990, including authority to declare martial law. At the end of January 1991 joint army–

police patrols were instituted in nearly 500 cities (except in Armenia, Estonia, Georgia, Latvia, Lithuania and Moldavia), ostensibly to combat crime. Special-purpose squads, the Black Berets (originally formed in 1987 in Moscow) were also widely deployed. Gorbachev's views on secession coincided with those of the KGB, Party hardliners and military reactionaries, represented in the Congress of People's Deputies by the *Soyuz* faction. In January the army was ordered to arrest draft dodgers, but local commanders also lent support to pro-Moscow communists in Lithuania and Latvia who were attempting to stage coups and install fraudulent Committees of National Salvation. The repression culminated in January and February with the deaths of seventeen civilians in Vilnius and Riga. Media condemnation of the killings, notably by *Moscow News*, *Komsomolskaya Pravda* and *Moskovski Komsomlyets*, led to newsprint and broadcasting restrictions.

In the face of western denunciations, protest strikes and demands from MPs and demonstrators for the government to resign, Gorbachev still had room for manoeuvre. He refused to back the National Salvation Committees, criticised military intervention in politics, announced an enquiry into the deaths in the Baltic republics, and withdrew some of the security forces from areas of tension. This was regarded by the menacing colonels in *Soyuz* as a betrayal. Indeed, Gorbachev demonstrated that he was not so much a prisoner of the reactionaries as a Soviet traditionalist in the way he manipulated power as the head of a bureaucratic oligarchy.[6] This, and the fact that nationalist and democratic demands are not amenable to bargaining for material gain, suggest that perhaps a grand Marshall Plan would not have made much difference to the way the sovereignty confrontation was handled, though it could have eased the path to economic reform.

But the split with the radicals became critical. Prominent liberals signed an article in *Moscow News* which accused the regime of stooping to crime. Boris Yeltsin, President of RSFSR, claimed that the use of Russian troops against the citizens of other republics was unlawful, and further suggested that Russia might need its own defence forces, an expensive idea later retracted. In March 1991, Yeltsin's demand for Gorbachev's resignation and a 'metaphorical war' on the Soviet leadership was echoed by large demonstrations in cities across the country and by striking coal miners in the Ukraine and elsewhere. Yeltsin was accused by conservatives of fomenting civil war, and Marshal Sergei Akhromeyev wondered who was engineering a coup – the guardians of the Soviet constitution or Yeltsin and the separatists.[7]

The draft Treaty of Sovereign Republics, published on 8 March

1991, proposed a new federation in which the constituent republics could establish independent diplomatic relations, join international organisations and secede under strict conditions. The central government would retain the functions of defence, foreign policy and co-ordination of law enforcement. But power would be shared, in some unspecified way, in relation to conscription, the definition of foreign policy, the federal budget and the use of precious minerals and foreign currency reserves. The negotiators could not even agree on the name of the new federation, since some republics had ceased to be Soviet or socialist. Negotiations on the treaty were boycotted by the Baltic republics and Georgia, but by mid-1991 the RSFSR and eight other republics accepted its basic terms.

The Union referendum of 17 March enabled a simple majority of voters throughout the state to countervail large majorities for independence in individual republics. The question: 'Do you consider it necessary to preserve the USSR as a renewed federation of equal sovereign republics in which human rights and freedoms of all nationalities will be guaranteed?' made little sense. As critics argued, no-one would want to vote against human rights and there was no definition of 'renewed', merely an implication that the Soviet Union would be preserved. The Baltic republics had already secured overwhelming majorities for separation in independent plebiscites in February and March 1991, and boycotted the central poll, as did Armenia, Georgia and Moldavia. Additional questions in Ukraine and Uzbekistan, asking whether people wanted full independence, produced majorities in favour. And Yeltsin took advantage of a vote in the RSFSR which led to his direct election as its President in June. This new political legitimacy induced Yeltsin and Gorbachev to co-operate more closely. Although Gorbachev could claim a majority for his 'centrism', paradoxically the narrow margin of his success gave him a respite to attack hardline communist power in the Kremlin.

Implications for European security

The upswing in repression and military influence was regarded in the rest of Europe as a major setback to the Helsinki process. CSCE states called for a review conference to discuss the Baltic situation – which the Soviet Union rejected as interference in its internal affairs. The European Community suspended aid and economic negotiations. However, although European states called for a peaceful transition to independence in the Baltic region, they stopped short of recognising the republics as sovereign states. Germany, Poland, Hungary and Czechoslovakia clearly wanted to avoid giving Moscow an excuse for slowing down Soviet troop withdrawals. But three other factors also inhibited foreign reactions: the need for Soviet support against Iraq, the Helsinki Agreement's respect for existing state borders, and anxiety about what the ultimate effects might be. It was not necessarily in the interests of the rest of Europe to see the Soviet Union plunged into wars of secession. Dismemberment would no doubt open the way for more effective economic reforms, because republics would be free of the CPSU's leading role of stifling the profit motive, but where would the process of disaggregation stop? The Yakutsk people in the RSFSR and the Ossetians in Georgia, for example, were also provoking their parent republics with demands for independence. For Europe as a whole, fragmentation would multiply the problems of monitoring existing arms control agreements and reaching new ones. Any proliferation of nuclear weapons among new sovereign states would also be a retrograde step for European security.

Gorbachev reclaimed the trust of western governments by rejecting further use of force in the Baltics and disavowing any return to the stagnation of the past. Shevardnadze's successor as Foreign Minister, Aleksandr Bessmertnykh, told the Ministerial Committee of the Council of Europe in February 1991 that the Soviet Union would adhere to the Council's Cultural Convention (though for the time being not its Human Rights Convention and the Court of Human Rights). In the spring the European Community restored emergency aid and in the summer, persuaded by federal reform and Gorbachev's economic plans, the G7 capitalist states agreed to ease Soviet entry into the world economy.

Martial law and a revival of authoritarian repression were the apparent aims of conspirators in 1991. Hardliners, such as the KGB Chief Viktor Kryuchkov, revived cold war rhetoric and linked foreign interests to the secession movements. Military officers were beset by problems of low morale, a manpower cut of 500,000, and desertions and draft dodging on an extraordinary scale. They resented the unilateral arms control concessions, the retreat from Eastern Europe, and NATO's continued existence after dissolution of the Warsaw Pact. In January 1991 the military could claim a victory. Although the Supreme Soviet cut the defence budget request by 2 billion roubles, it still represented a 28 billion roubles increase over 1990. Justified as a product of inflation, it also reflected an artificial repricing of equipment and was designed to protect the military-industrial complex from conversion and cuts.[8] The army and vested interests in the military-industrial sphere must be counted as major obstacles to *perestroika*.

In addition, almost immediately after signature of the CFE Treaty, problems surfaced over alleged Soviet contraventions. Three motorised infantry divisions were reassigned to coastal naval units and thousands of tanks and other weapons were moved east of the Urals. The Soviet General Staff pointed out that naval units had been excluded on western insistence, and argued that the reclassification and equipment removals occurred legally, before the treaty was signed in November 1990.[9] Rather than reverting to cold war confrontation, it seems probable that the military were making the best of a bad deal, contrary to the general thrust of Foreign Ministry policy. Although the Soviet Union cannot exert much leverage in this area, and the 'contraventions' were disallowed by the West and revoked, this hiccup serves as a signal to the West that in any future negotiations the Soviet Union will not make concessions as readily as it did in 1990.

A successful coup in August 1991 would have certainly destroyed the integrationist trend and brought a chill into peaceful Soviet–European relations. But it was unlikely that Soviet military leaders would have been able to solve the country's domestic problems, or detract attention from them, by reverting to confrontation with the West. The military are unlikely to be galvanised into an attempt to restore control over Eastern Europe for it would hasten the disintegration of their own state. In fact whatever their private sentiments, the higher echelons of the military establishment declared their support for military reforms, the German settlement and the withdrawal of forces from Eastern Europe – though there were obstacles to a smooth retreat such as the lack of accommodation for troops at home and Czechoslovakia's demand for hard currency transit payments.[10] In March 1991 the Supreme Soviet ratified the political parts of the German agreement on the 'temporary stay and removal' of Soviet forces.

Moreover, the Gorbachev era had changed the context in which the instruments of control have to operate. Symptomatic of this was the entirely novel debate, in February 1991, conducted by a Soviet Parliamentary Committee on a bill to define the operations of state security agencies (though the bill vests oversight of the legality of KGB operations in the Soviet President and Procurator-General). The effect of Gorbachev's early reforms had been 'to destroy the old docility that made totalitarianism possible'.[11] Faith in the old system had gone, marked by continued falls in the CPSU's membership, splits and, in mid-1991, the Central Committee's ditching of Marxist–Leninist dogmas.

A stable Europe depends on a relatively smooth reconstruction process in the Soviet Union. This may not be possible in the 1990s. However, neither a new federation nor a core group of republics based on the RSFSR is likely to be actively confrontationist in its weakened condition. By contrast, internal repression, economic and social strife would increase the flood of political and economic refugees. Such instability in the current Soviet domain has already put pressure on the capitalist community of Europe. Not only has the Soviet crisis drawn Poland, Czechoslovakia and Hungary closer together, it also led these front line states to redouble their efforts to secure a rapid integration with western institutions.

Ripples from the Gulf

The crisis in the Gulf, caused by Iraq's invasion of Kuwait on 2 August 1990, was bound to seem detrimental to European security interests – though many of the anxieties it aroused about Coalition casualties were not realised. Five effects on European security can be identified.

First, the Gulf crisis exposed inadequacies in the co-ordination of Western European security policy. Initially the crisis shook confidence about achieving common security positions. In particular, there was a chorus of dismay from the European Parliament, the President of the Commission and French, Italian, German and Belgian Ministers about the EC's lack of credibility during the crisis. However, the fact that, on the ground at least, the war itself was mercifully short may have limited any corrosive effect on the process of West European integration.

Public and government reactions to the crisis revealed the constraints of national interests and traditions. The majority of Europeans were initially opposed to the use of force, notably in Germany, Spain, Italy and Belgium. The British appetite for conflict was sharper than most, though opinion throughout Europe swung behind the military option after attempts to negotiate broke down in January 1991.[12] Apart from popular concerns about American war aims, about the possibility of military escalation and heavy Coalition casualties, and about long-term ecological damage, governments were wary of disrupting relations with parts of the Arab world with which they had strong economic and migrant connections. Many governments, especially the German, were also deeply concerned that a war would have a disastrous effect on the West's ability to cope with the problems of security within Europe. France, Germany, Spain and Italy, as well as Algeria and the Soviet Union, were at the forefront of diplomatic efforts to avert war after the failure of US–Iraq talks on 9 January. Although, following the resignation of the French Minister of Defence, French forces were not only placed under US–Saudi command, but also committed to a deep invasion of Iraqi territory, other states adopted distinctive positions to avoid getting directly involved in fighting, though their naval vessels played important roles in protecting the sea-lanes. As the air war entered its second week and the costs mounted, so burdensharing arguments developed. Anti-EC opinion in Britain alleged that the other members of the Community were unreliable, and took solace from a situation which appeared to confirm nationalist prejudices.

Yet some convergence had been achieved in Western Europe in spite of national idiosyncrasies and differences in the level of support for military and diplomatic initiatives. There was unanimous support among EC governments for the UN resolutions and for enforcing sanctions against Iraq. Paradoxically, too, the Gulf crisis gave a new impetus to proposals for political union and institutional changes which would facilitate common European approaches, including the development of independent European defence obligations. Ultimately, the Gulf war revealed that EC governments were concerned that their differences during the crisis had detracted from unity, and there was little difficulty in agreeing to enhance crisis management. The EC reacted more adroitly to the Slovenian crisis. Debate over the Gulf thus became a step towards improving co-ordination.

However, the issue of military responsibility looked set to grow more contentious. The Secretary-General of NATO, Manfred Woerner, opened a debate within NATO about losing the distinction between area and out-of-area activities, by giving the alliance a 'variable geometry'. Threats from outside Europe, by states with new ballistic missile technology for example, posed a new order of risks which required an imaginative and less restrictive geographical framework.[13] But, as Bill Park's chapter indicates (this volume), the further from the old central front that NATO's attention wanders, the more difficult it would be to get agreement for the new strategic concept being drafted for the autumn of 1991.

The relationship between the EC and the WEU, as detailed by Juliet Lodge in chapter 4 above, was given greater salience by the Gulf crisis. Building on its valuable experience of maritime peacekeeping during the Iran–Iraq war, the WEU had organised the presence in the Gulf of thirty-nine ships from seven European countries, and this gave heart to fusionists. Jacques Delors, for example, urged that the WEU should become a 'melting pot for a European defence embedded in the Community' and equipped with a multilateral rapid intervention force by 1995.[14] But such a proposal widened the gap between the Atlanticist perceptions of the United States and Britain on the one hand, and the integrationist perceptions of continental Europe on the other. The United States welcomed the Europeanisation of defence but warned the Europeans not to set up an oppositional camp to NATO.[15] The United Kingdom, having ignored the Western European Union when it was revived by a French initiative in 1984, now saw it as a potential *bridge* between the EC and NATO. The logic of Britain's geostrategic position dictated that Prime Minister John Major repair the damage caused by Thatcherite negativism. His support for an evolutionary approach to a common security policy called for consensus and the recognition of America's pivotal role.[16]

The second major impact of the Gulf conflict was to affect Germany's crucial stabilising function in the new European order, a function which would be doubly afflicted if the special relationship between the Kohl and Gorbachev Governments was terminated by a reactionary coup in the Kremlin. In fact the danger of Germany's diplomatic isolation in the Gulf crisis was averted by burdensharing solutions. In response to allied pressure, Germany pledged contributions of over DM12 billion for military operations, and as part of NATO's Ace Mobile Force sent to Turkey, albeit reluctantly, some old Alpha jet aircraft which lacked the range to attack targets in Iraq.

More seriously, the war sharpened the domestic German debate about the role of the Bundeswehr under the constitution. Article 24–2 of the Basic Law of 1949 states the German Federation can 'join a system of mutual collective security for the maintenance of peace', either in Europe or among the nations of the world. Deployment of troops outside the NATO area or in a UN peacekeeping role was certainly not envisaged until after reunification. Then, it seems, a political consensus was developing to amend the constitution to allow involvement in peacekeeping. This was shattered by the Gulf crisis. Whereas the Social Democrats now wanted German military participation abroad restricted constitutionally to UN or CSCE peacekeeping and election monitoring, the Kohl Government was prepared to interpret the existing constitution in such a way as to allow German minesweepers to work in the Gulf under the auspices of the WEU.[17] Until the issue is clearly resolved it is difficult for Germany to take a lead in promoting European defence integration.

In a broader sense, too, the Gulf crisis also came at an unfortunate time from the German point of view. The Kohl Government was deeply engaged in an economic mission to help the East Europeans, was admitting some 300,000 refugees, paying for the return and relocation of Soviet troops, and attempting to overcome the divisions of Germany. As Hans-Joachim Spanger indicated in his chapter (above), the absorption of the former GDR is likely to prove onerous and to take between five and ten years. Unification costs obliged the Bonn Government to impose a 'Fatherland tax' increase of 7·5 per cent. The eastern *Länder* and cities were bankrupt, the labour and export markets were in a condition of collapse, and it was becoming increasingly difficult to police strikes and social unrest.

A third impact of the Gulf crisis was to reinforce Europe's security interests in the Mediterranean which was already an area of concern because of migration from North Africa, a flourishing traffic in drugs, and the need to strengthen economic links between Southern Europe and North Africa. On the eve of the Gulf crisis, Spain had proposed a Mediterranean CSCE sub-grouping, and a separate CFE arms control agreement for the region. Whilst there are grounds for optimism about human rights, in view of significant changes on this score in Algeria, Mediterranean arms control is unlikely to make much progress because inevitably it would have to include naval systems. The United States and other NATO countries will be even less inclined to accept naval restrictions after the Gulf crisis than they were beforehand. Indeed, by far the greater part of the Coalition's forces were shipped through the Mediterranean during the Gulf crisis. The importance of the Mediterranean as a strategic link was also reflected in an adjustment to the US command structure which combined the Atlantic and Indian Oceans in one region. It is quite probable, therefore, that the American maritime presence in the Mediterranean will not be as severely affected by defence cuts as other force projection capabilities. NATO's centre of gravity may also be said to have shifted to its southern flank.

Fourth, the impact of the Gulf crisis on the two superpowers indirectly affected European security. Although the United States emerged from the war confident and demonstrably supreme in military technology, the crisis added to the pressure on Europeans to do more for their own defence. Before the crisis, in fact, Pentagon planners had been preparing to reduce the European presence and develop Third World fire-fighting capabilities within a smaller defence budget. In general terms the Gulf conflict reinforced this policy. The defence budget request submitted to Congress on 4 February 1991 for FY 1992 was $291 billion, or $3·7 billion less in real terms than in 1991. Six active army divisions and ten active and reserve air force wings were to be cut. Various large procurement programmes would terminate, and global force projection would be affected by the US Navy's contraction from 545 vessels in 1991 to 451 vessels by the mid-1990s, a significant retreat from the 600-ship objective of the mid-1980s. The net domestic economic effects of the

Gulf conflict are not easily assessed because the estimate costs will be offset by Allied contributions and the stabilisation of oil prices. Even so, insistence on making others pay reflected US unease about the strain on American resources. At a time when the US federal budget deficit was nearing $400 billion in 1991 and the economy was deep in recession, the Gulf war seemed to bear out the argument that the United States would have to choose between burdens because it was becoming over-extended.[18]

The Gulf conflict was a special case in which US leadership was unavoidable, the Soviet Union was preoccupied, the UN malleable, oil access essential and the aggressor particularly blatant and brutal. American prescriptions for security will not necessarily be accepted by others, nor will the United States have the resources to act as policeman. According to critics of force projection, US military power is no longer needed abroad to deter Japanese and German rearmament and it is not credible to defend the world against 'instability and unpredictability'. The most likely conflicts in Europe, such as hostilities between the Yugoslav republics or between Yugoslavia and Albania over Kosovo, would be irrelevant to US interests. Henry Kissinger argued that in general terms in the future, American forces should be employed 'only for causes for which we are prepared to pay'.[19]

In this regard, finally, the Gulf conflict threw doubts on co-operation between the Soviet Union and the West. In the early weeks of the Gulf crisis, Bush spoke of the vision he shared with Gorbachev of multinational responsibility for freedom and justice. 'Clearly,' he said, 'no longer can a dictator count on East–West confrontation to stymie concerted U.N. action against aggression.'[20] Three months later, against the background of Soviet consultations with Iraq, Senator Bill Bradley described US–Soviet co-operation as being in 'a very serious stage of disintegration'.[21]

In the Soviet Union there was widespread anxiety lest the Gulf conflict spread, raising the spectre of a second Afghanistan and the involvement of Soviet Forces. Conservatives went further and argued that the Soviet Union should not allow the destruction of a power with which it had a Treaty of Friendship or accept the presence of US forces in the Middle East near Soviet borders. In addition, Soviet military advisers, already impressed by US offensive capabilities after visiting an aircraft carrier in 1988, were likely to draw military lessons from the Gulf conflict which would lead them to demand new air defences, more cruise missiles and high-technology precision-guided weapons. As already suggested, a Soviet military adventure in Europe seems unlikely. But an arms race in new technologies could alter western perceptions of Soviet intentions, especially if accompanied by the development of offensive doctrines to reflect new technological capabilities.[22]

Gorbachev's role as a peacemaker was an abject failure, for Saddam Hussein was implacable until long after the United States had decided on a military solution to the crisis. Nevertheless, Soviet diplomatic support for the Coalition established a claim for participation in any post-war regional security discussions. The Foreign Minister, Bessmertnykh, even extracted an acceptance from the US Secretary of State, James Baker, that any Middle East security system must include a reconciliation for the Palestinians. This particular *démarche* was disavowed by the White House. Quite apart from any peacemaking there is no doubt, also, that the United States must deal with a Soviet Union that will protect its own 'backyard', perhaps by reasserting influence in Iraq and Iran. All the same, Moscow's policy of safeguarding or extending influence in the Middle East is hardly likely to be achieved at the expense of securing the greater advantages of co-operation with the West in Europe.

Summary

The lessons of the Gulf crisis tended to confirm and reinforce, rather than overturn, our perceptions of change in European security. The diplomatic crisis and subsequent conflict can be reasonably interpreted to emphasise that there are limits to 'superpower' clout, that Europe will have to look after itself, that Germany will have to come to terms with a more extensive military/peacekeeping role, and that a European security community cannot be a fortress against the outside world. The interlocking crises in the Soviet Union, on the other hand, have the capacity to jeopardise both the improvement in interstate relations and transnational security developments such as the spread of democratic values. Nevertheless, the fragmentation of the Soviet polity which was occurring at the beginning of the decade was less likely to produce a concerted state-directed military threat to the rest of Europe than a messy overspill from ethnic violence.

Conclusions

This book has focused on the roles of organisations and states in shaping European security, and on the processes which have been employed, for it is somewhat easier to envisage the factors which will shape the future of

European security than the kind of system established, if any, by the year 2000. It has been shown that the 1990s began with considerable strains being exerted on the web of European security relationships. These arose not only from the Soviet Union and the Gulf, but also from economic dislocation in Eastern Europe and the threat of hostilities between ethnic groups in the Balkans, most seriously in Yugoslavia. East Europeans had gained democratic rights but were sliding towards impoverishment and a revival of ethnic and national animosities. Such strains are likely to be a feature of the remainder of the decade, presenting security threats which are more complex than those perceived during cold war confrontation, but less apocalyptic than a system-threatening war. To some extent the forces of disintegration and instability in the East can be offset by forces of assimilation and integration in the West. However, policy-makers should aim to achieve something more secure than a cold peace in which rules are recognised, crises managed and major war avoided, but in which co-operative behaviour is curtailed by resentment and permanent instability. If, as seems reasonable, the ideal end-goal of European policies should be the establishment of a pan-European security community, what developments might be fostered? Several factors which would shape an idealised community can be identified.

- European security cannot be ensured without inputs by the United States and the Soviet Union, as Bertel Heurlin argued in chapter 2 above. But both these powers will have to accept roles defined, not by rivalry with each other, but by a complex web of connections which are designed primarily in and for Europe, including structures like the EC.
- Cold war instruments need to adapt to a changed context if they are to be useful. NATO requires a reconfiguration of its military activities within Europe, to present a minimum deterrent and a defensively orientated strategic concept. Eventually, it might supervise its own dissolution, with the US–Europe security link maintained in some other framework. In the short term, however, there clearly needs to be co-operation between the European and Atlanticist institutions, especially as both the CSCE and NATO have crisis management functions.
- Pan-European organisations which had little or no function in sustaining cold war militarism, such as the Council of Europe and the CSCE, should acquire greater powers with parliamentary oversight, in order to support human rights, confidence-building, economic co-operation and disarmament. Their roles need to go beyond bridge-building to address the legitimate values and interests of all European states. The CSCE also has a responsibility to promote peaceful change.

The Helsinki Final Act recognises existing frontiers but allows for negotiated disassociation of a constituent part of a member state.

• A key factor in containing and reducing instabilities will be the reorientation of military forces and the redeployment of resources from military to civilian purposes. Proposals for arms reductions include cutting CFE equipment categories by a further 50 per cent, eliminating short-range (under 500 km.) nuclear forces, the curbing and monitoring of arms transfers, and the inclusion of air and naval forces in future negotiations.[23] Such negotiations are bound to be more complex, however, not just because the most easily verified reductions have already been made, but because bloc-to-bloc talks are no longer feasible. However, defence reorientations to make large-scale offensive operations and territorial aggrandisement unmanageable, and the creation of European Defence Community-type forces to reduce national autonomy, would contribute to unilateral or regional arms reductions.

• Specific regimes for Europe, such as the CSBM regime analysed by Manfred Efinger and Volker Rittberger in their chapter, are essential to bind states together through norms and processes which not merely reduce tension but enhance co-operation.

• To go further than the monitoring of elections, human rights and arms control agreements, European institutions might consider the provision of peacekeeping forces to contain local conflict. As with UN peacekeeping, however, the problems of finding the right mix of military competence and political acceptability are likely to bedevil any such interventions, except on an *ad hoc* basis and by the invitation of parties to a dispute, including the local competent authority.

• Policies of deterrence and economic leverage exercised by western states can reinforce behavioural norms, but states seeking assimilation into a security community must have some hope of being rewarded. The conditions traditionally imposed by the IMF on borrowers have frequently created resentment and instability. Leverage needs to be calibrated to take the legitimate security interests and values of supplicants into account, and to be balanced by interim goals and schedules which symbolise progress towards assimilation.

• With the demise of bipolarity, many of the alignments in Europe are likely to be regional. Therefore, regional arms control arrangements might be appropriate in the post-bloc Europe. More broadly, regional subsystems such as the *Pentagonale* should be fostered as a means of undermining the significance of borders, defusing ethnic disputes and reducing the growing distinction between a core western community and a marginalised periphery.

- Europe's security will grow in new dimensions as non-military transnational processes, of the kind discussed in Owen Greene's chapter above, are strengthened. Realist perspectives, which look to the redistribution of power between states for a new and stable balance in Europe, underestimate the potential of transnationalism in promoting stability. The anarchy of state sovereignty will not be swept aside, but constrained sovereignty and shared sovereignty on issues affecting security cannot be avoided.

Adrian Hyde-Price outlined four reconstructed polarities and alignments, any one of which might settle into a regulated system. His chapter also emphasised that although cold war military structures lost their monopolies over security, the process of reconstruction is likely to be evolutionary. This accords with the view of some Soviet scholars, and reflects an understanding that political constellations tend to revolve more quickly than alterations in power capabilities.[24] Indeed, strong voices are heard for moving slowly as a hedge against a return to cold war postures and to allow time for new arrangements, such as German unification, to be properly absorbed. However, undue prevarication in remoulding the European security system to cope with the pressures of disintegration in the Balkans, Central and Eastern Europe and the Soviet Union could make those pressures more severe.

In an analysis of post-war settlements, K. J. Holsti has offered a peacemaker's guide to the prerequisites for stability, in which the key constituents are: a system of international governance based on justice; opportunities for assimilation; a system of deterrence; mechanisms for conflict resolution and norms concerning the use of force; procedures for peaceful change, and anticipation of conflictual issues.[25] Such stabilising features are already present, at least in embryo, in the post-cold war Europe. In concluding that there is significant potential for moving beyond a cold peace in the rest of the decade it is worth noting an additional factor for stability. The transition from cold war has not been propelled by an imposed peace settlement. The voluntarily-accepted agreements and processes which accompanied the revolution in Europe formed a reasonable basis on which to remould the European security system.

Notes

1 'The spectre of dictatorship', *The Observer*, 23 December 1990, p. 19.
2 'Helping Mr Gorbachev', *The Economist*, 23 June 1990, pp. 16–17; Group of Seven Report, 21 December 1990.

3 'The rise and fall of perestroika', *The Economist*, 19 January 1991, pp. 51–3.
4 *The Times*, 13 February 1991, p. 1. The radical leadership of the RSFSR was implicated in a scheme to sell resources and 140 billion roubles for $7·5 billion to be used by the RSFSR to buy consumer goods.
5 Boris Kagarlitsky, 'When we are ruled by paralysis', *Dagens Nyheter*, reprinted in *Guardian Europe*, 15 February 1991, p. 21. For a discussion of the Soviet variety of controlled capitalism, see Nicholas Spulber, *Restructuring the Soviet Economy: in Search of the Market*, Michigan, University of Michigan Press, 1991.
6 Col. V. Alksnis, 'Moscow welched on us', interview in *Argumenti i Fakti*, no. 4, January 1991 (Novosti tr.). Alksnis advocated a junta, without Gorbachev or Yeltsin, to save the Motherland, in *Komsomolskaya Pravda*, 10 January 1991 (Novosti tr.). On Gorbachev's use of power, see 'An interview with Andrei Sakharov', *New York Review of Books*, XXXV, 22 December 1988, pp. 28–9; Archie Brown (ed.), *Political Leadership in the Soviet Union*, London, Macmillan/St Antony's, 1989.
7 Marshal Sergei Akhromeyev, interview in *Sovietskaya Rossia*, 7 February 1991 (Novosti tr.).
8 S. Bobrovski, 'Tanks hit us in our pockets', *Komsomolskaya Pravda*, 11 December 1990 (Novosti tr.).
9 Col.-Gen. B. Omelichev, 'We pursue an honest and principled policy', interview in *Krasnaya Zvezda*, 16 February 1991 (Novosti tr.). The Soviet Union wanted to exclude auxiliary troops in civil defence and security for the rocket forces.
10 Gen. M. Moiseyev, 'The agreement with Germany is working', interview in *Trud*, 5 March 1991 (Novosti tr.); Dimitri Yazov, interview in *Pravda*, 23 February 1991 (Novosti tr.).
11 Michael Howard, 'The remaking of Europe', *Survival*, XXXII, no. 2, March/April 1990, p. 100.
12 'Divided Europe nails its colours to the fence', *The Observer*, 3 February 1991, p. 15. Pre-war opinion was also divided about use of force in the United States where the Senate voted by a narrow margin to accord war powers to the President.
13 Manfred Woerner, address to the North Atlantic Assembly, London, 29 November 1990.
14 Jacques Delors, Alistair Buchan Lecture, IISS, London, 7 March 1991; Roland Dumas, interview in *Le Monde*, 11 March 1991.
15 Hon. William Taft, address to the IISS, 8 February 1991.
16 'I want us to be at the very heart of Europe', *The Times*, 12 March 1991, p. 8.
17 Thomas M. Wandinger, 'The German discussion on the use of German armed forces in peacekeeping operations', paper for Peacekeeping Seminar, Department of Politics, University of Newcastle-upon-Tyne, 19 March 1991; Dieter S. Lutz, *Basic Law, Security and Peace, Armament and Disarmament*, Institut für Friedensforschung und Sicherheitspolitik, Hamburg, September 1989, p. 31.
18 See, e.g., Stephen Van Evera, *Journal of Strategic Studies*, XIII, no. 2, June 1990, pp. 1–51; Christopher Layne, 'Continental divide: time to disengage in Europe', *The National Interest*, Fall 1988, pp. 13–27; Jane M. O. Sharp, *Europe After an American Withdrawal: Economic and Military Issues*, Oxford, Oxford University Press/SIPRI, 1990.
19 Henry Kissinger, 'America cannot police the world forever', *Los Angeles Times*, reprinted in *The Times*, 12 March 1991, p. 14; Center for Defense Information, 'The US as the world's policeman?', *The Defense Monitor*, XX, no. 1, 1991, pp. 1–8.
20 George Bush, address to Congress, 11 September 1990 (USIS text).
21 Cited by Martin Walker, 'New Moscow nightmare for Pentagon', *Guardian*, 15 January 1991, p. 9. Also, the long-anticipated completion of the START Treaty

was further delayed by disagreement on technical matters, such as rules for monitoring Soviet mobile missile production, but finally signed in July 1991.

22 John Erickson, cited in 'Gloom for the Russians in Gulf weapons toll', *The Sunday Times*, 3 March 1991, supplement p. xv.

23 Hans-Dietrich Genscher, 'German responsibility for a peaceful order in Europe', in Adam Rotfeld and Walther Stützle (eds.), *Germany and Europe in Transition*, Oxford, Oxford University Press/SIPRI, 1991, p. 25; Jonathan Dean, *Meeting Gorbachev's Challenge: How to Build down the NATO–Warsaw Pact Confrontation*, New York, St Martin's, 1989; Frank Blackaby, *The 'Comprehensive Concept' of Defence and Disarmament for NATO from Flexible Response to Mutual Defensive Superiority*, London, British American Security Information Council, 1990, pp. 8–11.

24 Morten Kelstrup, 'On the structure and political system and scenarios for the future of Europe', paper for European Consortium for Political Research, Bochum, 2–7 April 1990; Sergei A. Karaganov, 'The year of Europe: a Soviet view', *Survival*, XXXII, no. 2, March/April 1990, p. 126.

25 Kalevi J. Holsti, *Peace and War: Armed Conflicts and International Order 1648–1989*, Cambridge, Cambridge University Press, 1991, pp. 336–9.

Postscript

In the Soviet Union, the respite which Gorbachev had won for 'centrism' lasted barely four months. The attempted coup of 19 August 1991, which occurred during the production of this book, intensified the Soviet crisis and, incidentally, reinforced our analysis of the European security outlook. Military restructuring in Europe, consolidation of confidence-building and progress towards a security community, and the growth of non-military security issues will occur in the context of a 'one-plus-four' international system (though one of the four is more likely to be Russia than the Soviet Union, and the global role of the United States without a Soviet adversary is as yet undefined).

Within the Soviet Union, the coup had a cathartic effect, achieving in its collapse all that it had been designed to prevent: dismemberment of the empire, dissolution of the Communist Party as a governing system and emasculation of the internal security apparatus. The conspirators in the KGB, CPSU and the armed forces overestimated their control over the instruments of coercion and underestimated the impact on the urban populace of six years of political reform. Further, they left radicals at liberty to rally popular resistance – notably Yeltsin, Shevardnadze, and the Mayor of Leningrad/St Petersburg, Anatoly Sobchak. On his return from the Crimea, Gorbachev accepted responsibility for having elevated the coup leaders, including his deputy Gennady Yanayev, Prime Minister Pavlov, Defence Minister Yazov, KGB chief Kryuchkov and Supreme Soviet Chairman Anatoly Lukyanov. But there was also a failure of policy. Gorbachev's vacillations in trying to maintain a consensus for reform satisfied neither radicals nor hardliners because 'centrism' lacked a synchronised economic plan. Much of *perestroika* was improvised and reactive. Gorbachev's failures thus made a coup likely, but his attacks on the Brezhnev system also made the August coup untenable. The crisis, however, further undermined his own political position, marked by his subservience to Yeltsin, his resignation as General Secretary of the Party and his relegation to the role, without a genuine political mandate, of inter-republic referee in a transitional State Council. All the same, the Gorbachev leadership lasted far longer than Western commentators had insistently predicted throughout his ascendancy in the 1980s.

It is perhaps unsurprising that the profound political alienation of the Soviet people, evident by 1990, should have found an outlet in romantic chauvinism. The Baltic republics cut loose and were duly admitted to the United Nations. In a new Union accord voted by the Congress of People's Deputies on 2 September 1991, other republics agreed to negotiate about a residual central role for economic co-ordination, defence and security. Their aim seems to be to achieve a more natural integration of interests. But with perhaps as many as thirty republics and regions claiming internal independence, economic barriers are likely to grow and instability, fuelled by nationalist and ethnic unrest, increase. In this regard suspicion was voiced, especially in the Ukraine, about the future hegemony of the Russian Federation. Apart from Yeltsin's unconstitutional, decree-happy assertion of authority after the coup, his dismissal of 'Stalinist borders' and subsequent claim to a monopoly of nuclear weapons, there is cause for concern in the potential for unrest among Russians living in neighbouring republics who will look to the Russian government for protection.

As the warfare in Yugoslavia has demonstrated, the ability of West Europeans to influence the course of ethnic conflict is limited. The saving grace is that there is little prospect of a military threat to general European security. There was much loose talk about a revival of the cold war when the hardliners took temporary control in Moscow. But the junta was unlikely to have posed a competent threat to Eastern Europe or the West, having accepted, albeit resentfully, the changed strategic environment.

For Western Europe, the coup failure provided another opportunity to weigh the demands of economic security. The NATO members had worked overtime to re-design military structure and strategy, but the G7 capitalist club (United States, Japan, Germany, France, Canada, Australia and the UK) had offered Gorbachev nothing of substance after their meeting of 17 July 1991. The 'wait and see' policy, a hangover of cold war economic ideology in the United States and Britain in particular, was exposed as inadequate and lacking in vision. Henceforth, any attempt to revive a 'Grand Bargain' (aid in return for radical economic reform) would face the prospect of dealing with fragmented polities. The weakness of central authority, widespread civil disorder and inter-republic economic competition may not threaten the West directly, but it challenges the rest of Europe to pursue alternatives to a 'cold peace'.

Further reading

Bialer, Seweryn (ed.), *Politics, Society and Nationality Inside Gorbachev's Russia*, Boulder, Colo. and London, Westview, 1989.

Buzan, Barry, *People, States and Fear: The National Security Problem in International Relations*, Brighton, Wheatsheaf, 1983.

Buzan, Barry *et al.*, *The European Security Order Recast: Scenarios for the Post-Cold War Era*, London, Pinter, 1990.

Caligaris, Luigi, *European Defence: Hopes, Challenges, and Debates*, Oxford, Brassey's, 1990.

Carpenter, Ted Galen (ed.), *NATO at 40: Confronting a Changing World*, Lexington, Lexington Books/Cato Institute, 1990.

Coker, Christopher (ed.), *Shifting into Neutral? Burdensharing in the Western Alliance in the 1990s*, London, Brassey's, 1990.

Dahrendorff, Ralf, *Reflections on the Revolution in Europe*, London, Chatto and Windus, 1990.

Dawisha, Karen, *Eastern Europe, Gorbachev and Reform*, Cambridge, Cambridge University Press (2nd edn), 1990.

de Nevers, Renée, *The Soviet Union and Eastern Europe: The End of an Era*, Adelphi Paper 249, London, Brassey's/IISS, 1990.

Eavis, Paul (ed.), *European Security: The New Agenda*, Bristol, Safer World Foundation, 1990.

Freedman, Lawrence (ed.), *Military Power in Europe*, London, IISS, 1990.

Gambles, Ian, *Prospects for West European Security Cooperation*, Adelphi Paper 244, London, Brassey's/IISS, 1989.

Halliday, Fred, *The Making of the Second Cold War*, London, Verso, 1983.

Harle, Vilho (ed.), *European Values in International Relations*, London, Pinter, 1990.

Harle, Vilho and Iivonen, Jyriki (eds.), *Gorbachev and Europe*, London, Pinter, 1990.

Harle, Vilho and Sivonen, Pekka (eds.), *Europe in Transition: Politics and Nuclear Security*, London, Pinter, 1989.

Hyde-Price, Adrian, *Beyond the Cold War: Four Scenarios for the Year 2010*, London, Sage, 1991.

Independent Commission on Disarmament and Security Issues [Palme Commission], *Common Security: A Programme for Disarmament*, London, Pan Books, 1982.

Kaldor, Mary and Falk, Richard (eds.), *Dealignment: A New Foreign Policy Perspective*, Oxford, Basil Blackwell/UN University, 1987.

Kaplan, Lawrence S., *et al.* (eds.), *NATO After Forty Years*, Wilmington,

Scholarly Resources Inc., 1990.

Kennedy, Paul, *The Rise and Fall of the Great Powers: Economic Change and Military Conflict from 1500 to 2000*, New York and London, Random House and Unwin Hyman, 1988.

Keohane, Robert O., *International Institutions and State Power*, Boulder, Colo., Westview, 1990.

Lodge, Juliet (ed.), *The European Community and the Challenge of the Future*, London, Pinter, 1989.

Luard, Evan, *International Society*, London, 1990.

Lucas, Michael R., *The Western Alliance After INF: Redefining U.S. Policy Towards Europe and the Soviet Union*, London, Lynne Rienner Publishers, 1990.

McCauley, Martin, *Gorbachev and Perestroika*, London, Macmillan/School of Slavonic and East European Studies, 1990.

Niou, Emerson M. S., *et al.*, *The Balance of Power*, Cambridge, Cambridge University Press, 1989.

Prins, Gwyn (ed.), *Spring in Winter*, Manchester, Manchester University Press, 1990.

Pugh, Michael C. and Williams, Phil (eds.), *Superpower Politics: Change in the United States and the Soviet Union*, Manchester, Manchester University Press, 1990.

Rittberger, Volker (ed.), *International Regimes in East–West Politics*, London and New York, Pinter, 1990.

Rizopoulos, Nicholas X., *Sea-Changes: American Foreign Policy a World Transformed*, New York, Council on Foreign Relations, 1990.

Rollo, J. M. C. and Roper, John, *The New Eastern Europe: Western Responses*, London, RIIA, Chatham House Paper, 1990.

Rotfeld, Adam and Stützle, Walther (eds.), *Germany and Europe in Transition*, Oxford, Oxford University Press/SIPRI, 1991.

Rudney, Robert and Reychler, Luc (eds.), *European Security Beyond the Year 2000*, New York, Praeger, 1988.

Russell, J., *Environmental Issues in Eastern Europe: Setting an Agenda*, London, RIIA, 1991.

Smith, Dan (ed.), *European Security in the 1990s*, London, Pluto, 1989.

Spulber, Nicholas, *Restructuring the Soviet Economy: In Search of the Market*, Michigan and Manchester, University of Michigan Press, 1991.

Thomas, Caroline, *The Environment and International Relations*, London, RIIA, forthcoming.

Väyrynen, Raimo (ed.), *The Quest for Peace: Transcending Collective Violence and War Among Societies, Cultures and States*, London, Sage/International Social Science Council, 1987.

Waever, Ole *et al.* (eds), *European Polyphony: Perspectives Beyond East-West Confrontation*, London, Macmillan, 1989.

Wallace, W. (ed.), *The Dynamics of European Integration*, London, Pinter/RIIA, 1990.

White, Stephen, *Gorbachev in Power*, Cambridge, Cambridge University Press,

1990.

Young, Oran R., *International Cooperation: Building Regimes for Natural Resources and the Environment*, Ithaca and London, Cornell University Press, 1989.

Zwick, Peter, *Soviet Foreign Relations: Process and Policy*, Englewood Cliffs, NJ, 1990.

Index